Praise for
The Girl's Still Got It

"This is by far the most interesting, encouraging, and applicable book on Ruth I've ever read. Liz is brilliantly profound as she makes the Bible come alive in a fresh, enlightening way. I kept finding myself saying, 'I didn't know that!' Plus, Liz's trademark wit makes this book so much fun to read. I give this book my highest recommendation."

—Lysa TerKeurst, *New York Times* best-selling author
of *Made to Crave* and president of Proverbs 31 Ministries

"Liz Curtis Higgs is one of the most amazing teachers of God's Word that I have ever experienced. Her in-depth knowledge of the Scriptures, gifting as a communicator, and personal relationship with the Lord make her unmatched in the ability to take biblical truth and make it applicable to anybody."

—Priscilla Shirer, *New York Times* best-selling author
of *The Resolution for Women*

"Liz has a profound gift. She can pull back the curtain of history, and suddenly we are weeping with Naomi, kneeling beside Ruth, and celebrating a God who redeems our stories in outrageously beautiful ways. You will love this book!"

—Sheila Walsh, author of *God Loves Broken People*
(and those who pretend they're not)

"Liz is authentic, hilarious, and theologically substantive. Every time I have the privilege of hearing her teach or reading something she's written, I come away with a bigger, clearer picture of Jesus. Her new book about an Old Testament girl named Ruth—which is ultimately about God's redemptive affection for all of us—is a must read!"

—Lisa Harper, author of *Stumbling into Grace*

"Liz Curtis Higgs has done it again! With her thorough research, spontaneous wit, and extraordinary attention to every detail of Ruth's life, Liz will have you laughing and crying at the same time while being challenged with poignant choices that apply to your own life. This book sings of hope, redemption, and lasting joy. I highly recommend it for personal and small-group study."

—CAROL KENT, author of *Between a Rock and a Grace Place*

"Liz's genius, sensitivity, and humor are reflected on every page. I've taught the book of Ruth many times, but, oh, did Liz introduce me to insightful, ancient cues that deepened what I thought I knew. You're going to fall in love with *The Girl's Still Got It*—and with Liz!"

—JAN SILVIOUS, author of *Same Life, New Story*

"I love Liz. I love Ruth. Put them under the same roof, and you have my full attention. Liz is the consummate storyteller, and Ruth is a woman with a story worth knowing. It worked for me. Big time!"

—PATSY CLAIRMONT, author of *Stained Glass Hearts*

"Liz has certainly still got it! You'll laugh, learn, and love Liz's contemporary parallels to Ruth and Naomi. She brings them alive, vividly helping us identify with their hopes and hurts. Like us, they faced enormous storms, but also—and Liz makes this so clear—they learned to trust the Lord of the Storm. Liz's astounding research will teach you valuable history—yet all the while you'll feel like you are curled up with a novel."

—DEE BRESTIN, author of *The Friendships of Women*

"Liz Curtis Higgs has taken this remarkable story and made it come alive! With delightful humor and well-researched insight, Liz presents Ruth's story as it truly is—the story of you and me. For we, too, have been chosen and deeply loved by a Kinsman-Redeemer who went to such extravagant lengths that he left heaven and interrupted eternity just to make us his own."

—JOANNA WEAVER, author of *Having a Mary Heart in a Martha World*

"The first time I heard Liz Curtis Higgs speak, I fell in love with her wisdom, her grace, and especially her infectious laughter. It has been the very same for me with this book. She had me at the first sentence, bent over the pages, underlining like a crazy woman, writing notes in the margins, and laughing out loud along with her. Liz writes with the mind of a scholar, the heart of a novelist, and a beautiful wit. I cannot wait to huddle my girlfriends around our kitchen table and study *The Girl's Still Got It.*"

—ANGELA THOMAS, author of *Do You Think I'm Beautiful?*

Praise for the
Bad Girls of the Bible series

"Popular storyteller Higgs takes a look at the vamps and tramps of the Bible, searching for the lessons these wicked women have to teach. Higgs retells these biblical stories with rollicking humor and deep insight as she teaches about the nature of sin and goodness."

—PUBLISHERS WEEKLY

"Liz takes—with humility and humor—the evangelical message and puts it in a lens that anybody can look through. A truly remarkable accomplishment."

—RELIGION & ETHICS NEWSWEEKLY

"Everything touched by Liz Curtis Higgs turns to humor and encouragement. Higgs connects each of her Bad Girls with her readers. A refreshing look at Bible characters we don't hear much about."

—CHURCH & SYNAGOGUE LIBRARIES

"Higgs is such a fine writer. She invites us to see 'badness' not as something 'out there' but as something within. The key, needless to say, lies in pulling the right lesson from each bad example. And Higgs is superb at it."

—DESERET NEWS

The
Girl's
Still
Got
It

LIZ CURTIS HIGGS

Best-selling author of *Bad Girls of the Bible*

The Girl's Still Got It

Take a Walk
with Ruth *and the* God
Who Rocked Her World

WATERBROOK
PRESS

THE GIRL'S STILL GOT IT

All Scripture quotations, unless otherwise indicated, are taken from the Holy Bible, New International Version®, NIV®. Copyright © 1973, 1978, 1984 by Biblica Inc.™ Used by permission of Zondervan. All rights reserved worldwide. www.zondervan.com. Scripture quotations marked (ASV) are taken from the American Standard Version. Scripture quotations marked (AMP) are taken from the Amplified Bible. Copyright © 1954, 1958, 1962, 1964, 1965, 1987 by The Lockman Foundation. Used by permission. Scripture quotations marked (CEV) are taken from the Contemporary English Version. Copyright © 1991, 1992, 1995 by American Bible Society. Used by permission. Scripture quotations marked (KJV) are taken from the King James Version. Scripture quotations marked (MSG) are taken from The Message by Eugene H. Peterson. Copyright © 1993, 1994, 1995, 1996, 2000, 2001, 2002. Used by permission of NavPress Publishing Group. All rights reserved. Scripture quotations marked (NASB) are taken from the New American Standard Bible®. © Copyright The Lockman Foundation 1960, 1962, 1963, 1968, 1971, 1972, 1973, 1975, 1977, 1995. Used by permission. (www.Lockman.org). Scripture quotations marked (NCV) are taken from the New Century Version®. Copyright © 1987, 1988, 1991 by Thomas Nelson Inc. Used by permission. All rights reserved. Scripture quotations marked (NKJV) are taken from the New King James Version®. Copyright © 1984 by Thomas Nelson Inc. Used by permission. All rights reserved. Scripture quotations marked (NLT) are taken from the Holy Bible, New Living Translation, copyright © 1996, 2004, 2007. Used by permission of Tyndale House Publishers Inc., Carol Stream, Illinois 60188. All rights reserved. Scripture quotations marked (NRSV) are taken from the New Revised Standard Version of the Bible, copyright © 1989 by the Division of Christian Education of the National Council of the Churches of Christ in the USA. Used by permission. All rights reserved. Scripture quotations marked (YLT) are taken from Young's Literal Translation.

Trade Paperback ISBN 978-1-57856-448-4
eBook ISBN 978-0-307-72955-2

Copyright © 2012 by Liz Curtis Higgs

Cover design by Kelly L. Howard; cover photo by A. Green/Corbis

Published in the United States by WaterBrook, an imprint of the Crown Publishing Group, a division of Penguin Random House LLC, New York.

WATERBROOK® and its deer colophon are registered trademarks of Penguin Random House LLC.

Library of Congress Cataloging-in-Publication Data
Higgs, Liz Curtis.
  The girl's still got it : take a walk with Ruth and the God who rocked her world / Liz Curtis Higgs. — 1st ed.
    p. cm.
  Includes bibliographical references (p.   ).
  ISBN 978-1-57856-448-4 (alk. paper) — ISBN 978-0-307-72955-2
  1. Bible. O.T. Ruth—Criticism, interpretation, etc. I. Title.
  BS1315.52.H54 2012
  222'.3506—dc23
                    2012006654

Printed in the United States of America

20 19 18 17 16

SPECIAL SALES
Most WaterBrook books are available at special quantity discounts when purchased in bulk by corporations, organizations, and special-interest groups. Custom imprinting or excerpting can also be done to fit special needs. For information, please e-mail specialmarketscms@penguinrandomhouse.com or call 1-800-603-7051.

For my mother-in-law,
Mary Lee Higgs,
with heaps of love
and my deepest gratitude

CONTENTS

"In the days
when the judges ruled..."

RUTH 1:1

Great Sea

Jordan River

AMMON

Jericho ●   Plains of
              Moab

Jerusalem ●

Bethlehem ●   ▲ Mount Nebo

Wilderness of Judea

Hebron ●   Salt
                Sea

                        Arnon River

JUDAH

                        M O A B

N E G E V   Zoar ●

             Zered Brook

Which Girl's Still Got It?

Ruth & Naomi

R uth's definitely got it. Yes, *that* Ruth. The one in the Bible. And her mother-in-law, Naomi? She's still got it too. So do you, beloved.

What do I mean by "it"? Value. Significance. Vibrancy. Worth. Something vital and meaningful to offer, no matter how many times you've been around the block.

Look at Ruth. Even thirty-two centuries later, her shining example of bold-ness and faithfulness still blows us away. Why don't we take a walk in her san-dals and see where the Lord might lead us and how he might use us?

Resist the urge to say you're too old, too young, too busy, too scared, too worn out, too washed up, too *anything* to be useful to God. Truth is, you've always been part of his love-the-world plan. Need proof? From the day he formed you in your mother's womb, God has watched over your every step, making sure you got where you needed to go.

When you stumbled, it was God who steadied you.

When you fell, it was God who rescued you.

When you lost your way, it was God who carried you home.

Why? Because he knows you fully, loves you completely, and holds you close to his heart. God will never give up on you, my sister. You claim a special place in his Big Picture.

As the book of Proverbs says, "You can make many plans, but the LORD's purpose will prevail."[1] Count on it. As surely as we know how the book of Ruth ends—happily—God knows how your story is going to unfold.

We don't use the phrase *divine providence* much anymore, but here's what it means: "God is there, God cares, God rules, and God provides."[2] How comforting to know that we're never alone and never unloved, that Someone powerful is in charge and looking out for us. The book of Ruth is a crash course in Sovereignty 101, with God whispering all through it, "Trust me!"

Okay, but *trust* is an easy word to say and a hard thing to do. It took a decade of Bad Girl foolishness before I understood how good and trustworthy God is. The refrain of one classic hymn never fails to bring a lump to my throat (not good when you're trying to sing):

> Jesus, Jesus, how I trust Him!
> How I've proved Him o'er and o'er!
> Jesus, Jesus, precious Jesus!
> O for grace to trust Him more![3]

Yeah, that last bit. Gets me every time.

From childhood Naomi learned to trust the Sovereign God of Israel. Ruth discovered his faithfulness a bit further down the road. Some of us are only now realizing what it means to live in the circle of God's embrace and at the absolute center of his will.

I'm still getting my head around it. Maybe you are too.

Suppose we hang out with these ancient sisters for a season and see what they can teach us about God's steadfast love. First, we need to figure out how to transport Naomi and Ruth into the present. Or project ourselves into the distant past.

Hmm...

TIME TRAVEL WITHOUT THE DELOREAN

If only we could jump into a time machine! Instead of simply reading about biblical history, we could live it. Rather than merely studying maps and books, we could see, touch, and experience that long-lost world firsthand. Wouldn't that be something?

H. G. Wells created a device for his Time Traveller out of nickel, ivory, and quartz. Doc Brown sent Marty McFly back to 1955 in a plutonium-powered DeLorean. I'm thinking we'll employ something God designed—our imaginations—and toss in a healthy measure of old-fashioned research. (No worries. That's my gig.)

Page by page I want us to *go* there—to Moab, to Bethlehem, to the days of Naomi, Ruth, and Boaz. We'll tarry in the corners of their homes and listen to their conversations and consider every word of every verse until we can say, "I *totally* get the book of Ruth. And I see what God is trying to teach me through this rags-to-riches redemption story—he has a plan for my life."

Girl, does he ever!

Before we step back in time, here are three things you're going to love about the book of Ruth.

First, it's a guaranteed great read.

A combo of "literary art and theological insight,"[4] these four chapters in Scripture have "enchanted every age,"[5] including our own. I've pored over Ruth's story in fourteen translations and a hundred books and commentaries, and I still get tears in my eyes when the women of Bethlehem sing out, "Praise be to the LORD, who this day has not left you without a kinsman-redeemer."[6] Yes, yes, yes!

Plus, the book of Ruth has all the stuff English majors swoon over: fascinating parallels, flashbacks, and clever repetition. Watch for all the uses of *return* (*shubh* in Hebrew) and *favor* (*hesed*). Very cool. Scottish theologian Sinclair Ferguson said, "Like the stories we loved to hear again and again in childhood, the pleasure of this one lies partly in spotting the clues."[7] We'll be regular Nancy Drews before we're done.

It's also a deliciously chatty story. In the New International Version nearly *sixty* of the eighty-five verses include dialogue. Lots of "she said, he said."

Love it.

Second, wait until you find out how this true story began.

Though Jewish tradition gives Samuel props for writing the book of Ruth,[8] most modern scholars don't agree. It's a timing problem, since the book ends with David's name. Everyone reading it three millenniums ago would have smiled and nodded, recognizing the famous ruler. Yet Samuel died before David became king around 1010 BC, meaning Samuel's authorship is improbable.[9]

Instead, the book of Ruth was likely composed around 1000 BC,[10] a century or two after the actual events. Could be it was written even more recently than that, anywhere from 1000 to 500 BC,[11] depending on who's doing the research.

Guess who preserved the account of Naomi, Ruth, and Boaz until it was finally recorded? Storytellers.

Accomplished troupes knew all the favorite songs and familiar legends and shared them at public gatherings and festivals.[12] Since the book of Ruth began in poetic, oral form and circulated that way for ages,[13] these storytellers of old kept Ruth's history alive by carefully memorizing every word, then recounting the much-loved tale wherever people hung out, especially around the spring or at the town gate.[14]

Don't panic! This is still God's Word, a work of the Holy Spirit. Through the centuries the Lord used ordinary people to bind his truth onto stone, clay, papyrus, leather, parchment, copper, potsherds, and silver.[15] Yet many of the ancient texts, those God-breathed words, were spoken long before they were written.

Ruth's story is so skillfully arranged, so beautifully narrated, we can easily imagine a gifted storyteller standing before an audience, commanding everyone's undivided attention from the opening words: "And it came to pass in the days of the judges…"

That third thing you'll love?

The book of Ruth is all about our biblical sisters. They don't simply make an appearance or hover in the background; it's a women's story through and through. Some commentators go a step further, believing the Naomi-Ruth saga was "passed on by a guild of women storytellers."[16] Other scholars suggest "the writer was a woman."[17]

Oh my. Not only *spoken* by women but also *written* by a woman?

Well, we know songs written by women are included in Scripture. Miriam exhorted the assembled, "Sing to the LORD, for he is highly exalted."[18] Deborah declared in her own voice and words, "Wake up, wake up, break out in song!"[19] And Mary sang with all her heart, "My soul glorifies the Lord."[20]

If God placed those lyrics in the hearts and mouths of our sisters and saved them for eternity in his Word, might he also have entrusted a woman writer to faithfully preserve the story of Ruth?

Not trying to convince you, dear one. Just tossing it out there.

After three thousand years we can't be certain "whether the real author was male or female."[21] But we can be sure of Jesus, "the author and perfecter of our faith,"[22] who has written his name across our hearts and whose eternal Word is true.

THIS ONE'S FOR THE GIRLS

We can also be certain of this: women matter a great deal to God. No book of the Bible demonstrates that more powerfully than Ruth.

Here are seven you-go-girl truths that jumped out at me as I read her story.

Two women command the leading roles.

You won't find another book like it in Scripture. Brief scenes featuring only women are rare; Mary's visit to Elizabeth in Luke 1 comes to mind. But a story that has two female leads plus a whole chorus of sopranos and altos? Remarkable to find a book of the Bible so "unusually woman-centered both in language and in plot."[23] Not only that, they're strong, intelligent women who, as they say in Hollywood, can carry a film.

Naomi and Ruth are complex and distinctive, not stereotypes.

They represent two nationalities, two religions at first, two generations, and two very different personalities. No need to ask who's speaking when you read their words. The Bible is filled with Good Girls and Bad Girls, often contrasted with each other. In Proverbs we find archetypes of the wise woman and the foolish woman,[24] the kindhearted woman and the immoral woman.[25] But in Naomi and Ruth we see *real* women, even flawed women, who change and grow throughout their journey.

The story is told from a female viewpoint.

I wouldn't dare call Scripture chick lit, but the book of Ruth "seems to reflect a female perspective."[26] A male commentator wrote those words, and he's absolutely right: we see all the early scenes through the eyes of Naomi and Ruth. Even when Boaz appears, his dialogue is solely about helping these two women. (Like something straight from the Lifetime channel, you know?)

Naomi and Ruth are cooperative instead of competitive.

When Sarai and Hagar take the biblical stage together in Genesis 16, it is *not* pretty. Same thing with Rachel and Leah in Genesis 30, and Hannah and Peninnah in 1 Samuel 1. Regular catfights, all. Yet in the book of Ruth, we find a young woman and her mother-in-law walking in the same direction (imagine that!) and seeking the same goals: putting food on the table and keeping the family name alive. Ruth looks out for Naomi from the start. Later Naomi looks out for Ruth. Go, team!

These women make things happen rather than wait for things to happen.

Instead of playing the passive-aggressive card, Naomi and Ruth are in the game. They talk and act independently of men and do what needs to be done. Often in biblical narrative things happen *to* women—sad things, even horrible things. Yet these two take their future into their own hands. You'll soon find "it is female assertiveness which drives the story's action."[27] When tragedy strikes their household, Naomi and Ruth don't sit moping in Moab, hoping someone will rescue them. They go, they do, they seek, they find—with God leading the way.

The women are strong, and the men are mostly...um, weak.

Just sayin'. Even when Naomi and Ruth burst into tears, "neither woman strikes the reader as weak, helpless, or lost."[28] In contrast, the men die, are unnamed, or shirk their responsibilities. Spiritually, emotionally, and physically, the men in this story (other than Boaz, of course) pale in comparison to our stalwart sisters.

Females are continually discussed, acknowledged, and praised—by name.

The number of nameless women in Scripture is legion. The woman at the well,[29] the bleeding woman,[30] the slave girl who predicts the future[31]—the list goes on and on. Yet our female leads in Ruth are all named. Additional name-dropping takes place near the end of the narrative when Tamar, Rachel, and Leah are spoken of in glowing terms—and by the *men* of Bethlehem, no less. These men saw with their own eyes that the Israelite faith was "cherished, defended, and exemplified by women."[32]

Suffice it to say, Naomi and Ruth were important to God's people. And God meant the world to Naomi and Ruth. They turned to him for provision, honored him through their obedience, and blessed him with their words.

OUR FIRST, OUR LAST, OUR EVERYTHING

Why study the girls (and guys) of the Bible? Because they help us understand God's character. Through the fickleness of his people, he reveals his unchanging nature. Through their neediness, he demonstrates his compassion. Through their rash behavior, he exhibits his patience. Through their sinful choices, he shows us what mercy looks like. Through their bitter complaints, he proves his capacity to love the unlovable. Through their disloyalty, his faithfulness shines.

However fitting it may be that this book of the Bible has Ruth's name on it, make no mistake: this is the Lord's story, and he alone claims center stage. As one commentator wrote, "It is God's actions we are to learn about, not a series of admirable human qualities."[33] Exactly so. Our desire as believers isn't to be more like Ruth; it's to be more like Jesus. With each admirable thing Ruth does, we'll see the Lord's hand at work.

God doesn't have a speaking role or make a physical appearance in the book of Ruth, but we'll sense his constant presence, steady as a heartbeat. When we reach the final page, I hope that instead of saying, "Wow, what a woman!" we'll be saying, "Wow, what a Redeemer!"

One more thing, sis. Take a minute to check out the resources in the back of this book in case you'd like to use them while you read: a short list of

Discussion Questions for book clubs; a longer Study Guide for more in-depth, chapter-by-chapter Bible study; and a recommended reading list for those of us who like to dig even deeper.

Now then, I promised you a journey in a time machine. With hearts engaged and Bibles in hand, let's travel back to 1200 BC, give or take a few decades, and meet King David's great-grandmother as a young woman in her midtwenties.[34]

Wait. Is that Ruth wearing an ugly black thingy?

Oh dear. I hadn't expected to find her like *this*.

One

Off to a Rocky Start

*T*he girl doesn't need a big *R* embroidered on her tunic to give her away. See that graceful posture? And that tender expression on her face? Gotta be our Ruth.

Looks as if we've come at a bad time, though.

Beneath the blazing desert sun, large stones mark the outlines of two fresh graves, with earthen mounds covering the bodies. Two husbands, buried on the day of their passing—a must in a country this hot.[1]

Just as well no one can see or hear us. I never know what to say at funerals, and all my words of comfort sound like clichés. So we stand with our backs pressed against the rough trunk of a date palm tree and watch two young widows and their grieving mother-in-law face the darkest day of their lives.

All three women are wearing coarse sackcloth, woven from goat's hair and dyed black.[2] Makes me itch just looking at them. But then, this day isn't about comfort or fashion. Sackcloth is worn as a sign of repentance or mourning.[3]

Father God, are they aware of your presence? Are they even now whispering your name?

If you've buried the love of your life, you understand at a deeply personal level what Ruth is going through: the numbness, the heartache, the emptiness.

She stands a few steps back lest her tunic brush against her husband's burial mound and leave her ceremonially unclean,[4] at least in her mother-in-law's eyes. A major nuisance, that Mosaic Law: "anyone who touches a human bone or a grave...will be unclean for seven days."[5] *Seven days?* It's amazing people attended funerals in Israel with that risk hanging over their heads.

Ruth's sister-in-law, Orpah, is wailing, tears coursing down her cheeks. Behind them stands Naomi, resting her hands on their shoulders. Offering solace, perhaps. Or leaning on them for support.

Easy enough to figure out how Orpah and Ruth got here: this is their hometown. But how did Naomi, a daughter of Israel, end up in a graveyard on the outskirts of a nameless settlement in Moab, where the people worship the evil god Chemosh? The answer is what screenwriters call the *back story*, the details from a character's past that shape her present and hint at her future.

As it happens, the book of Ruth opens with Naomi's back story, squeezing ten years into five short verses. While our sisters tarry in the hot sun, paying their respects, we'll get the goods on this midlife matriarch. More than one writer thinks the book of Ruth should be called "The Book of Naomi."[6] Let's see why.

ACT ONE, SCENE ONE

In the days... *Ruth 1:1*

Well, that's an exciting start. No, really. Back then these few words told the listeners that trouble was on the horizon, with a happy ending sure to follow.[7] The best kind of story. Whether rendered "now it came to pass" (KJV) or "long ago" (NCV) or "once upon a time" (MSG), this simple Hebrew phrase signaled the audience: you are going to love this!

...when the judges ruled,... *Ruth 1:1*

That's our time frame, somewhere between 1220 and 1050 BC,[8] during the Iron Age (not to be confused with an indie rock band from Austin, a tattoo parlor in Saint Louis, or steel-toed boots—but who's Googling?). Though we can't be certain, the story of Ruth probably falls chronologically between Ehud and Jephthah,[9] two of the many guys mentioned in Judges.

The final verse of Judges sums things up: "In those days Israel had no king; everyone did as he saw fit."[10] Uh-oh. When people do their own thing, it's seldom a good thing and almost never a God thing. Like rebellious children, the people of Israel "refused to give up their evil practices and stubborn ways."[11]

Those were seriously chaotic years, "a bleak, dark time of disobedience on the part of God's people."[12]

Then, like an oasis in the desert, Naomi and Ruth's story appears as a welcome relief from all the warfare and savagery. We'll find no signs or wonders, no parting seas or burning bushes, no dens of lions or fiery furnaces. The only miracles in the book of Ruth are changed lives.

Best. Miracles. Ever.

Of course, it wouldn't be much of a story if everything went smoothly. Instead, Naomi and her family face one disaster after another, beginning with a scenario that would surely strike fear in my heart.

> …there was a famine in the land,… *Ruth 1:1*

Not just a few days without food. Israel was utterly ravaged, and the people were starving—Naomi and her family included.

Various troubles can bring crops to a halt. Too little rain in the growing season, too much rain in the harvest season, and hungry locusts and caterpillars in any season. However, this famine was no "accident of history but the outworking of God's covenant promise"[13] made generations earlier to Abraham.

By the time of our story, Abe's descendants are playing fast and loose with God's favor. A constant refrain echoes through the book of Judges, which spans more than three hundred years: "the Israelites did evil in the eyes of the LORD."[14] I mean, those exact words appear *six times*. How stubborn can people be?

Sorry, Lord. I know the answer to that one all too well.

God takes no pleasure in our suffering. But he takes even less pleasure in our unfaithfulness. When the Israelites of old "forsook the LORD, the God of their fathers," worshiping instead the gods of their Canaanite neighbors, they "provoked the LORD to anger."[15]

How deeply did his anger burn? Hot enough to singe the ground.

The last biblical famine had occurred during Joseph's time, and God had put that one in motion too: "He called down famine on the land and destroyed all their supplies of food."[16]

That sovereignty thing in action? Right. God really is in charge, and he really does know what he's doing. The famine in Egypt made a way forward for

Joseph "till the word of the LORD proved him true."[17] And that same famine, terrible as it was, brought Joseph's brothers to his door for a God-ordained reunion.

Whenever heartache, loss, disappointment, stress, or any of the other stuff we hate comes our way, it helps to remember that hard times are purposeful, meant to refine and redirect us. They're not arbitrary or random, and they're definitely not cruel. If I'm going to suffer, at least let it be for a good reason. Make that a God reason.

If we start thinking, *A loving God wouldn't do that,* we miss the truth recorded in his Word and the seeds of hope planted deep in our parched soil: God loves us too much to let us starve spiritually.

That's why this famine struck Israel.

Unfortunately, Naomi wasn't humbled yet. Merely hungry, like her husband.

MAN, OH MAN

...and a man from Bethlehem in Judah,... *Ruth 1:1*

No name is given here, just "a certain man" (KJV) from Bethlehem. Find Jerusalem on the map, then head south five or six miles along the eastern ridge of the central mountain range, and there it is: O little town of Bethlehem. Before the famine this man and his family would've gazed across richly cultivated expanses beyond the town gate: fields of wheat and barley, groves of olive trees, and vines laden with grapes. Bethlehem was the "granary of the country."[18] Even the word *Bethlehem* in Hebrew means "house of bread" or "house of food."[19]

But those days were over.

...together with his wife and two sons,... *Ruth 1:1*

One husband, one wife, two sons. They sound like the Cleavers on *Leave It to Beaver,* the perfect suburban family. Still no names given for our Bethlehem bunch. Not Ward, not June, not Wally.

And that place they called home, that "good and spacious land, a land flow-ing with milk and honey"?[20] With the cows dying and the bees no longer buzzing, Bethlehem had lost its curb appeal. We can almost see this husband and father longing to feed his family, eying the land east of Bethlehem, wondering if the grass might indeed be greener on the other side of the Jordan River.

>...went to live for a while... *Ruth 1:1*

Kinda vague. How long did they plan to stay? Did they take a moving van—well, caravan—with all their household goods? Or did they tie spare tunics around their waists and hit the road? This much is clear: they got outta Dodge.

People today regularly move from place to place. Except for the hassle and expense, relocating is a perfectly fine thing to do. But for an Israelite family to abandon their clan and leave the land of God's blessing and provision was a grave sin.[21] A holy no-no. They weren't just turning their backs on Bethlehem and its people; they were turning their backs on God. As Warren Wiersbe, a seasoned Bible teacher, put it, this man from Bethlehem "walked by sight and not by faith,"[22] dragging his family down with him.

If their departure from Judah was the first shoe, dropping with a heavy thud, their unseemly destination was the other shoe.

>...in the country of Moab. *Ruth 1:1*

Remember our storyteller holding the audience spellbound? The crowd just let out a collective gasp: "Not *Moab*!"

Yup, Moab. The last place—I mean the *very* last place—this family from Judah should've headed. The porous soil of Moab might have been good for growing things, and the moist winds from the Mediterranean may have watered the fields and pastures, but Moab was still off-limits for Israelites. Strangers in a strange land, they couldn't even buy property there.[23] They could only find lodging. And food.

The apostle Paul's words, written centuries later, suit this foolish family to a T: "their god is their stomach."[24] Couldn't they trust the God of Israel to provide their next meal? Not this gang. Too hungry for that.

If only we could've stolen their passports, made sure they set off the metal detectors while going through security, or had a TSA agent pull them aside for a pat-down—anything to stop these travelers from crossing the border.

But their stomachs were growling at the thought of all that yummy food. Can I just say, I get this? *Groan.*

WHERE'S MAPQUEST WHEN WE NEED IT?

Once the foursome left Bethlehem, we have no record of exactly where in Moab they landed or what route they took to get there. Ancient Moab wasn't very big—roughly twenty-five miles across and thirty-five *or* sixty miles north to south,[25] depending on what year it was and how well the Moabites succeeded in battling their northern neighbors. Check out our map in the front of the book to chart the route this hungry family might have traveled.

The area that Scripture calls "the plains of Moab by the Jordan across from Jericho"[26] is open and rolling, irrigated by streams winding through the shallow valleys.[27] Archaeologists have identified several dozen small settlements in Moab.[28] This family of four might have plunked down their luggage anywhere.

There *is* something significant about not knowing where they settled. It wasn't home, was never meant to be home. The precise location doesn't matter, then or now.

They "went to sojourn in the country of Moab" (KJV). 'Nuff said.

WHAT'S SO BAD ABOUT MOAB?

In the story of the prodigal son, the young man "set off for a distant country."[29] That description fits Moab too: unfamiliar, foreign, dangerous, and a long way from home. A place to be avoided, especially by Israelites.

In later years the prophet Jeremiah would speak of Moab's "overweening pride and conceit, her pride and arrogance and the haughtiness of her heart."[30] Even worse, Moab trusted in its "deeds and riches"[31] and "defied the LORD."[32]

What was this religious Israelite family thinking, moving to such a place?

They were thinking about olive oil, grapes, pomegranates, figs, and amber honey. About wine, lamb, roasted grain, and raisins. About bread, warm from a clay oven. About water, fresh from the streams that flowed from Moab's eastern hills.

They weren't thinking about the people, the Moabites.

But they should've been. Here's why.

Moab was born of (shhh) incest.

Jesus once cautioned his disciples, "Remember Lot's wife!"[33] Who could forget a woman who turned away from her family—and from God—only to become a pillar of salt?[34] She was a Bad Girl of the Bible, all right, and her two daughters were worse.

When Lot fled from Zoar with his girls and settled in a mountain cave, the older daughter suggested to the younger, "Let's get our father to drink wine and then lie with him and preserve our family line through our father."[35] A really, *really* Bad Girl.

Some nine months later, when the older daughter gave birth to her father's son—yes, her own brother—"she named him Moab; he is the father of the Moabites of today."[36]

Moab had a reputation for promiscuity.

The women (how I hate to say this!) were one of the main reasons for the country's bad rep. Despite God's warnings not to fraternize with pagans, the men of Israel "began to indulge in sexual immorality with Moabite women, who invited them to the sacrifices to their gods."[37] Bet you can guess God's response to the men's apostasy. "And the LORD's anger burned against them."[38]

Moab couldn't even spell *Welcome Wagon*.

When the Israelites passed by Moab during their exodus from Egypt, the Moabites refused to feed them. So Moses came down hard on them, saying, "No Ammonite or Moabite or any of his descendants may enter the assembly of the LORD, even down to the tenth generation. For they did not come to meet you with bread and water on your way."[39]

Yet where did this Israelite family go looking for bread and water?

Moab. Go figure.

Moab honored every god but the one true God.

The Moabites worshiped a whole bunch of gods "alongside their principal god, Chemosh."[40] Ugh. That "vile god of Moab,"[41] to whom they made human sacrifices.[42] No wonder God didn't want his chosen people mixing it up with Moabites.

Why dwell on the evils that awaited our sojourners in Moab?

Because *Ruth was a Moabitess.* A pagan, an idol worshiper, a woman whose family roots were twisted with incest, "a member of a cursed race."[43] She was hardly the sort of woman Israelite parents would want their sons to marry.

Even so, our God—our utterly amazing, truly forgiving God—chose Ruth as the great-grandmother of King David, firmly placing her in the lineage of Christ. Just as God chose flawed and fallible us to be his children, his heirs.[44]

Think of it! Such love, such grace, such mercy…

Oh bother. Now my eyes are watering. And I'm getting ahead of myself.

First, we need to wind up our back story so we can rejoin Ruth and company in the graveyard. They're still weeping, yes? Poor dears. Why do I never remember tissues?

Meet the Family

> The man's name was Elimelech, his wife's name Naomi,…
> *Ruth 1:2*

Finally we learn their names. The storyteller grabbed our attention with their plight—the famine, the hunger, the flight to Moab—before revealing their identities. We've already marked them as people whose faith in God was flagging. Now we'll see who they really were, since in the ancient Near East, a person's name often described his or her character.[45]

Elimelech means "my God is king."[46] Clearly his parents expected great things from their boy. When Elimelech married and fathered two sons, he did his folks proud. When he turned his back on Israel, Elimelech's name didn't change, but apparently his allegiance did.

His wife, Naomi, was also given a promising name. Depending on whom you ask, *Naomi* means "pleasant,"[47] "my delight,"[48] "lovely,"[49] "my joy,"[50] or "sweetness."[51] A tasty name. Scrumpdiddlyumptious.

Tough to live up to, though. If your name is Joy, you know what I'm talking about.

I wonder how *pleasant* Naomi was about leaving Bethlehem. How much *delight* she felt, bidding her friends farewell. How *sweetly* she regarded her husband when they passed through the town gate, bound for Moab.

Stay in Bethlehem? Risk starving their bodies.

Move to Moab? Risk starving their faith.

Given that choice, many of us would put bodily comfort above spiritual commitment. At least that's how it looks at my house. I might miss church now and again, but I never miss Sunday dinner.

How does the Lord put up with us? Same way he put up with Naomi, helping her discover, through various trials and errors, the difference between giving lip service to religion and embracing God with her whole heart.

That's one reason we're taking this journey; we need to learn the difference too. In a culture where it's easy to play at church and hard to stem the tide of secularism, we could use a fresh reminder of how much God loves his followers and how far he's willing to go to redeem us.

Now that we've met mom and dad, it's time to check out the kids.

> …and the names of his two sons were Mahlon and Kilion.
> *Ruth 1:2*

Israelite parents often named their children based on what was happening around the delivery or what sort of future they imagined for them.[52] Either Naomi struggled in childbirth, or her newborn sons were punier than average, because their names were not very encouraging.

Mahlon means "weakling,"[53] "mild,"[54] or "sickness" or "infertility."[55] His brother, Kilion—sometimes spelled *Chilion* (AMP)—was in equally bad shape. Mom and dad called him "pining,"[56] "consumptive,"[57] "sickly,"[58] "perishing,"[59] or "comes to an early end."[60]

Pitiful. Just pitiful.

I'd be chasing down one of those judges and demanding a name change. But I doubt *chasing* was part of the lads' vocabulary. Nor was running, jumping, swimming, or diving. Mahlon and Kilion were not "strong male figures who could take over their father's role."[61] Instead, they were weakness personified. When I teach the book of Ruth, I call 'em Wimpy and Frumpy.

Maybe they really needed that food in Moab. Some multivitamins might've helped too.

> They were Ephrathites from Bethlehem, Judah. *Ruth 1:2*

Those Ephrathites were likely an aristocratic clan[62] with high social standing.[63] A family of means, then. Three generations later God's Word states, "David was the son of an Ephrathite named Jesse."[64] Same clan, same place.

But we're a long way from that cheery finale.

> And they went to Moab and lived there. *Ruth 1:2*

That's not an echo. That's our storyteller driving home a point. *They went to Moab.*

For vacay? No way.

This family "settled" (NCV) in a land where they had no business being. The language and culture of Moab and Israel were similar,[65] but Moab was no place like home. As veteran radio pastor J. Vernon McGee phrased it, "When you get away from God, that's when trouble comes."[66] Preach it, brother.

T-R-O-U-B-L-E

> Now Elimelech, Naomi's husband, died, and she was left
> with her two sons. *Ruth 1:3*

I doubt Naomi saw this coming, unless—like father, like sons—her husband was sickly as well.

The Bible gives us zero description of their time in Moab and no clue how long they lived there before death came knocking. We know only this: the patriarch of the family never returned home to Judah.

What happened to the guy? Was it old age? Some nasty plague or foreign disease for which he had no immunity? Or did dwelling where he didn't belong weaken Elimelech's heart?

The rabbis of old saw his death as divine punishment. But however ill-advised Elimelech's departure from Judah was, the book of Ruth doesn't point out any specific wrongdoing worthy of death. Nor did Jesus use the man's demise as a cautionary tale, as he did with Lot's wife: "Remember Naomi's husband!"

We're left with what's recorded in Scripture: Elimelech died. Period.

A surprise to Naomi maybe but not to God. He knew what would happen in Moab, just as he knows the first and last days for each of us: "All the days ordained for me were written in your book before one of them came to be."[67] I don't want to know precisely when I'll step from this world into the next. But I'm relieved God knows and ordained it so.

Our story has just taken a dramatic shift. In a single verse Naomi became the head of her household. Elimelech is now described as *her* spouse, and Mahlon and Kilion are *her* sons. Even though they were old enough to marry, their care and provision fell on Naomi's grief-bent shoulders.

I wonder why Naomi didn't go back home to Bethlehem? Maybe the famine hadn't lifted in Judah. Maybe she'd grown comfortable in Moab. Maybe the thought of making that long journey without her husband was more than she could bear.

Or maybe her sons had found a reason to stay put. Actually, two reasons.

They married Moabite women,... *Ruth 1:4*

Man, that was fast. The storyteller hardly let us catch our breath, let alone mourn Elimelech, before these young men claimed Moabite wives. No word of their courtship, no description of their wives' appearance or personalities or social standing. Not even a statement of who married whom.

Since fathers were usually the ones who arranged marriages for their sons and paid a bride price, or *mohar,* to the father-in-law,[68] good old mom must have handled the negotiations and coughed up the cash.

But why would Naomi yoke her Hebrew sons to pagan wives?

Could be she wanted two extra pairs of hands to care for Wimpy and Frumpy. Or more help around the house. Or the comfort of female companionship. Or real estate, if the brides' dowries included land the family could farm.[69]

But what Naomi *definitely* wanted was grandsons to carry on Elimelech's name and to provide for her someday. That meant wives for her sickly sons. Any wives. Even Moabite wives.

Come meet the women wedded to Mahlon and Kilion.

NAME THAT BRIDE

…one named Orpah and the other Ruth. Ruth 1:4

Orpah is mentioned first, probably because she was older. Or because our storyteller wanted to save the best for last, since Orpah has little to recommend her. One scholar translated Orpah's name as "disloyal."[70] Traditionally, her name has been translated as "obstinacy" or "the Stiff-Necked One," but the true meaning remains a mystery. At least if Orpah were stiff necked, she couldn't follow the example of Lot's wife and look back!

Then there's Ruth, whose name has several possible meanings, all of them positive: "lady friend,"[71] "faithful friend,"[72] "to drink one's fill,"[73] or "the act of seeing" or "sight."[74]

Whatever her name means, you won't find another Ruth in the Bible.

TRAGEDY, PART 2

After they had lived there about ten years,… Ruth 1:4

We're talking a rough estimate here, not ten calendar years to the day. A long time, in other words. Long enough that Naomi may have forgotten all about going home to Judah.

Scholars can't agree if the ten-year clock started ticking when the family arrived in Moabtown or when the sons married. We'll let the PhDs hash out that one. I want to know what these people were doing for a decade. Not a single hour is described. Were their lives that boring?

Meanwhile, a different sort of famine visited the family. The sons of Elimelech married, but no children came. "Instead of empty stomachs, there are empty wombs."[75]

From Naomi's viewpoint that was what mattered. Not the number of years, but the number of grandsons. In those days men were never at fault for failing to produce children; it was the women who were assumed to be infertile.[76] Did Naomi blame her daughters-in-law? Or blame herself for choosing these Moabite women for her sons?

Hearing the phrase "ten years" would've made our ancient Hebrew audience nervous, remembering barren Sarai a few centuries earlier and how she solved *her* infertility problem: "after Abram had been living in Canaan ten years, Sarai his wife took her Egyptian maidservant Hagar and gave her to her husband."[77]

Rachel did the very same thing,[78] and so did Leah,[79] with no mention of waiting anything like ten years. That's how desperate women were in this ancient culture that measured a woman's worth by her ability to produce sons.

For the record, Naomi's daughters-in-law aren't called "barren" in Scripture. Instead, Naomi's sons are the ones named "infertility" and "sickly." It seems they couldn't produce life, nor could they hang on to it.

…both Mahlon and Kilion also died,… *Ruth 1:5*

We know. We're looking at their graves right now.

With Naomi's back story all told, we've returned to the scene at hand, eying this heartbroken mother who just buried her only children.

Oh, Naomi.

Like their father, her sons have simply expired. No cause of death is given. The Amplified Bible emphasizes they "died also, both of them," which sounds as though they died one right after the other or—perish the thought!—together.

Whether it's because her sons took Moabite brides, or because the young men were weakened by illness, or simply because their time on earth was finished, the fact is, they're gone. Since the Bible doesn't offer any explanation here, we'll resist the urge to fill in the blanks.

Naomi remains in Moab, suffering "a triple blow to the heart."[80]

> …and Naomi was left without her two sons and her husband.
> *Ruth 1:5*

Though some translations, like this one, include her name, the word "Naomi" doesn't appear in the Hebrew text. Just "the woman." No wonder. In her faintly lined features, devoid of expression, we can see Naomi has lost her identity. None of her names suits her any longer. Not "pleasant" or "sweetness" or "lovely" or "joy."

Her earthly roles are gone as well. She's no longer a wife, no longer a mother. A woman who has lost her husband is a widow. But "we have no word for a mother whose children die,"[81] just painful adjectives to describe her heart: crushed, broken, shattered.

During my rebellious teen years, I was so convinced my parents had grown weary of me that I once asked my father in a sharply defiant voice, "What if I die before you do?" With unaccustomed tenderness and a sheen in his eyes, he murmured, "That would be the worst day of my life."

I was shocked by his response. And deeply moved.

In typical teenage fashion I never let him see how his answer affected me. But his unexpected revelation took root in my heart: I would be missed, even mourned.

Now, as a mother of two grown children, I cannot imagine how Naomi felt when she became "the woman without."[82] Did she announce her sons' deaths to her neighbors by immediately beginning to wail, the usual practice?[83] You'd have heard my cries halfway to Egypt. Did she close her sons' eyes and give them each a parting kiss, as custom required?[84] I fear I might have begged the townsfolk to wrap my body in a linen cloth and bury me with my children.

All through history women have suffered as Naomi did. In the recent World War II movie *Defiance,* a Russian mother watches in horror as her husband and two sons are shot, one after the other. Devastated, she falls to her knees and pleads with their assassin, "Kill me too!"

We understand. How could any woman recover from such loss? How could she go on?

Yet women do survive. They do go on.

You may know such a woman and admire her strength. You may *be* such a woman who lifts her head each morning and says, "My flesh and my heart may fail, but God is the strength of my heart and my portion forever."[85]

When we bury loved ones, we remind ourselves that this life is not the end, that heaven is assured for those who love the Lord Jesus, and that "whoever believes in him shall not perish but have eternal life."[86]

But look at our grieving Naomi. She doesn't have the hope of John 3:16 to comfort her. She thinks this life is everything and beyond death is nothing but a shadowy nether world known as Sheol in Hebrew.[87] The ancient Israelites knew that God was eternal, but when family members died, they were believed to be gone forever since there was "no assurance of life after death in early Israelite history."[88] In the words of Job, "As a cloud vanishes and is gone, so he who goes down to the grave does not return."[89] If people expected to live beyond the grave, they had to do so through their sons, who carried on the family name.

A FINAL FAREWELL

Now we get why having sons was such a big deal and why our Old Testament sisters would do *anything* to help their husbands father a son: that was their definition of eternal life. To Naomi's way of thinking, she has lost *three* generations of men since she has no hope of grandsons.

Even from this distance we sense her agony as she holds a knife above her right breast, the sharp blade glistening in the sun. No, no, it's not what you think. She is rending her garment as a token of grief, an ancient custom. We can hear the fabric tearing. A handbreadth, no more.[90] Formal mourning will stretch on for seven days, with neighbors bringing food, then hanging around to eat the best dishes. Some things never change.

Sadly, we can watch our sister Naomi, but we can't console her. Looks like the other mourners aren't doing a very good job of it either.

The truth? Only God can help Naomi now. Perhaps no author has phrased it better than Frances Vander Velde: "God was loving Naomi all the while that He was leading her through the shadows."[91]

That's the lesson Naomi will soon learn and in which we can take solace. She is not alone, will never be alone. Her faith is battered but not abandoned. Her posture may sag, but she's still standing. Her future looks cloudy, yet God can sweep away those clouds with a brush of his hand.

The girl's still got it. Despite all appearances to the contrary, she still has God's steadfast love to cling to. And things will get better for Naomi.

Much-loved commentator Matthew Henry wrote, "When death comes into a family it ought to be improved."[92] I had to read that twice to grasp what he was saying. Since death changes a family, what if the family changed for the better? Not right away, of course, but eventually, when the pain recedes and hope lifts its head once more?

My mother's death from emphysema, late in my twenty-third year, was the beginning of my journey back to the family I'd all but ignored and the Savior I'd almost forgotten. For months following her funeral, I cried every time I got into the car, so deep was my grieving. In the depths of my sorrow, I started asking hard questions for which no answer could be found apart from a Sovereign God.

I ran from the truth, as rebels do, burrowing deeper into my Bad Girl pit, which merely magnified my sense of loss. When friends and lovers proved unfaithful, my family did not. They still embraced me, still loved me.

My cries for help were eventually heard by two new believers who'd just climbed out of their own dark pits and knew where to point my Bad Girl self: straight into our Savior's arms.

I'm not suggesting the Lord ended my mother's earthly life for my benefit. Not for a minute. I simply mean God used the sorrow in my life for his good purpose. And for mine.

He will do the same for our Naomi. She is no longer a wife, no longer a mother, but she's still God's precious daughter. And she's still a mother-in-law, a relationship that will define the rest of her life and rescue her from despair.

As for us, you'll be relieved to hear that the worst of the story is over. No more funerals. No more anguish. (Okay, there's some major whining ahead, but we can handle that.)

Time to brush the sand off our skirts and follow the shuffling crowd home.

Ruth = The Gentile - The Great Grandmother of David.
Israel under Judgement.

Ruth In Real Life: SHEILA

"In the beginning I did not feel accepted by my mother-in-law because I had a history, a past, of which she did not approve. The unfortunate day came when her daughter—my sister-in-law—grew very ill and passed away. Standing by my mother-in-law at the funeral home, I promised that, although I could not replace her child, I would always take care of her. Since then we've become more like a mother and daughter. I cannot imagine my life without my mother-in-law any more than I can imagine my life without my husband."

"Now it came to pass" - usually means trouble! Followed
          by Deliverence & Happy ending.

13 Famines   1. Cannan in Abrahams Day
              2. Cannan in Iasics Day 3.   Ruth
              3. Cannan in Jacobs Day   — Cannon during the Judges.
              4. Cannan in Davids Day
              5. Cannan in Elijahs Day
              6. Cannan in Elishas Day
              7. Samaria in Elishas Day
              8. Cannon in Elishas Day
              9. Jersalem in Zedekias Day
              10. Cannon in Nememiahs Day
              11. An unknown Land
              12 Roman Empire in Pauls Day

Ruths story was from
the early part of the
Judges.

Elimelech means "my God is King"
Orpah means "kind or fawn"
Ruth means "Beauty"

Note: Long Life was
promised if the
Law was obeyed

Two

Coming or Going?

A goatskin tent.

Somehow I hadn't imagined Naomi roughing it like this, even if her family did leave Bethlehem in a hurry. Had she known they'd spend a decade here, Naomi might have insisted on leasing a fixer-upper with solid walls. Fabric partitions offer some privacy, though not at the moment with so many neighbors milling about. The funeral was nearly a week ago, yet the grieving continues.

We've claimed two seats—small woven mats—near the open side of the tent, where we can catch a faint breeze. Several mourners stand in clumps, whispering, while others nibble on salty cheese shaped into small, hard cakes.

Most women are wearing some shade of blue with a row of embroidery outlining their modest V necks. It's easy to pick out the well-to-do Moabites, with their animal-skin sandals and their long hems sweeping against the rough woolen carpet. Garments are held in place with simple bronze pins—the latest Transjordan fashion. In contrast, the laborers are barefoot and wearing shorter robes, which are easily tucked into the girdles around their waists while they're working.[1]

Not far from us sit Naomi, Orpah, and Ruth, their heads bowed. People kneel to speak with the two younger women, all but ignoring Naomi. Losing a son is not unusual in this time and place. But two married sons without issue? Folk stare at our widowed sister as if *cursed* were written across her forehead.

One phrase travels around the tent like a swirl of sand: "Now what?"

Good question.

What would your next move be if you were living in a foreign country and had lost your husband and grown sons? Would you settle there permanently and honor their memories? Or return home to face a vacant house, an empty bank account, and neighbors who might keep their distance?

Even if I was wealthy and that foreign city was Paris, I'd have to go home. Want to go home. Need to go home.

It's clear Naomi's heart is already turning toward Bethlehem. Over the last few days, we've often caught her gazing westward across the Salt Sea, eying the Judean hills. During meals she has seemed distracted and disconnected from those around her. Her sleep has been restless, her nights short, her grief palpable.

All at once a servant darts into the tent and heads straight for Naomi, then whispers something in her ear. The news must be good. Naomi's expression has brightened, and she's reaching for her daughters-in-law, clearly eager to share what she's learned.

We lean forward in anticipation. Of all the words spilling from Naomi's lips, the one that stands out is *Yahweh*.

EARS TO HEAR

When she heard in Moab that the LORD... *Ruth 1:6*

Hit the Pause button, and let that sink in. If Naomi *heard*, then she must have been listening attentively, her ears still tuned to the Lord's voice even after ten long years away from the Promised Land. Her sons may have married Moabite girls, her neighbors may worship Chemosh, but Naomi's wounded heart still belongs to the Lord, who made very sure his daughter in distant Moab heard the good news: God is in the House of Bread!

> ...[he] had come to the aid of his people by providing food
> for them,... *Ruth 1:6*

God had not only "visited" (KJV); he'd also "come to help" (NCV) and had "blessed his people in Judah by giving them good crops again" (NLT). The shouts of joy in Bethlehem must have startled the birds from their nests. *Food!*

This is the first of two God incidents framing the story. He's always present and often discussed, but here he shows up in a tangible and life-altering way. After enduring years of barrenness across the land, the people of Judah are discovering plump grapes on the vines, clusters of olives nestled in the trees, and barley ripening in their fields. The famine has ended, "not by chance but by God's providential hand."[2]

Naomi's face is radiant as she shares the glad tidings with her daughters-in-law. When she says, "his people," we hear the conviction in her voice. *My people. My God.* Naomi is more than ready to reclaim both her national identity and her personal one.

Interesting that God sent news to Moab rather than sending grapes and olives. Like the prodigal son, Naomi must return home to be nourished. No small message there.

As for the Lord's feeding us, I'll try not to go overboard, but the parallels are…well, delicious.

When God brought his people out of Egypt, he "satisfied them with the bread of heaven."[3] Then God helped his people in Judah by "giving them bread."[4] Later Jesus would tell his followers, "I am the bread of life. He who comes to me will never go hungry."[5] Bread is a mainstay of the human diet, the staff of life, filled with the health-giving whole-grain nutrients our bodies need.

The lesson for Naomi and for us couldn't be clearer: we have no life apart from God. We can't even bake our own spiritual bread! It must come from God's hand—like his grace, like his Son, who said, "For the bread of God is he who comes down from heaven and gives life to the world."[6]

Naomi found food to eat in Moab, but the word *bread* is never used to describe it. Moab is malnutrition. Moab is lifelessness. Moab is death. Instinctively, Naomi knows she must quit this town before it kills her.

In the same way and for the same reason, you and I need to leave the Moabs of our own making.

You know what I'm talking about.

Whether it's a place we don't belong or a relationship going in the wrong direction or an activity we're ashamed of or a habit that's strangling us, we need to get out of Moab.

Never mind how we got here. The bus is leaving, sister. Grab your purse.

GO, NAOMI

> …Naomi and her daughters-in-law prepared to return home
> from there. *Ruth 1:6*

Love the word "prepared." Getting ready to get ready—that's how I roll.

I can't travel anywhere, not even for a weekend, without creating a packing list. My husband, Mr. Throw-Whatever-in-a-Suitcase, teases me, but we seldom get where we're going and say, "Oh no! We forgot _____."

The Bible doesn't give us any details, but you can bet these women will carefully prepare for their journey. Naomi is the expert; she's traveled this road before. Now that she "got herself together" (MSG), she's also getting her stuff together: her best tunic, an extra pair of sandals, and her woolen cloak, all tied up in a neat bundle. No point dragging household goods across the Jordan. Hard enough to ford the river without a cooking pot strapped to her back.

As Orpah and Ruth follow her example, we notice how quiet they are. But then, they aren't returning home, are they? Just the opposite. They're leaving their families, their friends, and their gods and moving to a foreign country.

Have Naomi's daughters-in-law ever ventured past Moab's border? Probably not. Men go abroad for warfare or trade, while women stay home and keep the oil lamps burning. That's what makes Naomi's plan so daring. Three women traveling without husbands or sons to protect them and without servants to attend them? Very risky.

Good thing the Lord is their trail guide.

A simple Hebrew word appears in this verse. And the next verse. And the one after that. Plus nine more places—all in the first chapter of Ruth. Depending on the translation, *shubh* (sounds like "shoove") is rendered in Ruth as "return," "turn again," "go on," "go back," "brought back," or "turn back." I'm all for variety in writing, but when this story was told orally, the same *shubh* spoken twelve times in quick succession would've had quite an impact.

Why? Because *shubh* is the main Old Testament word for "turning back to God's covenant grace and mercy—for repentance, for conversion."[7] An audience repeatedly hearing *shubh* would've gotten the message: go back, go back, go back to God.

I need that message every day, every hour, every minute. When my imagination travels down crooked paths or my less-than-lovely qualities raise their ugly heads, the Holy Spirit gently prods me, *Turn around, Liz.*

As for Naomi, she's turning her back on Moab and its false gods, "leaving behind her the graves of those she loved,"[8] and going home.

> With her two daughters-in-law she left the place where she had been living and set out on the road that would take them back to the land of Judah. *Ruth 1:7*

A light breeze lifts the veils from their foreheads as the three start westward on foot. Patches of wildflowers blanket the fields ahead. In a nearby orchard the fig trees are covered with pale leaves and tiny fruit.[9] Out of respect, Orpah and Ruth follow a step behind Naomi, their leather sandals the same color as the sandy ground beneath them.

I want them to have donkeys. Nice, docile ones with firm backs and steady gaits. But the Bible doesn't mention donkeys in this story. Or horses. Or camels. Or any other four-footed means of transportation. The author Edith Deen thinks they traveled "partly on foot, let us suppose, and partly on donkeys."[10] The word "suppose" gives me pause, especially when another source tells us they journeyed on foot.[11] In any case custom dictated that men rode and women walked.[12]

Guess we'll be walking, then.

If we mean to get out of Moab, we gotta do whatever it takes. Though obedience is seldom an easy road, it helps to know the One leading the way: "It is the LORD your God you must follow, and him you must revere. Keep his commands and obey him; serve him and hold fast to him."[13]

We've got it: follow, revere, obey, serve, and cling to God.

Desert dwellers often sojourn well into the night since it's cooler.[14] However unsafe that may feel to us twenty-first-century girls, we're setting out on an early spring evening before the first stars appear in the sky.

Neighbors are standing in the doorways of their houses, silent and wary, watching the women depart. The Moabite settlement Naomi has called home has no outer walls, no public buildings, and no fortifications. Only silos for storing grain and a series of low houses built around central courtyards.[15]

As we leave the town behind, the apostle Paul's road trips come to my mind: "I have been in danger from rivers, in danger from bandits, in danger from my own countrymen, in danger from Gentiles; in danger in the city, in danger in the country…"[16] *Eeek.* All we can do is put one foot in front of the other and pray as we head for the Jordan River, many miles in the distance.

When she last traversed this road, Naomi was at least a decade younger and had two sons and a hubby to handle her luggage. This time she has one small bundle tied securely across her shoulders and two daughters-in-law with the same. Fig cakes and dried meat will have to suffice for food, with fresh water from the stream we're following west.

In our first hour we pass a handful of other travelers, heads bent as they trudge by. All three women have remained dry eyed, although Naomi has a troubled look about her.

She slows her steps before coming to a full stop.

Then Naomi said to her two daughters-in-law,… *Ruth 1:8*

Hold it. We've spent only "a short while on the road" (MSG). What's the problem? And where exactly are we?

One scholar thinks Naomi paused before they descended into the Jordan Valley.[17] Another suggests they were about to ford the Arnon River.[18]

From where I'm standing, it appears we're in the middle of nowhere, the sun is sinking toward the horizon, and Naomi looks as if she's having second thoughts.

About Face

…"Go back, each of you, to your mother's home." *Ruth 1:8*

Her daughters-in-law are wide eyed, as are we. *Go back?*

This is *so* not right. Naomi made Orpah and Ruth gather their worldly goods, bid their friends and relatives farewell, and follow her down this lonely road. Now she's changed her mind? The woman must be menopausal.

If Naomi intended to travel alone, she could've said so before they started packing. Or waited until nightfall, then slipped between the tent flaps, leaving them behind. Anything is better than pulling a switcheroo like this one, tossing out that *shubh* word. "Go, return" (KJV). You heard her, girls. "Go back home" (NCV).

Either Naomi is cruel and manipulative, which we don't find elsewhere in this story, or she's having a hot flash and is too weepy to think straight. See that damp forehead? Those mottled red cheeks? Dead giveaway.

And what an emotional appeal she makes! "Don't you want to go back home to your own mothers?" (CEV). Though the phrase *father's house* is more common, *mother's house* "is natural in her mouth, and has more tenderness in it."[19] That tenderness is working. Orpah and Ruth look undone. Maybe they're remembering their equally menopausal mothers dabbing their eyes back in Moabtown.

What stopped Naomi in her tracks other than hormonal hysteria? I think that from the time they left home until they reached this stopping point, Naomi has been picturing the Bethlehem welcoming committee.

If she trudges into her hometown without husband or sons, she'll find total sympathy.

If she shows up with two Moabite daughters-in-law, she'll face certain hostility.

It's not that Naomi doesn't care for these girls. I believe she does. But not enough to weather the scorn of her former neighbors, especially when she'll need their help to start a new life.

Naomi tells her daughters-in-law none of this, of course. Here's what she offers them instead.

SHE SAID, *"HESED"*

> "May the LORD show kindness to you, as you have shown to your dead and to me." *Ruth 1:8*

Naomi may be urging them to go home, but at least she's determined to do the right thing. As the matriarch and spiritual head of this little household, she's speaking a blessing over them.

When I threw a bridal shower for Beth, the young woman who's now our daughter-in-law, I went overboard (as usual) with fancy cupcakes from the bakery and decorated trays piled with fruit and veggies. Our home was (almost) spotless, the October weather was gorgeous, and everything went like clockwork.

What does Beth remember most from that day? My simple blessing at the end.

With our eyes closed none of us could see the clean house or the snazzy refreshments. Instead, the Holy Spirit made himself at home in our family room. By the time I reached "amen," the bride-to-be had tears in her eyes. So did her mother. So did I.

It's heartening to think our words might matter to the next generation, just as Naomi's did to her daughters-in-law.

The literal translation of Naomi's blessing is "May Yahweh do with you *hesed.*"[20] A powerful word, it means "faithful goodness,"[21] "loyalty, reliability, kindness, compassion,"[22] and "lovingkindness."[23]

People can be reliable and kind, but *hesed* is really a God word. When he faithfully blesses those who've done nothing to deserve it, that's *hesed.* When he fulfills a promise that costs him dearly, that's *hesed.* When his Son hung on the cross for our sins, that was *hesed* in its fullest and deepest expression.

As for the kindness Naomi's daughters-in-law have shown to her dead sons, maybe the girls followed the burial rituals required by Israelite law: purifying the bodies with water, preparing them with oils, then wrapping them in linen shrouds.[24] If these young Moabite women willingly provided such services, Naomi is right to bless them.

By the look on her face, she's not done yet.

> "May the LORD grant that each of you will find rest in the home of another husband." *Ruth 1:9*

Looks like she's passing the baton. *Here, Lord. You take care of 'em.* Except Naomi is asking the God of Israel to bless her *pagan* daughters-in-law with new *pagan* husbands?!

Must be those raging hormones. Or a desperate cry for help.

After ten years in Moab, Naomi and her family have seen their resources dwindle to zip. She can't meet their daily needs, let alone provide dowries. And so she wishes her daughters-in-law "rest," meaning "security, love, comfort,"[25] in someone else's house. Naomi is setting them free, giving them permission to press on with their lives and marry again.

> Then she kissed them... *Ruth 1:9*

An I-love-you kiss? Not so much. More like a formal "gesture of farewell."[26] Her blessing, benediction, and bon voyage all rolled into one.

Here come the tears.

> ...and they wept aloud... *Ruth 1:9*

A really *loud* kind of "aloud." A full-blown, full-volume lament. No surprise. The girls have been on edge all day, with their lips pressed into thin lines and their eyes glassy. All they needed was a reason to weep, and Naomi has certainly given them one as they huddle beneath a darkening sky. Their men are gone forever. Now here's another final separation.

Does Naomi have tears in her eyes as well? I can't quite tell, though her chin is trembling. Maybe the girls leaked first. But who can remain unmoved, especially when this is how they respond?

> ...and said to her, "We will go back with you to your people."
> *Ruth 1:10*

Orpah and Ruth speak in unison as if they'd anticipated this turnaround and practiced their response beforehand. Do they really want to move to Judah? Maybe remaining loyal to their husbands is the way things work in their culture, and never mind "till death us do part."

Of course, the girls could be saying what they think their mother-in-law wants to hear. Believe me, I get this, both as a daughter-in-law and as a mother-in-law. "When Mama ain't happy, ain't nobody happy" isn't just a worn-out slogan from the nineties. It's a fact. Who hasn't told a woman wearing an apron,

"No, no, your Thanksgiving turkey was delicious this year," just to keep peace in the family?

Then, too, following Naomi may be more appealing than living with mom and dad again. I moved back home after my first year of college and lasted all of six months before I threw caution and my tiny savings to the wind and escaped to my own apartment. Even if you love your parents, once you've lived away from home, it's mighty hard to go back.

In ancient Israel a young widow returning home became either "an added burden to her family or a servant for her brothers' wives."[27] Both options sound awful. And who's to say their families will take them back? Having been married to Israelites, they may have few prospects for another husband. Better to travel west with their mother-in-law and cast their lot with her people.

Naomi Does a No-No

But Naomi said, "Return home, my daughters." *Ruth 1:11*

We hear a faint sharpness to her tone and our fifth *shubh* of the story. "Turn again" (KJV). "Go back" (MSG). I'm getting the idea Naomi really doesn't want the girls to join her. The jut of her chin is as pointed as her words.

> "Why would you come with me? Am I going to have any more sons, who could become your husbands?" *Ruth 1:11*

What do you sense in Naomi's voice? Frustration? Weariness? A longing to be alone? Maybe their presence is more irritating than comforting, a reminder of the loved ones she's lost and of the fertility she no longer possesses. "I cannot give birth to more sons" (NCV), Naomi chides them.

I also hear an unspoken dig: *I had sons, but you did not.*

Some of us know well the heartache of infertility. Others have been blessed with a child or two yet long for a larger family. Then one day in our late forties or early fifties, any possibility of carrying a child in our womb quietly ends.

We keep those blue (or green or pink) boxes on our bathroom shelves a few months longer, just in case. Finally we know that season of our lives is over.

With a certain sadness we pack up all the monthly paraphernalia, realizing we'll never need it again.

For Naomi, menopause represents yet another death, another door closed forever. She's so distraught she doesn't even let her weeping daughters-in-law speak before she gives another command, more emphatically this time.

> "Return home, my daughters;…" *Ruth 1:12*

Naomi begins to pace, the hem of her tunic flapping about her ankles. The endearment doesn't soften what she means for them to hear: "On your way, please!" (MSG). She's run out of sons and out of options. She's also run out of patience.

> "…I am too old to have another husband." *Ruth 1:12*

How old is too old? Most scholars put Orpah and Ruth in their midtwenties and Naomi in her forties, beyond the fertile childbearing years. No hope of a second wedding, then—not in that era, when a bride's value was measured by the health of her womb.

> "Even if I thought there was still hope for me—even if
> I had a husband tonight and then gave birth to sons—…"
> *Ruth 1:12*

Naomi is the one with tears in her eyes now, convinced she'll sleep alone this night and every night. Her speech sounds rushed, and her anguish pours out unchecked.

> "…would you wait until they grew up? Would you remain
> unmarried for them?" *Ruth 1:13*

She knows better, of course. These young women can't wait fifteen years to marry again. Naomi is boxing them into a corner, giving them no choice but to return home.

Go back, go back, go back.
With night approaching, the drama escalates.

> "No, my daughters. It is more bitter for me than for you,…"
> *Ruth 1:13*

We knew this was coming: the my-pain-is-worse-than-your-pain ploy. Put a group of fractious women in a room together, and they can play this sorry game of one-upmanship for hours. "Sorry that happened to you, but listen to what happened to *me…*"

Mrs. Pleasant has left the building.

In her place stands a miserable woman whose life is "much too sad" (NCV) for her daughters-in-law to share. Literally, Naomi is "bitter-souled"[28] as she speaks the language of lament, later captured by the prophet Jeremiah: "Bitterly she weeps at night, tears are upon her cheeks."[29]

Orpah and Ruth have remained silent throughout their mother-in-law's diatribe—overwhelmed by their emotions and hers—until at last Naomi offers an explanation for her suffering.

A Shocking Confession

> "…because the LORD's hand has gone out against me!" *Ruth 1:13*

Her words strike a blow to the chest, bruising the heart.

Naomi, you can't mean this.

Oh but she does. A different translation doesn't help things. Naomi is still saying, "The LORD himself has raised his fist against me" (NLT).

I once knew a man who raised his fist against me. It was not an idle threat. He sent me into work the next morning with my face battered and my spirit broken. I was nineteen. And though I was naive and foolhardy, I did not deserve such treatment. No woman does. Ever. For any reason.

When I read Naomi's words, I feel almost sick, remembering the pain and the shame of that relationship and how much he hurt me, using only his hand.

Please, Lord. Please tell us your hand is not like that man's.

It is not, beloved.

The Hebrew phrase *yad-yhwh,* rendered here as "the LORD's hand," points to something great and vast, "a mysterious, unpredictable power."[30] Naomi has seen and felt that power, and it has shaken her to the core. In the words of Moses, "O Sovereign LORD, you have begun to show to your servant your greatness and your strong hand."[31]

God does not lift his hand against Naomi to wound her. He lifts his hand to stop her. Naomi has lived the last decade with her back to the Lord, making her home among pagans and marrying her sons to Moabite wives, who—if they'd given birth—would surely have raised her grandchildren to worship Chemosh.

So God held out his hand. *Enough.*

Naomi, like most of us, is a slow learner. She lost almost everything before she realized what she had: a relationship with the one true God. Naomi would have nodded in understanding had she heard Job say, "Have pity on me, my friends, have pity, for the hand of God has struck me."[32] Same hand, same God, same sorrow, and same hope.

Sinclair Ferguson reminds us, "God does not guarantee our comfort."[33] A hard truth. We *love* to be comfortable. We *pray* to be comfortable, asking the Lord to give us lives that are pain-free, debt-free, and hassle-free with as few red lights and speed bumps as possible.

God makes no such promises.

Instead, he is "the God of all comfort, who comforts us in all our troubles."[34] The Lord's way of comforting us isn't by making our troubles go away; it's by being *with us* in the midst of those troubles. "I will never leave you nor forsake you"[35] trumps any friendship pledge, any loyalty clause, any family bond, any signed contract, even any marriage vow.

Naomi is in that hard place—unable to escape her pain, yet aware of God's presence. She understands who he is as she never has before. That's what suffering does; it grinds away our pride and self-sufficiency. It also prepares our hearts for the blessings to come. As author Linda Hollies wrote, "When we are down to almost nothing, God is up to something bigger than we can ever imagine."[36] Amen, sister.

Feeling the weight of the Lord's hand upon her, our female Job must rest in the knowledge that God is strong enough, wise enough, and compassionate enough to see her through. The hand that presses against Naomi is also guarding her path and guiding her home.

Her daughters-in-law have not yet claimed this God as their own, but considering the number of times Naomi speaks his name in Ruth's book, we can only imagine how often the Lord has been mentioned in their household over the years. With her final words, "GOD has dealt me a hard blow" (MSG), Naomi is testifying to God's power, however much it grieves her to confess it.

> At this they wept again. *Ruth 1:14*

Orpah and Ruth have seen for themselves the cost of trusting Naomi's God and so pour out their grief once more. Will their well of tears never run dry? I almost can't bear to watch, yet it seems rude to look away.

THE ROAD HOME

We've reached a major turning point in our story. And where do we find ourselves? Standing at a crossroads, with Moabtown behind us and the Judean hills in the distance. The symbolism is timeless, understood by every generation. It seems a decision must be made. A road must be chosen.

Naomi has repeatedly asked her daughters-in-law to go back home. She's also shown them what pledging allegiance to her all-powerful God may require of them. Which way will they turn? Toward Moab or toward Judah? Toward Chemosh or toward the Almighty? Toward the certainty of their old home or the uncertainty of a new one? This isn't a fork in the road; "the two paths led in opposite directions."[37]

While Ruth's soft weeping continues, Orpah dries her cheeks with the sleeve of her tunic, a look of resignation in her eyes. Naomi slowly nods, whether in agreement or mere acceptance, we can't be sure.

After a lengthy pause Orpah leans closer and murmurs something in Naomi's ear. We don't need to hear the words. Her actions say enough.

> Then Orpah kissed her mother-in-law good-by,… *Ruth 1:14*

Oh my, oh my.

Naomi kissed her daughters-in-law earlier. Now Orpah is responding in kind. In their culture a kiss is appropriate when honoring a dignitary, greeting a friend, or parting company.[38] Though the word "good-by" doesn't appear in the Hebrew text, it's implied by her gesture.

Can't help noticing that Orpah has no farewell kiss for Ruth. Instead Orpah turns almost immediately, hiding her face from us. Shame? Guilt? Or relief?

She appears eager to retrace her steps, not looking over her shoulder as she departs in haste, the bundle of clothes on her back bouncing up and down as she strides along the rock-strewn road. As one commentator said of Orpah, "She may go sobbing on her way back, but she goes."[39]

Good Girl, then? Or Bad Girl?

We hardly know the woman. Seems unfair to judge her motives, though I'm curious what compelled her to turn back, to choose "the familiar, the temporal."[40] Is she more practical than Ruth? Is the home she's returning to more prosperous or her future brighter? Is she the prettier, more accomplished daughter-in-law who's certain to find another husband? Maybe she's had an offer to host a daytime talk show. (Sorry, Oprah.)

This is certain: Orpah is doing what her mother-in-law asked her to do. She's the obedient one. Nothing wrong with her behavior "except that it is not *hesed*."[41] She is faithful to herself and to her Moabite gods. Period.

With her good-by kiss, "Orpah walks out of biblical history."[42] She never again surfaces in the pages of Scripture. We don't even know if she makes it back home.

But we know who remains with Naomi: her other daughter-in-law, Ruth, a young widow who has yet to make a move or speak a single word on her own.

Oh baby. Is *that* about to change.

Ruth In Real Life: MARY

"Many years ago the Holy Spirit revealed to me that I didn't *really* love my mother-in-law. I confessed this sin and repented to God. I asked him to help me let his love flow through me. I started visiting her more often and helping around the house. I also started telling her regularly that I loved her. She eventually came to faith in Christ! I felt that I had failed the Lord regarding her for so many years. Yet in such a short time, God did a marvelous work in her heart."

Three

A Wow of a Vow

2-18 chp 3&4

Ivy clings to brick walls. Plastic wrap clings to bowls (at least in the commercials). And nylon fabric clings to anything.

But people who cling—emotionally or physically—can make things difficult. Especially if you're trying to shake them loose.

Just ask Naomi.

> …but Ruth clung to her. *Ruth 1:14*

Yes, we can see that. She's holding Naomi's hand and resting her head against Naomi's shoulder. In every translation, from "clave" (KJV) to "clung tightly" (NLT), Ruth is stuck like glue to Naomi's side.

Some might consider Orpah the stronger daughter-in-law at this point, holding her head up and walking away, while Ruth hangs on for dear life. "She clings. She needs."[1] Unwilling to go back, unable to go forward, Ruth simply holds on whether Naomi wants her to or not.

Gotta confess. I get uncomfortable when people get clingy.

When I was a harried young mother with a four-year-old in nursery school and a two-year-old at home, I tried to make the most of those limited school hours by straightening the house, doing laundry, washing the dishes—you know the drill. My toddler daughter followed me from room to room, tugging at my jeans, my shirt, whatever her little hands could grab.

At one point when I bent over a basket full of dirty clothes, she tried to jump onto my back and nearly succeeded in knocking me over. A clever mother would have laughed and made a game of it. A patient mother would have ignored her chores and paid attention to her child. A kind mother would have understood what was needed and offered a big hug.

But I was not clever or patient or kind that day. I was irritated and tired and inexcusably mean as I shouted, "Get off my back!"

My poor daughter. She sat down at once and began to cry, frightened by my tone of voice. Mortified, I quickly scooped her up in my arms and apologized profusely, realizing what I'd said. Not "Climb down, please" or "Don't knock Mommy over." Oh no. I'd spilled out my frustration and put my feelings into words without weighing the impact.

Give me some space. Leave me alone. Get off my back. All those awful things mothers try not to even *think,* let alone say.

Please, please forgive me, Lord.

He did, because he loves me. So did my daughter, because—bless her sweet self—she loves me too.

Love was the reason she wanted to be near me that day. Love is also why Ruth is clinging to Naomi. The Hebrew word implies "firm loyalty and deep... affection."[2] It's the same word used in Genesis to describe marriage: "a man leaves his father and his mother and clings to his wife."[3]

A serious commitment on Ruth's part has prompted a serious effort by Naomi to push away her daughter-in-law. Frowning, Naomi tries to wriggle free, her brow tightly creased, her emotions easily read. *Get off my back.*

BAD GODS OF THE BIBLE

> "Look," said Naomi, "your sister-in-law is going back to her
> people and her gods. Go back with her." *Ruth 1:15*

Orpah is still well in view when Naomi nods in her direction. "Behold" (KJV), "see" (NRSV), she tells Ruth, adding a double whammy of *shubh.* "Go with her" (MSG).

Buried in the middle of Naomi's statement are three little words that stop my heart: "and her gods." One scholar thinks this might refer to "the household gods or the icons representing the ancestral dead."[4] No improvement there, not when God's people were warned, "Do not make cast idols."[5] Orpah may have married an Israelite man, but she's still worshiping her Moabite gods. Her heart belongs to Chemosh and company.

Yet what has Naomi done? The woman who just prayed a blessing over Orpah in the name of the God of Israel? After sending Orpah home to her false gods, Naomi is now encouraging Ruth, "You should do the same" (NLT).

Naomi, Naomi, what are you thinking?

Have you given up on your Moabite daughters-in-law and decided they're not worthy of your attention? Or do you care only about getting home to your people and your God, and never mind what happens to these young women? It's as if "she has no desire to convert Ruth."[6]

How easy it is to find fault with Naomi even as I ignore the Holy Spirit gently reminding me of times I've kept my faith to myself. Rather than share the gospel with foreign travelers seated next to me on a plane, I rationalize, *They come from a different country, a different culture, a different religion. They have their own gods. They aren't interested in what I have to offer.*

Maybe not, but God is very interested in them! Our commission is to "go and make followers of all people in the world,"[7] including those who worship other gods. We begin by listening to them, learning from them, and loving them until—at God's bidding and in his perfect timing—we have the joy of seeing them sink into his embrace.

Does Naomi genuinely care about this Moabite daughter-in-law who's still clinging to her? More to the point, do you and I care enough to reach out to our own family members who've yet to receive God's gift of mercy?

Open our eyes, Lord. Open our hearts. While those we love are still near, give us the courage to tell them about you.

To be fair to Naomi, there's another possible explanation for her words.

We know that she's heard of God's provision in Bethlehem and that she's going home to his people. What if she's been testing her daughters-in-law in a roundabout way, finding out if they are willing—on their own—to leave their Moabite gods and follow the God of Israel? Not because she's asking them to, but because she's asking them *not* to?

At our house if I had a hard time getting our kids out the door, I'd say,

"Forget it. We'll stay home." Never failed to get them up and moving. Might Naomi be practicing reverse psychology, 1200 BC–style?

Alas, we can't read Naomi's mind or probe her heart. We can't be certain why she keeps pushing Ruth away. We can only watch and see how Ruth responds.

BUT...BUT...BUT

It's one of the most common words in the Bible, popping up in the NIV translation nearly four thousand times. It's also one of the most vital words in Scripture, because it often serves as a hinge, opening or closing a door.

> But Ruth replied,... *Ruth 1:16*

Naomi keeps saying, "Go back."

God's Word says, "But..." That single, small word changes everything.

Ruth is not going to do what Naomi has asked. She's not going to be obedient. She's not returning home, not returning to her old gods. Even now, as Ruth stands before Naomi, as she lifts her chin and meets her mother-in-law's gaze, we can tell something big is happening.

The Spirit of God is moving through Ruth like wind, like living water. This quiet, almost invisible young woman is changing before our eyes. She's being cleansed, filled, and made new. Her olive skin is glowing; her dark eyes have a spark we've not seen before. She isn't making a choice about whether or not to follow her mother-in-law. No, "this decision is about God."[8]

Ruth is moving forward according to plan. Not her plan, and definitely not Naomi's plan. God alone ordained and orchestrated this sacred moment. Ruth's great-grandson will one day write, "The plans of the LORD stand firm forever, the purposes of his heart through all generations."[9] Naomi and Ruth are woven into those plans. So are you, my sister. Long before Naomi and Ruth walked the earth, God's plans for you were already in place.

Ruth isn't a time traveler like us. She knows nothing about a man named Boaz waiting in Bethlehem. She knows only that she is compelled to follow Naomi home. God is at work in the heart of this brand-new believer, so freshly minted she shines like gold, like sunlight.

As Ruth opens her mouth to speak, we prepare our hearts for "the most determined, the most decisive, the most unhesitating confession of love in all literature."[10]

> ..."Don't urge me to leave you or to turn back from you."
> *Ruth 1:16*

Her voice is thick with emotion. "Don't beg me" (NCV), "don't ask me" (NLT), "don't force me" (MSG), she pleads. Just listening to her, I can barely swallow for the lump in my throat.

Ruth is easily her mother-in-law's match in conviction. Her heartfelt entreaty rings with "integrity and authority."[11] And she's making it personal, using the word "you." Ruth's entire focus is on Naomi as she tightly clasps her hands, forcing her mother-in-law to look at her.

We can't take our eyes off Ruth either. My, oh my. Where is all this passion coming from? She hasn't invoked the name of her dead husband, Mahlon, so it's not about him. And Naomi certainly hasn't made her welcome on this journey. Yet Ruth tosses *shubh* right back in Naomi's lap, saying, "Do not press me...to turn back" (NRSV).

Naomi's mouth is hanging open. Clearly she wasn't expecting this.

Before Naomi can respond, Ruth makes a bold vow.

HERE WE GO

"Where you go I will go,..." *Ruth 1:16*

Not an inch of wiggle room in this promise. No small print, no conditional clauses. If Naomi shoots back, "How 'bout Egypt?" Ruth will ask for directions.

I've heard more than one dewy-eyed bride speak Ruth's words while gazing into her bridegroom's handsome face: "Whither thou goest, I will go" (KJV). The lines are poetic, "like an exquisite ritual."[12] But here's what makes Ruth's vow so extraordinary: she's not talking *to* or *about* a man. "In a world where life depends upon men,"[13] she's pledging to follow her mother-in-law, who by all appearances doesn't want her along for the ride.

What's compelling Ruth, do you suppose? A sense of duty? Or is it "a voice we cannot hear"[14] calling her home?

"...and where you stay I will stay." *Ruth 1:16*

Or, if you prefer, "where thou lodgest, I will lodge" (KJV). Sounds like a great ad campaign for Holiday Inn.

No doubt Ruth heard about Bethlehem during her time with Mahlon, but she's never seen the place. She seems to care little about where she's going as long as she is with Naomi. Ruth has "committed to love her for the long haul"[15] and asks for nothing in return, not even Naomi's mutual affection.

Nor does she beg Naomi, "Don't leave me." Instead, Ruth promises, "I won't leave you."

And the girl's just getting started.

"Your people will be my people..." *Ruth 1:16*

Whoa. Big step there. It's one thing to leave your home and quite another to leave your culture—permanently. Ruth is promising to adopt the laws, traditions, dialect, foods, customs, folklore, and history of Israel, turning her back on the only life she knows and embracing a world she has yet to experience.

Naomi lost her identity without meaning to. Ruth is willfully flinging hers aside.

Foreign missionaries do this on a daily basis, knitting their lives with a different people group for as long as the Lord allows. They may keep a mailing address in their home country and return on furlough every few years, but the place where they serve becomes the place that feels most like home.

When I think of Allison in the Dominican Republic, I think of a beautiful young woman who is American by birth yet wholly Dominican at heart. She would say without hesitation, "These are my people." Except she would say, *"Esta es mi gente."* Her gestures, her expressions, her manners are those of her Dominican sisters. Allison is not simply *with* them; she's *one* of them.

I believe that's what Ruth has in mind here. Total immersion.

Pocahontas, who embraced the Christian faith in the early seventeenth century, is oft quoted as saying, "Let the white man's country be my country, and his kindred my kindred."[16] We certainly hear an echo of Ruth in the Native American's stirring words.

We must do the same, accepting, even embracing, the whole body of Christ as family. Matthew Henry reminds us, "If they be his, they must be ours."[17] *Ouch.* This one cuts me to the quick as I think of the times I've shaken my head at other Christians and discounted them because they didn't think, look, or behave as I do.

Yet Ruth is about to meet a whole nation of people who are different from her, and, sight unseen, she's happy to claim them. We're called to do likewise for our brothers and sisters: "Dear friends, since God so loved us, we also ought to love one another."[18]

Lord, help us love others the way you do. Unabashedly. Unconditionally.

That's what Ruth does. She loves Naomi. She embraces Israel. And then she takes a giant leap of faith.

THE BIG ONE

"…and your God my God." *Ruth 1:16*

Somebody shout, "Hallelujah!"

Everything's been building toward this. A bold confession. A transformation from darkness to light. A simple, stark, powerful example of "how God sovereignly works to bring someone to faith."[19] Ruth glows like a candle against the evening sky, like a psalm come to life: "Commit your way to the LORD…. He will make your righteousness shine."[20]

Long before Ruth was born, the Lord pledged to his chosen ones, "I will walk among you and be your God, and you will be my people."[21] Maybe Naomi carved those words into their tent poles in Moab or painted them across their goatskin walls even as she planted them in Ruth's heart. Over the years Naomi has had plenty of time to teach her daughter-in-law about the covenant with Abraham and the Exodus with Moses. She's also had countless Sabbaths to show Ruth what a life devoted to Yahweh looks like.

Still, only the Lord himself could "put the desire in her heart to choose him."[22] And choose him Ruth does. Her smile broadens as tears stream down her face.

Your God my God.

Naomi's cheeks are dry, though, and her expression is stoic. It seems a Moabitess has "more passion for Israel's God than has the child of the covenant."[23]

Complacency can happen in any generation. We take our eyes off the eternal. We forget what we believe or why. We doubt the sincerity of a new Christian, thinking she doesn't know the difference between devotion and emotion. I'm ashamed to say I've been there. I've also stood on the other side of the great divide between lost and found and know what that looks like too.

When I embraced God's grace as an adult, I was saddened to meet people who'd been in church for years yet had little excitement about the Lord or his Word. Always on the lookout for believers who were as gung-ho about God as I was, I arranged lunch with a woman employed by a Christian organization, certain I'd found a kindred spirit. The moment we were seated, she grabbed the menu and said, "Enough about Jesus. Let's talk about something else."

Sigh.

Perhaps Ruth feels the same disappointment when she looks into Naomi's eyes. Yet her words don't falter, and her conviction doesn't wane. She has turned away from the gods of Moab and so "dethrones Chemosh for ever."[24]

Speaking of farewells, Ruth has plans for her final resting place too.

THE BURIAL PLOT THICKENS

"Where you die I will die, and there I will be buried." *Ruth 1:17*

Why is a woman in her midtwenties worried about her funeral? Because among ancient peoples, being buried in one's ancestral homeland was a must-do.[25] Yet here's our righteous Ruth, not only promising to stay with Naomi all her days and remain in Judah after her death, but also pledging to be buried there—"the ultimate commitment."[26]

Back in the day, the patriarchs and their matriarchs—Abraham and Sarah, Isaac and Rebekah, Jacob and Leah—all ended up in the same cave, "deeded to Abraham by the Hittites as a burial site."[27] That's how important it was for family to be interred together and on their own land. For Ruth willingly to be buried in foreign soil is another above-and-beyond pledge on her part.

We see a flicker of response from Naomi on this one, a slight softening of her features. As a childless widow, she has legit concerns about what might happen to her body when she dies.[28] Without Ruth to take care of her, Naomi "might suffer an improper or disgraceful burial—a shameful tragedy in the ancient Near East."[29]

I'm counting on our grown kids to take care of such things, though it's helpful to determine arrangements beforehand so they don't have to make all those hard decisions on their own. My list is short: I want the cheapest coffin available and a bagpiper in a kilt playing "Amazing Grace." Beyond that, it's all good.

Have you given much thought to where you'll be buried someday?

If you've moved a time or two, will it be the town where you were born or the place you're living now? Guess the real question is, where's home? For those who love the Lord, heaven is our true home. A marked grave is merely a place for loved ones to gather in remembrance. Ruth is making sure that when people come to mourn her, her grave will be beside Naomi's.

After making six stunning vows to her mother-in-law, Ruth winds things up with a seventh vow to God, "an ancient form of imprecation."[30] Before she speaks the words, Ruth takes a deep breath. I'm already holding mine.

> "May the LORD deal with me, be it ever so severely, if anything
> but death separates you and me." *Ruth 1:17*

No wonder Naomi is shuddering.

Having just claimed Naomi's God as her own, Ruth is giving him free rein to deal severely with her—to curse her if he chooses—should she leave Naomi's side. Even after watching her mother-in-law suffer, Ruth boldly says, "I ask the LORD to punish me terribly if I do not keep this promise" (NCV).

Yikes. God has a history of dishing out some pretty intense punishment. He covered Egypt with frogs, turned dust into gnats, afflicted people with festering boils, and sent a plague of locusts to devour every growing thing.

Ruth is either the most courageous woman who ever walked the earth, or she trusts the Almighty completely, knowing he'll make sure her vows are fulfilled now that she's stamped his name all over them. "Naomi painted the future very dark," wrote author John Piper, yet "Ruth took her hand and walked into it with her."[31]

Nothing in Ruth's or in Naomi's cultures requires such an enormous sacrifice from a daughter-in-law. Nor is Ruth's loyalty based on seeking her mother-in-law's approval or earning some future reward. Instead, "her actions are grounded in the Hebrew concept of *hesed*,"[32] that gift of loving-kindness we've already heard about and will be watching for in the chapters to come as we follow this brave young woman, who has spoken her last word in Moab.

It's easy to see why her commitment "has placed her among the immortals."[33] Yet we know where the supernatural power to love Naomi, follow Naomi, and support Naomi comes from. After all is said and done, "grace is always God's last word."[34]

THE SILENT TREATMENT

Now it's Naomi's turn. Wonder what *she's* been thinking.

> When Naomi realized that Ruth was determined to go with her,... *Ruth 1:18*

Ruth has so "firmly made up her mind" (NCV) there's no point discussing it. Her mother-in-law has apparently decided "any more words would be wasted."[35] So Naomi zips her lips.

> ...she stopped urging her. *Ruth 1:18*

She stopped all right. Naomi "left speaking" (KJV), "said no more" (NRSV), and "gave in" (MSG). Gifted wordsmith Walter Wangerin calls Naomi's silence "a howling solitude."[36]

What's up with Naomi? Is she angry, fearful, exhausted? All of the above, judging by her body language. Another writer saw her as "sullen, depressed, beaten down"[37]—whether by her losses, her loneliness, or her God. If only Naomi understood that God's intent isn't to *beat* her up but to *lift* her up. Having Ruth by her side isn't a burden; it's a blessing.

But Naomi can't see clearly at the moment. I'm not talking about bifocals, even if she is fortysomething. What Naomi needs is a new way of looking at God's providential care. Ruth's willingness to support her is part of that provision.

Naomi's nonresponse feels downright rude. "No warm embrace, no loving words of gratitude"[38]—in truth, no words at all. The very next verse of the story will put us in Bethlehem, suggesting "Naomi withdrew into silence for the rest of the trip."[39]

Ever travel with someone who's angry or upset and the way the person handles it is to stop talking? *Arrgh.* Maybe he or she sees silence as a calmer, more peaceful approach. I think it ramps up the tension. The atmosphere grows heavy with unspoken words and unexpressed thoughts and unnecessary angst.

That's what we're seeing now as Naomi and Ruth start down the road together while "the curtain falls on this dramatic scene."[40] They're not talking or touching or exchanging glances, and we're "left to imagine that Naomi's silence continues."[41]

At least both women are headed in the same direction: home.

Ruth In Real Life: MARTE

"At the beginning of my relationship with my mother-in-law, there was a slight frost around her. I tried so hard to thaw the ice created by her difficult life and circumstances. I dearly wanted to win her approval and love. First I prayed, then told her outright that I wanted our relationship to build and grow like Naomi and Ruth's. My request was simple, heartfelt, honest, and sincere; she melted! We grew closer and closer over the years. I stayed by her side in her last days at the hospital, holding her hand and sharing Jesus with her. Unable to speak, she lightly squeezed my hand. I felt so honored to have that privilege."

Four

Throw Out the Welcome Mat

*A*s homecomings go, this one leaves a lot to be desired.

So the two women went on until they came to Bethlehem. *Ruth 1:19*

That's it? All we get is "the two of them traveled on together" (MSG), heading toward "rumors of food and a future,"[1] with zero description of their journey?

Understand, I'm a novelist. I can make up stuff. We could have them sleep in a grove of olive trees for safety's sake, chat up a caravan driver over breakfast, and prepare to ford the Jordan by tucking the hems of their tunics inside their girdles. (No, not *that* kind of girdle; I mean the broad sashes around their waists.) While we're at it, let's have a few wild animals cross their path. Lions and jackals and bears (oh my!) were common around the river gorge.[2] Or a traveling merchant might consider Ruth a worthy prize and make trouble for the women, since commentators agree it was a "daunting and dangerous trip."[3]

An adventure story? I'm in.

One little problem: I'm also a Bible teacher, and this is a nonfiction book. I really can't make up tons of stuff and add it to the narrative. Definitely not whole days of action and dialogue. What I can say is the women arrived safely. Mission accomplished. Still, there's no denying "Ruth is a story with many gaps."[4]

For example, we don't know how many miles or days this journey took. Scholars think the women traveled between seventy and one hundred miles and spent about a week on the road.[5] Whatever route they followed, it included "ascending mountains and descending into deep valleys."[6]

On foot? Wearing sandals? My toes hurt just thinking about it. I've traveled through the undulating countryside of Israel and climbed Jerusalem's winding streets—which, for the record, are all uphill—and I'm here to tell you, what these two women did without a map or a motor coach is beyond imagining.

Here's the happy news: if Naomi and Ruth's arduous journey isn't recorded in the pages of Scripture, you and I don't have to cover those endless miles in this book. Isn't time travel the best?

Next stop, Bethlehem.

O LITTLE TOWN…I MEAN, *REALLY* LITTLE

Some twenty-five thousand people live in modern Bethlehem. But in ancient days the population was a couple of hundred souls, max.[7] A teeny, tiny town.

The surrounding terrain is anything but flat. Caves extend beneath the surface, so the landscape is rugged—more heaving than rolling—with deep gorges filled with trees and vegetation and steep hills scraped bare by the wind, suitable only for small flocks of sheep and goats.

The town itself sits on a high ridge that provides a broad view of the Judean desert to the east and the purple mountains of Moab beyond the Salt Sea. Small houses cling to the hillsides, their white limestone walls shimmering in the heat. And the countryside is fertile, with terraced vineyards and fields of grain claiming every inch of arable land.[8]

As we draw closer, we can make out more details. The narrow stone houses of Bethlehem have flat roofs made of wooden beams, covered with brush and clay, and edged with a wooden parapet.[9] Ladders propped against the outside walls let women climb onto the rooftops for weaving and washing[10] while their children cavort in the street below.

Sandals worn to shreds, Naomi and Ruth trudge toward the town gate. A short passageway through the protective wall surrounding Bethlehem, the gate leads to a broad, open plaza. Stone benches line the area, along with a series of small alcoves where people escape the heat, buying and selling merchandise, settling legal matters, and, above all, dishing about their neighbors.

The arched entrance beckons like an old woman with her arms out-stretched. *Come in. Come home.* Only citizens have the right to pass through unchecked.[11] Naomi must wonder if she still qualifies. After all this time. After all that's happened.

A familiar tune, played on a flute made of bones,[12] floats toward them on the hot, still air. Just inside the gate a dozen women have gathered—friends, cousins, neighbors—all talking, laughing, and sharing their secrets. We already feel at home. But does Naomi? And what must Ruth be thinking? Their faces are too haggard, too dust covered to read.

Ruth falls back a step, letting Naomi lead the way.

When the women of Bethlehem catch sight of their old friend, they stare for a moment, then gasp, then shout. The flute music abruptly ends with a squeak. Astonished faces crowd the gateway.

If Naomi thinks she can slip into town unnoticed, that is *so* not happening.

> When they arrived in Bethlehem, the whole town was stirred
> because of them,... *Ruth 1:19*

"Stirred" doesn't fully paint the picture. Throw in words like "uproar" and "turbulent" and "confusion,"[13] and you'll have a better grasp of it. People spill out of their houses like water from a jar, and the crooked streets are "soon buzz-ing" (MSG). After ten years the citizens of Bethlehem may have given up on ever again seeing Naomi alive.

Well, she's here now.

> ...and the women exclaimed, "Can this be Naomi?" *Ruth 1:19*

"The women." No names, no ages, no descriptions. "Like a *choros* in a Greek play,"[14] they all sing out at once, speaking not so much to the newcomers as to each other. "Is this really our Naomi?" (MSG). Any number of emotions could be attached to these simple words, from "surprise and joy through doubt and uncertainty to consternation and concern."[15] You never know how you'll react when you see an old friend.

I once made a national television appearance on the West Coast and was taken aback when I arrived to find a studio audience (not the norm for Christian shows). As I walked past everyone, waving nervously, one middle-aged woman stood, smiled at me, and shared her first name. Though she didn't look familiar, I smiled back and told her I was glad to see her. Which I was, of course, though I couldn't quite place where we'd met before.

The next day an e-mail came. "Great to see you last night, Liz—"

My heart stopped.

This was the woman who'd introduced me to Jesus. Not a passing acquaintance. A dear friend, though I'd not seen her for two dozen years. Had I realized who she was, I'd have stopped at once, given her a hug, and arranged for coffee after the show. Now that opportunity was lost.

My first reaction was embarrassment at making such a foolish mistake. My second reaction was regret over missing the chance to reconnect with her. But my third reaction was fear: *Have I changed that much too?*

Perhaps the women in Bethlehem feel the same way when they look at Naomi. No doubt those ten years have done a number on Naomi's appearance. Add a week on the road without revitalizing serum or antioxidant moisturizer or ultrasmoothing primer...

Really, what can her friends in Bethlehem expect?

We expect people not to change. Clearly we don't, right? Looking in the mirror each day helps us make tiny mental adjustments, such that we don't notice how much we're aging until we see a photo of when we were younger and the truth stares back at us.

For Naomi, these women are her looking glass.

Seeing herself as they do—older but perhaps not wiser—Naomi finally loses it.

NO MORE MRS. NICE

"Don't call me Naomi," she told them. *Ruth 1:20*

No small talk. No "Hello, how are you?" No "Good to be back." Naomi's first words are a "blunt, explosive retort."[16] That is to say, she bites off their heads. "Don't call me Pleasant. Don't call me Delight. And don't you *dare* call me Sweetness!"

I'm intrigued when people dwell on the kindness and goodness of Naomi. We'll eventually see that side of her. But at the moment she's being brutally honest, and the truth isn't always pretty. Matthew Henry sums up her response: "I am no more pleasant, either to myself or to my friends."[17]

When I get like that—and, believe me, I do—I retreat, I withdraw, I hide. My friends are too precious to me, and I'd rather not wear out my husband with all my whining. Instead, I close the door to my writing study and bang on the keyboard, talking to God through clenched teeth. He listens patiently. He corrects gently. He loves unconditionally. He fixes what's broken.

Those repair sessions are better handled privately. Unfortunately for Naomi, she has nowhere to go and so blurts it all out publicly. "Call me not Naomi" (AMP).

One writer believes Naomi has sunk into a deep depression,[18] and I agree. Her lashing out is one of many symptoms. How could she *not* be depressed with scholars calling her "a doomed old albatross,"[19] "a forlorn relic,"[20] "a grim old crone,"[21] and a "bent, gray, wrinkled, and sorrowful" woman?[22]

Good grief.

Naomi is only fortysomething. Is she sorrowful and forlorn because of her situation? Sure. Exhausted from her journey? You bet. Menopausal? I'm convinced that's part of it. And she has to be close to starving. When our stomachs grumble, our mouths usually do too. But bent, gray, and wrinkled? That's not in the Bible, and that's not our Naomi.

The girl's still got it. But right now her joy and confidence are buried beneath several layers of pain. That's why Naomi rejects her pleasant name and chooses another one better suited to her plight.

"Call me Mara,…" *Ruth 1:20*

Go ahead and say it, honey: "Call me Bitter" (MSG).

Maybe she's thinking of the time Moses led God's people into the Desert of Shur: "When they came to Marah, they could not drink its water because it was bitter. (That is why the place is called Marah.) So the people grumbled against Moses, saying, 'What are we to drink?' "[23]

Bitter water, bitter people, and now a bitter Naomi. Like her ancestors in the desert, she's a grumbler, a whiner, a complainer, "consumed with self-pity and hopelessness."[24] We've met this woman; we've *been* this woman. Drowning in self-absorbed misery, we usually look for someone else to blame.

> "...because the Almighty has made my life very bitter."
> *Ruth 1:20*

If we thought Naomi spoke harshly about God at the crossroads in Moab, her tongue has grown even sharper on the long journey to Judah. Her old neighbors flinch when she says without apology, "The Strong One has dealt me a bitter blow" (MSG).

Bless you, Naomi, but we've already covered this. God doesn't hate you; he loves you. God doesn't have it out for you; he's looking out for you. No point blaming God or yourself for the tragic events in Moab. The reality is, they happened—and not apart from God's perfect will. His intent is "never to make us bitter—only to make us better!"[25]

On a sunny Tuesday afternoon with nothing weighing on my heart, I can quickly and easily affirm the truth of those words. *Not bitter, just better. Got it, Lord.* But when I'm hurting, when life's dark clouds start moving in, I don't want to hear such platitudes. *Get thee behind me, inspirational thoughts and motivational phrases. Let me enjoy my pity party a tad longer.*

Here stands our Naomi, wearing her poor-me party hat. And scowling.

> "I went away full, but the LORD has brought me back empty."
> *Ruth 1:21*

Literally, she's "empty-handed."[26] The women nod at one another. They can see Naomi's husband and sons are not with her and so don't press for details. Something to watch for as these chapters roll by: whether from shame or sorrow, Naomi and Ruth never mention their dead husbands by name.

Naomi's lament harkens back to the last time she was with these women.

"When I left, I had all I wanted" (NCV). Has she forgotten the famine? Her family left town because they *didn't* have all they wanted, though her hands were full, with a son in each one. Sadly, Elimelech and Naomi were also "full of themselves and their own plans,"[27] which turned to dust in Moab.

WHAT ABOUT RUTH?

Naomi has been speaking in singular terms—"me," "I," "my"—with her loyal daughter-in-law standing right by her side. Ruth isn't included in the conversation nor acknowledged in any way. Is it because she's a foreigner, a non-Israelite? Let's face it, "there was nothing kosher about Ruth."[28] She's very much a Moabitess.

Just when we think her mother-in-law is finally going to make a proper introduction, Naomi moans, "GOD has brought me back with nothing" (MSG). *Nothing!* This daughter-in-law, who abandoned all she knew and loved, is worthless to you? Naomi, how could you say such a thing?

(Don't you just want to shake the woman? Not hard, of course, but a little?)

Meanwhile, Ruth seems strikingly unaffected by her mother-in-law's snub. She knows she's not welcome in Bethlehem. And she certainly knows Naomi.

What a contrast between these two women—especially in the way they're handling things on this difficult day. The Word tells us, "Those who suffer according to God's will should commit themselves to their faithful Creator and continue to do good."[29] Naomi isn't there yet. But Ruth is.

We don't hear any complaining from her, any protests, any cries of "What about me?" Though she, too, lost a husband and is childless, Ruth isn't whining about her situation or pining for the life she left behind. Those who trust in a Sovereign God are willing to wait their turn.

I discovered something about that kind of patience when I was a brand-new believer. Exercising at a health club (what can I say—it was the eighties), I worked my way around the mirror-lined room, then had to stand in line for several minutes for my turn to use a popular piece of equipment.

When I finally stepped forward, a woman barged in front of me, then growled, "I don't have time to wait!"

As she took the seat that should have been mine, everyone within earshot was urging me, "Don't let her do that to you! Make her get up!"

The old Liz would have let this woman have it—not with actions, but with words. Cruel, sharp words. Instead, my new best friend, the Holy Spirit, took over. He gently but firmly closed my mouth, then filled me with a huge measure of peace and a light heart as I waited for the woman to finish.

That was the first day I knew beyond any doubt that God is *real*. He's living and active and powerful enough to re-create us in his image. While I was working on changing the shape of my body, God was changing the shape of my heart.

We already see him at work in Ruth's life.

Naomi is still resisting him.

Once More, with Feeling

"Why call me Naomi?" *Ruth 1:21*

She again rejects her pleasant name in case anyone missed it the first time. Not likely. It's "a cry of pain and a cry of help,"[30] and though Naomi's self-absorption makes me twitchy, I feel her anguish too.

"The LORD has afflicted me;…" *Ruth 1:21*

Many translations use more forceful language here, invoking a courtroom scene in which the Lord "testified against" (KJV) or "witnessed against" (NASB) Naomi. She feels the hand of his judgment and the heat of his purifying fire. It's pain with a purpose, but it's still pain. The only answer is to trust God through the process.

Can you do it, sweet Naomi? Can you surrender to his will?

The way Matthew Henry saw it, "So many calamities have been lost upon you if you have not yet learned how to suffer."[31]

Naomi is suffering. But is she learning?

"…the Almighty has brought misfortune upon me." *Ruth 1:21*

The Hebrew word *Shaddai*—rendered here "Almighty"—means "God the self-sufficient, God of the mountain, God of overpowering strength, God the destroyer."[32] Naomi does not doubt his strength, then. "In her view, there was no other force in the universe."[33] I wonder, though, if she doubts his love?

Her words remain caustic: "The Strong One ruined me" (MSG).

Just as Naomi couldn't respond to Ruth's generous speech, the women of Bethlehem remain silent. We see them shrink back, exchange glances, yet say nothing, made uncomfortable by their Israelite sister's tale of woe.

If Naomi only understood that "God is plotting for her glory."[34] When it's our story, we can't see the plot, can't pick out the dramatic highs and lows that will bring us to a satisfying end. For Naomi, "his purposes remain hidden."[35]

I'm reminded of the sermon illustration we've all heard dozens of times, describing life as a huge tapestry that God has flawlessly designed. He sees the beautiful finished piece while we see only the knots and stitches on the underside.

Stitches are especially meaningful when a physician is holding the needle. On one memorable trip I made to the ER, a doctor put a long row of stitches across the back of my head. Oh. My. Goodness. So much pain, and I couldn't even see what he was doing. Sometimes that's how life feels: all stitches, all pinpricks, and nothing to admire. I find myself whispering, "Lord, can't we have one small glimpse? Just to give us hope?"

Then I remember we have his Word. A finished work, a completed tapestry. Scripture gives us everything we need to see that Big Picture. Even thirty-odd centuries ago, Naomi could turn to the oral histories of Abraham and Moses to assure her of God's *hesed,* of God's love.

In Bethlehem she not only has God's ear; she also has caring neighbors, who are listening without serving as judge and jury. Job's friends offered all sorts of advice. Not Naomi's friends. They listen, they acknowledge, "they give her dignity in her grief."[36]

Though I *am* starting to worry. No one has stepped forward to offer Naomi and Ruth lodging. Do they have an empty house to return to? Since Israelite law required that land remain in the family, we can assume the two women have somewhere to lay their heads tonight. After ten years the place is probably a run-down, filthy mess—a sad but fitting home for our Naomi, who's "broken-hearted, desolate and poor."[37]

This is the nadir, the lowest point of the story. Ye olde storytellers would never have taken an intermission here, or they'd have lost their audience.

Welcome home? Not exactly.

> So Naomi returned from Moab accompanied by Ruth the
> Moabitess, her daughter-in-law, arriving in Bethlehem as the
> barley harvest was beginning. *Ruth 1:22*

Why state the facts again? To alert the audience and reader that this chapter of the women's lives is ending. None too soon, eh? We also have our last *shubh* of the chapter: "Naomi was back" (MSG). Plus a nod to Ruth's foreignness and to her supporting role (Naomi really did *not* return empty-handed). Finally, we receive one new and very important detail about the timing of their arrival: it's late April, "the beginning of the barley harvest" (MSG).

The first chapter of Ruth opens with a famine and closes with a harvest. Says everything, doesn't it? After this bleak season of Naomi's and Ruth's lives, hope is on the horizon.

Ruth In Real Life: SUSAN

"During my early years of marriage, when my husband and I had four children, my mother-in-law would call and say, 'I have fifteen (or twenty or thirty) minutes, and I am coming by to see my grandchildren, not you. Go shave your legs, take a long shower, run to the drugstore, whatever. I am not coming for you to entertain me.' What a gift for a mother of preschoolers! Many mornings I stood in the shower and prayed my mother-in-law would have fifteen minutes that day. Unfortunately, my father-in-law had a stroke last summer, and now I go by her house and offer her fifteen minutes, thirty minutes…"

Five

Out Standing in Her Field

W e're about to encounter one of my favorite words in the Bible, right up there with *but…*

> Now… *Ruth 2:1*

Like a conductor lifting a baton, "now" is a signal: prepare for a change. Could be an important character is about to be introduced, or some vital action may be about to unfold. It's like watching a play, and "at the beginning of the second act we hear the narrator from the wings."[1]

> …Naomi had a relative on her husband's side, from the clan of Elimelech,… *Ruth 2:1*

A "kinsman" (KJV), is it? Living, we hope. Our sisters have spent enough time in graveyards. Since this person is "connected with Elimelech's family" (MSG), perhaps he's in a position to help Naomi and Ruth financially. Meeting him now, before he steps on stage, is meant to fill us with "anticipatory delight."[2]

We're there. Tell us more, please.

> …a man of standing,… *Ruth 2:1*

A stand-up kind of guy. Who'd want otherwise? This relative is, by all accounts, "a mighty man of wealth" (KJV), "influential" (NLT), "prominent and rich" (MSG), and "important" (CEV). A perfect description of a larger-than-life hero, which this story and these women desperately need. Some men are rich yet not of high standing—today's headlines are proof—but this man is both wealthy *and* respected.

We like him already.

The same Hebrew phrase, *ish gibbor chayel,* is later used to describe Saul's father,[3] Jeroboam,[4] and David[5]—men of strength and valor. That word *gibbor* is often used of warriors and military men, hinting that our hero may have a strong body in addition to that strong bank account.[6] The ancients read it "mighty in the law," meaning this guy could be "mighty in the scriptures too."[7]

He certainly sounds more promising than Wimpy and Frumpy.

What shall we call this fine fellow?

...whose name was Boaz. *Ruth 2:1*

Good name, even if the meaning is kinda muddy. Could be "fleetness"[8] or "in him is strength."[9] As to who Boaz's parents were, everyone in Bethlehem knows yet seldom discusses the subject in polite company. His dad was Salmon, famous only for being the father of Boaz, and his mother was Rahab, famous for something else entirely.

That's right. The mother of Boaz was Rahab the harlot from Jericho. Imagine a "man of standing" having a mother whose job was...well, *not* standing.

Yet look at how much Rahab and Ruth have in common! Both were born as Gentiles yet chose to live among the Israelites. Both tossed aside their old lives and their old gods to follow the one true God. And just as Ruth made a confession of faith to her Israelite mother-in-law beneath the desert sky, Rahab declared her allegiance on a starry rooftop in the presence of two spies from the Israelite camp: "the LORD your God is God in heaven above and on the earth below."[10] Bring it, Rahab.

Meanwhile, on his father's side, Boaz is descended from Judah, whose daughter-in-law, Tamar, wore the garb of a prostitute and seduced him in order to continue the family line. Well, well. Further proof that God can and will use *anyone.*

Ruth knows nothing of this man or his background at the moment, but *we* know his story, which strengthens our trust in a Sovereign God. That small glimpse of the huge tapestry? We just got it with our sneak peek at Boaz.

Time for Ruth and Boaz to meet. (*Squeal.*)

RIPE FOR THE PICKING

And Ruth the Moabitess said to Naomi, "Let me go to the fields and pick up the leftover grain…" *Ruth 2:2*

The abruptness of this statement is a clue that "virtually no time has passed since the arrival of Naomi and Ruth."[11] Dawn has barely broken on their first morning in Bethlehem, and Ruth is already thinking about breakfast, lunch, and dinner. Same thing when you move into a new apartment and go buy groceries before you start unpacking. Food is always at the top of the to-do list.

We're standing in their reclaimed house, with its barren rooms and high, narrow windows. The simple lamp—a clay saucer filled with olive oil and a flaxen wick—barely lights one corner. Naomi is halfheartedly sweeping the dirt floor with a stiff branch, while Ruth bathes her hands and face using an earthenware bowl of water provided by a thoughtful neighbor. She's had time to shake out her tunic and brush her hair, but she's still called a Moabitess in this verse. A reminder of her foreignness, her vulnerability.

Even so, we see the resolute look in her eyes and hear the courageous note in her voice as she glances toward the door, then asks permission to head to the fields on the outskirts of Bethlehem. "Let me go, I pray thee" (YLT).

We never saw Ruth working in the grainfields of Moab. Is she accustomed to manual labor? Or merely willing to go out of necessity? Either way, gotta love this girl for getting out there. Work is not only how she'll provide food for the two of them; it's also a way of demonstrating her love for Naomi. "See! the harvest is calling me—your God is spreading for me, for you, a table in the wilderness."[12]

While we weren't paying attention, Naomi must have explained to her Moabite daughter-in-law how gleaning works in Israel. The Lord laid down the Law for landowners on this one: "do not reap to the very edges of your field or gather the gleanings of your harvest. Leave them for the poor and the alien."[13] Poor? Alien? That'd be Ruth. Harvesters were given special incentive to be generous: "so that the LORD your God may bless you in all the work of your hands."[14]

It was one of those win-win deals: harvester and gleaner were both blessed. But gleaning wasn't a handout. No steady diet of government cheese down by the river. Gleaning was hard work, allowing the alien, the fatherless, and the widow "a little more dignity than rummaging in garbage."[15]

My friend Evelyn once showed me how this gleaning thing functions in the here and now. She was always the first to arrive at our workplace—an hour before the front door was unlocked—so she used the alley entrance. Most mornings she passed a woman in ragged clothes digging in the Dumpster by the back door, looking for something to sell or eat. When Ev offered her money, the woman shot her a nasty look and muttered, "I don't need your money!" Ev knew better yet didn't want to trample the woman's sense of worth.

Her solution? Ev came to work a few minutes earlier each day and stuffed cans of food inside the Dumpster where this woman could easily find them. I've heard of collecting canned goods for the needy, but Ev took generosity a step—no, a leap—further. As it was once said of Ruth, she has "one of the truest hearts that ever beat in mortal clay."[16]

Ruth is not only faithful; she's brave. Anything might happen in the barley fields. She's a foreigner without a kinsman to guard her virtue, and she's a widow rather than a virgin, making her an easy target for the male harvesters. So she's choosy about where she'll glean.

"…behind anyone in whose eyes I find favor." *Ruth 2:2*

Not just anybody. Ruth is saying she'll follow only "after him in whose sight I shall find grace" (KJV). Only the one who deals in *hesed*. You'll remember that on the road home Naomi prayed, "May the LORD show kindness to you."[17] That's what Ruth is counting on—not the kindness of strangers, but the loving-kindness of one who'll look upon her with compassion.

Joseph had a similar experience in prison: "the LORD was with him; he showed him kindness and granted him favor in the eyes of the prison warden."[18]

Hesed begins in the heart of God, and that's what Ruth is hoping to find in the grainfields of Bethlehem: a godly landowner with mercy in his eyes.

On Her Own

After a long stretch of silence, her mother-in-law sighs heavily, then gives her consent.

> Naomi said to her, "Go ahead, my daughter." *Ruth 2:2*

Not "go back" this time, just "go." Rather a terse response. Naomi doesn't speak a blessing over Ruth or invoke the Lord's name or even wish her well.

Still, the word "daughter" brings a faint smile to Ruth's lips. Naomi is easing back into the role of mother and tucking Ruth firmly under her wing.

Odd that Naomi isn't going with her to glean in the fields. Especially since "two certainly would have been safer than one."[19] Was Naomi too tired? Too weak? Too emotionally wiped out? Was it improper for a woman her age? Was the work too hard for her? Was she worried about breaking a nail?

Embarrassment, or even shame, at the thought of her daughter-in-law gleaning beside Bethlehem's poor may be the reason. Or pride, the sin that often lurks beneath such emotions.

If Ruth is surprised to be departing for the fields alone, she does a good job of hiding it. With a light kiss on Naomi's cheek and a promise not to return empty-handed, Ruth walks into the sunlit courtyard, never guessing she's headed "right into the arms of Providence!"[20]

Since Bethlehem has no natural spring, the townsfolk rely on a cistern for their water.[21] Ruth follows a gaggle of women, all with large jars balanced on their heads, as they make their way out of town, eying her from beneath their cloth head coverings. A square of fabric, folded to shield the eyes, drapes over their necks and shoulders and is held in place with a plaited cord.[22] Ruth's fabric is threadbare, and the cord around her head is starting to unravel, but she's made herself as presentable as she can and meets their curious gazes with a tentative smile.

When the women stop to fill their water jars, Ruth scans the nearby fields and chooses the one that appears the most prosperous, with neatly planted rows of barley ripe for harvest and a fair number of people busy about their work. Just as we saw in Moab, there are no fences or boundaries lest an inch of ground be wasted.[23]

Ruth starts toward the field, glancing upward as if seeking the Lord's direction. Her pace never slows, and her feet never stray from the path until she enters the field, her gaze fixed on the edges. That's where Naomi told her she would find the stalks of grain that are hers for the taking by law.

> So she went out and began to glean in the fields behind the harvesters. *Ruth 2:3*

It's late April, meaning the rainy season has ended.[24] The tilled ground is soft beneath her sandals as she makes a beeline for the foreman. He's easy to pick out, sitting on a rocky protrusion, his tunic in good repair and a stout purse dangling from his waist.

Lowering her gaze as she approaches, Ruth waits until he bids her to speak. When she introduces herself, he grunts in acknowledgment. Tiny as this town is, everyone has heard about the unexpected appearance of Naomi and her foreign daughter-in-law. Then she asks him—politely, humbly—if she may glean among the sheaves. No need to prove she qualifies. Who would take on such a menial task if it weren't a dire necessity?

HARVEST TIME

Once given permission, Ruth stations herself behind the workers and takes a moment to observe how things are done. Strong-armed young men bearing hand sickles cut the ripe, standing grain with a practiced sweep of the blade. Then the workers behind them—mostly women and older men—gather the stalks and bind them into sheaves. Only after the paid laborers move forward can the gleaners—the destitute, the widows, the orphans—begin collecting the cut stalks of grain left behind.[25]

Ruth mimics their actions, bending at the waist, grasping a stalk of barley, then tucking it into the crook of her elbow. Down, then up. Down, then up. My back aches just watching her. The process is painfully slow. With others vying for the same stalks, it will take a full day of work to have much to show for her efforts. I'm wishing she had some kind of cloth sling hanging from her shoulder to hold the grain so she could have both hands free. Tomorrow she'll know to bring one.

As the sun moves higher in the cloudless sky, all the verses regarding seedtime and harvest come to mind, especially this one, which suits our hard-working Ruth: "Let us not become weary in doing good, for at the proper time we will reap a harvest if we do not give up."[26]

Laboring among the least in Bethlehem, our sister Ruth hasn't the slightest notion that someday her loving sacrifice will be recorded for all time. That her book—also known as "the Book of Lovingkindness"—will be read each year "on Shavuot, the ancient holiday that celebrates late spring harvest and the giving of Torah."[27] In the Old Testament it's called the Feast of Weeks,[28] and in the New Testament, Pentecost.[29] A sacred day on any calendar.

Imagine if Ruth knew the cherished spot she would someday hold in millions of hearts. Would she still be wiping sweat from her brow and getting dirt under her fingernails? Or would she toss aside her armload of grain and demand special treatment?

The very thought of her stamping around, saying, "I'm Ruth! Applause, please!" is ludicrous. But some of us do just that. Fearing we'll go unnoticed or be forgotten in seasons to come, we wave our banners high, tooting our own horns on Facebook or Twitter. "Please see me! Please see the good things I'm doing for God!"

Forgive our foolishness, Lord. Remind us daily of your Son's words: "Be careful not to do your 'acts of righteousness' before men, to be seen by them. If you do, you will have no reward from your Father in heaven."[30] Write it across our foreheads; engrave it on our hearts. In this age of shameless self-promotion (is there any other kind?), please help us sing your praises and not our own.

Though I said at the start that our goal isn't to be like Ruth, I'm beginning to rethink that. She's not worried about impressing others; she's focused on serving others. Gleaning barley, unseen and unheralded, she is exactly where the Lord intends for her to be. Fame for Ruth will come, but not by her own efforts. "Humble yourselves, therefore, under God's mighty hand, that he may lift you up in due time."[31]

Just Then

As it turned out,... *Ruth 2:3*

When the storytellers spoke those words, you *know* they winked at the audience. "It just so happened" (NCV) means it didn't "just happen" at all. The Hebrew phrase—literally "her chance chanced"[32]—points to the divine, letting us know our Sovereign Lord is at work on Ruth's behalf.

...she found herself working in a field belonging to Boaz, who was from the clan of Elimelech. *Ruth 2:3*

"Found herself" on Boaz's land, did she? Ruth may not know who Boaz is yet, but we do. No coincidence she landed here this morning! This second mention of Boaz's family ties "emphasizes his connection to Naomi,"[33] hinting of some provision to come. After suffering with these women through all their losses, we are eager to see them move from sorrow to joy.

It's already happening.

One of the field workers has turned to look over his shoulder and is nudging the guy next to him. A murmur moves through the ranks, and more heads turn, ours included.

Well, look who's here.

Just then Boaz arrived from Bethlehem... *Ruth 2:4*

"Just then," is it? As if Boaz appearing on this particular day at this precise hour is pure chance! The King James Version really grabs the Hebrew and runs with it: "And, behold, Boaz." We sense the storyteller saying, "Look! Do you see what is happening?"[34]

Yes, we do.

A distinguished-looking gentleman in a finely embroidered tunic is standing before his workers, arms outstretched, his expression open as well. Some bosses show up with a box of glazed doughnuts. Boaz has something far better to offer.

You Had Us at "Hello"

> …and [he] greeted the harvesters, "The LORD be with you!"
> *Ruth 2:4*

A few words, Boaz, and you've already stolen our hearts.

Strength, wealth, and influence are bonus features in a man, but what a woman really wants is a guy who's utterly devoted to God. A man she can trust with her whole self, body and soul. A man who takes to heart Paul's words: "Husbands, love your wives."[35] What John Piper calls "a God-saturated man."[36]

Some say the first recorded words of a biblical person reveal that individual's true identity. If that's so, Boaz clearly belongs to the Lord, because his holy name is the first thing we hear. "GOD be with you!" (MSG).

What would happen if your boss said those words when he or she walked into your workplace? Or the man in your life when he strolled through the door? Or your parents when they came over for a visit? How would it change the trajectory of your day if someone you love and respect spoke such a blessing over you?

Granted, these words aren't original with Boaz. Then and now it's a common way of greeting someone in the Near East, along with "God be gracious to you" and "Peace be with you."[37] Still, their familiarity doesn't diminish the meaning or sincerity behind Boaz's words. When my husband says, "I love you," I don't care how many billion times that phrase has been spoken; it still blesses my soul.

Grateful voices fill the air as Boaz's workers return the favor.

> "The LORD bless you!" they called back. *Ruth 2:4*

Unaware of what was expected of her—first day on the job and all that— Ruth is a half beat behind in offering a blessing to the new arrival. Her words, clear and strong, carry across the field, followed by the soft laughter of those around her.

Blushing, she quickly resumes her gleaning, not looking in the landowner's direction. He, on the other hand, is "arrested, caught, thunderstruck"[38] by the sight of this young stranger in his field. When he turns toward his foreman, we inch closer, hoping to catch some of their conversation.

Boaz asked the foreman of his harvesters,... *Ruth 2:5*

"Foreman." There's a word that seldom shows up in Scripture. It simply means the "servant that was set over the reapers" (KJV). At the end of the day, the foreman's task is to "call the workers and pay them their wages."[39]

Ruth isn't among the hired help. Her wages will be the barley she gleans—nothing more. But she's still answerable to the foreman, who gave her permission. And the foreman answers to Boaz, who has a question for him.

..."Whose young woman is that?" *Ruth 2:5*

Not *who* is she, but *whose* is she. Women in this culture belong to their fathers or their brothers or their husbands or their sons. Which is why Boaz is asking rather pointedly, "Whose girl is that?" (NCV).

"Girl"? She was a married woman!

This tells us that Boaz is older, not that Ruth is exceptionally young. From his vantage point all women under thirty are girls (right there with you, buddy). The Hebrew word, *na'ra,* can also mean "marriageable young woman,"[40] so perhaps Boaz is asking more than "to whom does this young woman belong?" (NRSV). Maybe he's really asking, "Is she spoken for?"

EYE OF THE BEHOLDER

The English poet Thomas Hood wrote of Ruth, "She stood breast-high amid the corn, clasp'd by the golden light of morn,"[41] with "corn" being the British word for any sort of grain. Is that how Boaz sees Ruth, as a vibrant young woman shining beneath the Judean sun? Or does he see more than the physical, the obvious? Does he see her strength of character by the way she helps those around her or her strength of commitment by her diligent labors?

Whatever he's thinking, Boaz hasn't taken his eyes off her.

Next time you're watching a drama, turn off the sound and notice where the camera lingers. Invariably it focuses on the actors' eyes. They acknowledge someone with an arched brow or swiftly avert their gazes or exchange meaningful glances, communicating their characters' true feelings more deeply with their eyes than through any words they might speak.

While Boaz gazes at Ruth, his manager fills in the details.

> The foreman replied, "She is the Moabitess who came back from Moab with Naomi." *Ruth 2:6*

At first I stifle a laugh. *A Moabitess who came from Moab? Well, duh.*

Then I realize anyone could travel from Moab. Ruth, however, is a native; she's a "Moabitish damsel" (KJV), a Gentile. Now I'm a little peeved. Did the foreman have to point out that Ruth is the foreign woman everyone's been talking about? *Humph.*

Our ruffled feathers are quickly smoothed by a wise commentator who notes, "This description emphasizes her foreignness, but it also may hint at her act of love and loyalty to her mother-in-law."[42] Okay, we're good with that.

When the foreman identifies Ruth as the one "who came back with Naomi" (NLT), Boaz lifts his eyebrows. He expected her to belong to a man, not a woman! Though Naomi is his relative by marriage, he doesn't bother to mention the family connection. After all, if he steps forward now and offers to provide for Naomi and Ruth, our story is over before it begins. That's not God's plan. Not Boaz's plan either.

We hold our breath, waiting to see what else the foreman might reveal.

> "She said, 'Please let me glean and gather among the sheaves behind the harvesters.'" *Ruth 2:7*

Yes, yes, we heard all that. Nice how the foreman relates their earlier conversation verbatim rather than putting it in his own words. He's also quick to praise her work ethic.

> "She went into the field and has worked steadily from morning till now, except for a short rest in the shelter." *Ruth 2:7*

You and I have spent most of the day in said shelter, a small covered booth where the fieldworkers take their meals and escape the midday sun.[43]

Translators can't agree whether Ruth labored nonstop or took a much-needed break. Some say, "She tarried a little in the house" (KJV); others think she's been working "without a moment's rest" (CEV). One commentator went overboard, sorting out the various interpretations under four headings: " 'Ruth takes a little rest'; 'Ruth does not take a little rest'; 'Ruth takes only a little rest'; and 'Ruth scarcely takes any rest.' "[44]

Whatever, people! The rest of the time (pun intended) she's been working. That's what matters to Boaz.

After pausing to speak privately with several of the men, he heads in her direction, a man on a mission. His bronze skin and firm stride make it difficult to pin down his age. Forty? Fifty? Sixty?

Ruth watches him approach, her features alert. Is he coming to welcome her? Or does he disapprove of a Moabite gleaning in his field?

She'll soon have her answer.

Ruth In Real Life: ASHLEY

"I knew he was my Boaz from the moment I saw him. He came to my YMCA for devotions and sang, badly. A man who would do that for kids was my kind of guy!"

Ruth In Real Life: COLLEEN

"As a young woman I prayed that God would send me a godly husband: a provider, a protector, and a man full of love. My husband continues to be the man I prayed for those many years ago. He is a fabulous father. He is our leader. He is our rock. He has been there for my family in times of financial need. I am thankful every day that, for once, I listened to God."

Six

A Different Kind
of Dinner Date

*T*he intensity of Boaz's expression might unnerve some women. Not Ruth. She tips her head in greeting, then meets his gaze.

So Boaz said to Ruth, "My daughter, listen to me." *Ruth 2:8*

Brother, we're *all* listening. The foreman, the harvesters, the gleaners, and most definitely Ruth.

How surprisingly tender those first two words are! The very ones Naomi used when she sent Ruth on her way this morning: "my daughter." Boaz is quickly assuming the role of a father figure, and rightly so with the family connections through Elimelech.

He lifts one cautionary finger, an age-old gesture. "Listen carefully" (NASB), Boaz says. Having ears to hear isn't enough. He wants her to pay close attention and heed his warning.

"Don't go and glean in another field and don't go away from here. Stay here with my servant girls." *Ruth 2:8*

Some fairly aggressive language: two *don't*s and a *stay*. "Don't even leave this field at all" (NCV), he insists. Literally, "you shall not wander."[1] Good thing our storyteller gave us a glimpse of Boaz's character a few verses back so we're certain he's a virtuous and godly man. Otherwise, we might find him overbearing, even controlling.

Clearly, Boaz doesn't want Ruth anywhere near the men. "Cleave to my young women" (YLT), he tells her. If he hasn't figured it out yet, she's good at cleaving.

Amid his strongly worded advice comes a subtle shift in Ruth's position. By urging her to "abide here fast by my maidens" (KJV), Boaz is treating her like one of his servants, which is a big step up from what she was a moment ago: an unpaid collector of scraps. For Boaz to "shepherd Ruth into the fold of his servant girls is an act of grace."[2]

Make that a beautiful, bountiful act of grace.

In a less than a day, Ruth has gone from foreign immigrant to trusted employee. This would be like moving—oh, let's say to Melbourne, Australia—with no money in your purse and no job prospects. The minute you arrive, jet-lagged and starving, you begin picking up trash at the Flinders Street Railway Station, hoping to find a few coins among the discarded coffee cups. Suddenly the CEO walks up and says, "Miss, I'd like you to start working for our railway division immediately. The hours are ten to six, the benefits are excellent, and our office staff will gladly arrange for your visa and help you get settled."

Crazy, right? Could never happen.

But that's exactly what's happened to Ruth. It's a miracle and nothing short of it.

It's also how God welcomes us into his family. He doesn't make us fill out a stack of forms or suffer through a probationary period. Once we belong to him, we're *in*. Not because of our goodness or worthiness, but because of his.

Thank you, thank you, thank you, Lord. We can never say it enough.

Ruth's eyes widen, trying to absorb this landowner's generous offer. Before she can respond, Boaz presses on with specific instructions.

> "Watch the field where the men are harvesting, and follow
> along after the girls." *Ruth 2:9*

It's her safety he's worried about. Since Bethlehem's fields are divided, not by hedges or fences, but by unplowed ridges, Ruth could easily stray from his property without knowing it and "find herself among strangers where Boaz could not protect her."[3] He's also making sure Ruth is surrounded by the girls and kept some distance behind the guys.

> "I have told the men not to touch you." *Ruth 2:9*

So *that's* what Boaz was discussing with the men a moment ago. Frankly, "told" is too gentle a translation. Boaz "charged" (KJV), "ordered" (NRSV), "commanded" (NASB), and "warned" (NCV) his male harvesters to keep their hands off Ruth. And "touch" dilutes the meaning as well. The Hebrew word is more often translated "bother" (NRSV), "molest" (AMP), and "harass" (MSG). It's a violent, physical word, alluding to the possibility of "sexual abuse."[4]

The threat is real in a culture where men do what is right in their own eyes. By offering to protect her, Boaz is already about the Lord's business. As Ruth's great-grandson will one day write, "O LORD, you will keep us safe and protect us from such people forever."[5] That's exactly what Boaz is up to.

He's also thinking about Ruth's comfort and convenience.

DRINK UP

> "And whenever you are thirsty, go and get a drink from the
> water jars the men have filled." *Ruth 2:9*

Startled glances dart about the barley field, and some of the laborers nervously shift their weight from one foot to the other.

Not only has Boaz extended a special privilege to Ruth, but by offering her water, he has also made a gesture of friendship, as when Rebekah met the servant of Abraham and "quickly lowered the jar to her hands and gave him a drink."[6] And when Jesus asked the Samaritan woman, "Will you give me a drink?"[7] he too was opening the door for conversation, which caught her off guard since Jews of that time didn't associate with Samaritans.[8]

In the same way, Boaz is throwing tradition aside by inviting a Moabite woman to drink from water jars filled by Israelite men. No wonder his workers are uneasy! Yet Boaz is careful not to provide too much assistance. Ruth must still glean, still get her hands and feet dirty, still sweat beneath the hot sun. Boaz is applauding and affirming her willingness to work, while keeping her physically safe.

Understandably, Ruth is blown away by his generosity.

> At this, she bowed down with her face to the ground.
> *Ruth 2:10*

A single, graceful movement. No fainting, flopping, or face planting. As Eugene Peterson describes it, "She dropped to her knees, then bowed her face to the ground" (MSG). Abigail humbled herself the same way before David,[9] and so did Bathsheba.[10] It was a demonstration of respect, awe, and gratitude.

Whenever I'm overwhelmed by God's loving-kindness, that's where I find myself: facedown. The first time I read Romans 5:8, sitting in a cold, drafty apartment many Februarys ago, my rebel heart was finally broken by this truth: "While we were still sinners, Christ died for us." Undone, I fell onto the open Bible before me and drenched the pages with my tears.

Bowing in the presence of grace is something we do instinctively by God's design: "Before me every knee will bow."[11] Ruth isn't worshiping Boaz, but she is honoring him, aware that his devotion to God is the source of his kindness to her.

Here's what I love about Ruth's pressing her hands into the soil at Boaz's feet: in the not-too-distant future, this ground will belong to her—as his wife! She can't for a moment imagine that happening. But God can. When you and I see nothing but dirt and sweat and work, God sees joy and fulfillment right around the corner. While we fret and worry, God says, "Trust me."

The crowd watches and listens as Ruth lifts her head and poses the question on all our minds.

> She exclaimed, "Why have I found such favor in your eyes
> that you notice me—a foreigner?" *Ruth 2:10*

Her voice catches on the last word, "foreigner." That's the heart of the issue. "I am not an Israelite. Why have you been so kind to notice me?" (NCV). In the

Hebrew text the words for "notice" and "foreigner" share the same consonants—*nkr*—at their root. So "a foreigner is one who is noticeable."[12]

Been there. When my teenage children and I visited Tokyo, we definitely stood out. My son is six foot two, my daughter had wavy brown hair down to her fingertips that year, and my size and shape are…well, not Asian. People were very polite, very kind, and very amused, giggling behind their hands. We were giggling too.

But in Israel circa 1200 BC, foreigners weren't funny. They were anathema.

Boaz's preferential treatment of Ruth the Moabitess is unbelievably bold. So is her question. "Her tone was direct, her self-confidence probably surprising to Boaz."[13] Rather than simply thanking him, she wants an explanation. Of Ruth's many character traits, "shyness is not one of them."[14] Though she'd married a man named Wimpy, she didn't share his personality.

What's going on here? Is Boaz making overtures toward Ruth? Is she flirting in return? Not yet. At this point he's being protective, and she's being inquisitive. But we do have "the beginning of a dialogue."[15] And a fine start it is.

You may be wondering if Ruth is lovely to look upon. If so, is that why Boaz noticed her?

BEAUTY AND THE BOAZ

Writers and artists over the years have painted Ruth with a flattering brush, describing her as a "radiant beauty of face and form" with "gleaming golden hair."[16] Golden hair? In Moab? Not buying that, nor "long, dark locks falling in ringlets over her neck and shoulders."[17] Ringlets? Really?

If you choose to picture a comely Ruth, then Queen Rania of Jordan, with her lightly freckled olive skin and striking dark eyes and hair, is a perfect example of a Middle Eastern beauty. And, of course, Ruth *is* beautiful in the same way all women are beautiful in the eyes of their Maker: uniquely created in his image,[18] made for his glory,[19] and designed to his specifications.[20]

Still, nowhere in Scripture is Ruth described as physically attractive. "She was never said to be beautiful," Matthew Henry reminds us, adding that her weeping, traveling, and gleaning probably "withered her lilies and roses."[21] (Don't you hate when that happens? Nothing to be done but plant new ones.)

The biggest clue that Ruth is average in appearance—and remarkable in every other way—is her astonishment at Boaz's interest in her. Beautiful women are used to being noticed. They don't say, "Why are you so good to me?" (CEV). Not unless they're being coy. They know why they've caught a man's eye.

Yet Ruth is taken aback by his attention. She's clearly not accustomed to being singled out, which also reveals something about Boaz's character. A man of wisdom and maturity, he's well aware that "beauty is fleeting,"[22] and he recognizes a woman of quality when he finds one. "A beauty of heart, a generosity of soul, a firm sense of duty"[23]—that's what Boaz sees when he looks at Ruth.

"What have I done to deserve such kindness?" (NLT) she wants to know.

We're curious too.

> Boaz replied, "I've been told all about what you have done
> for your mother-in-law since the death of your husband—
> ..." *Ruth 2:11*

Ah. Just as we suspected. It's her servant heart that Boaz considers praiseworthy.

Obviously somebody has been talking to him. Several somebodies, by the sound of it. "It has been explained and reexplained to me,"[24] Boaz confesses to her.

If Ruth is the talk of the town, her mother-in-law is the reason. No one but Naomi could know what Ruth has done for her since Mahlon's death. Maybe that conversation with the sisters at the city gate continued beyond what's recorded in Scripture. Maybe Naomi has had a steady stream of visitors, each one getting an earful about faithful, sacrificial Ruth.

Boaz certainly gets the details right.

> "...how you left your father and mother and your homeland
> and came to live with a people you did not know before."
> *Ruth 2:11*

Interesting choice of words. Like that marriage bit in Genesis, where the man "leaves his father and his mother."[25] We've heard those words in this story before. Boaz may be paying Ruth a huge compliment by comparing her to Abraham, to whom the Lord said, "Leave your country, your people and your father's household and go to the land I will show you."[26] By faith, that's what Abraham did. By faith, so did Ruth.

Here's what's fascinating about this little discourse: Boaz is telling Ruth what she already knows. Why would he do that? To show her how impressed he is. To make certain his eavesdropping workers know the truth and respect her, as he does. And to assure Ruth that her loyalty to Naomi "will amply serve in place of a genealogy."[27]

Ruth's history is of no concern to Boaz because it's of no concern to God. She's among the Israelites now. She's home.

Just as Boaz is looking to the future, we must do the same, beloved. Whatever we've done and wherever we've come from, let's claim this day for the Lord and move forward, leaving our past behind in Moab. Or Cleveland or Little Rock or Sacramento.

PAYBACK TIME

"May the LORD repay you for what you have done." Ruth 2:12

Maybe you've seen this sign posted in a church office: "Working for the Lord doesn't pay much, but the retirement plan is out of this world." That's our New Testament understanding of being rewarded in eternity: "Rejoice and be glad, because great is your reward in heaven."[28] But for the Israelites of old, rewards came sooner rather than later. "May your wages be paid in full by the LORD" (NCV), Boaz says, speaking a blessing over Ruth just as Naomi did earlier.

Boaz is praying the Lord will "repay" her, elsewhere rendered "complete," "make whole," "restore," "make good."[29] He doesn't mean a payment in grain or in gold. He's asking God to restore all that Ruth has lost or sacrificed and make her whole again.

Oh, sister. Can you feel it? Redemption is in the air!

The psalmist urges us, "Let the afflicted hear and rejoice."[30] Ruth wouldn't dare interrupt Boaz, wouldn't likely jump up and shout, but her face is glowing and her hope is showing, especially when Boaz offers almost the same blessing a second time, burnishing his words until they gleam with poetic beauty.

> "May you be richly rewarded by the LORD, the God of
> Israel,…" *Ruth 2:12*

Not just any old reward, but a rich one, a "generous bonus" (MSG). And not just any old god, but "Israel's caring covenant partner."[31]

> "…under whose wings you have come to take refuge."
> *Ruth 2:12*

Those outstretched wings are a comforting image, understood by all persons, through all ages, making us feel safe, warm, secure.

While I was working on this book, a stunning photo of a brightly plumed mother bird with a small chick tucked under each wing was bouncing around the Internet. Along with the verse that accompanied it—"He will cover you with his feathers, and under his wings you will find refuge"[32]—the photo conveyed a powerful message of "trust" (KJV), "shelter" (NLT), and "protection" (NCV), just as the words of Boaz draw a clear picture for Ruth.

If he knows she's seeking refuge with the God of Israel, he may also know what she pledged back at the crossroads: "your God will be my God" (CEV). Or perhaps some evidence of her newfound faith and the light in her eyes are enough to convince Boaz that Ruth shares his belief in the one true God. Naomi may not have given her daughter-in-law the affirmation she deserved on the road home, but it appears the woman has been touting Ruth's faithfulness nonstop since they arrived in town.

As the youngest of six kids, I've seen this movie. Daddy always bragged about us to others but seldom praised us in person. Just when we thought he hadn't noticed or cared that we'd done something right, we'd run into a neighbor who'd say, "Your father can't stop talking about you…"

That's our proud Naomi, boasting about her daughter-in-law.

As for Ruth, she's in no hurry to end her conversation with their generous neighbor.

Do Me a Favor

Now that she feels "seen, known, respected,"[33] Ruth slowly stands and meets his gaze, absently brushing the dirt from her hands.

> "May I continue to find favor in your eyes, my lord,"
> she said. *Ruth 2:13*

Ruth isn't concerned about Boaz changing his good opinion of her. She's extending an invitation to get to know her better in the days to come. "I hope I can continue to please you, sir" (NCV), she says, hinting at "a veiled desire to see Boaz again."[34]

Okay, something *is* happening between them. Even scholars agree that the dialogue between Boaz and Ruth fits "a common Hebrew literary convention, the 'betrothal type-scene.'"[35] The wealthy older bachelor, the impoverished younger widow—a match made in heaven. Yet unlike a Hollywood movie, this isn't about their strong physical attraction to each other. It's about their deeply shared faith.

Think that happens only in the Bible? I can tell you from experience, it happens in real life too. Though my hubby is a handsome guy, what drew me to him like a magnet was his love for the Lord, his compassion for people, and his knowledge of the Word. It's a different kind of sexy, but trust me, girlfriend, it's the real thing.

Now that Boaz has showered Ruth with compliments, it's her turn to heap praises on his head.

> "You have given me comfort and have spoken kindly
> to your servant—..." *Ruth 2:13*

Though her language sounds formal, in Hebrew it's far more intimate, more emotional. "To speak kindly" means "to speak upon the heart," a literal action involving "the tender gesture of speaking while leaning on the listener's breast."[36] Get the picture? Ruth not only heard Boaz's words; she felt his voice resonate through her body, as if his head were nestled...

Right! Well.

And to think she said this to him mere minutes after they'd met. And in public. Go, Ruth!

The girl's still got it, all right. Brave and honest and filled to the brim with *hesed,* she holds nothing back. The Message really captures her passion: "Oh sir, such grace, such kindness—I don't deserve it. You've touched my heart, treated me like one of your own. And I don't even belong here!"

Sounds like our Ruth, all right. As that last bit shows, she ends her speech with a reality check.

> "…though I do not have the standing of one of your servant
> girls." *Ruth 2:13*

Ruth doesn't overstep her bounds. She knows her place: at the bottom. "I'm not even one of your servants" (CEV), she admits. Because of Naomi's family ties, she is in fact much *more* than a servant in relation to Boaz, but she doesn't know that yet. And he's not talking.

I mean, he's *really* not talking. Boaz has fallen silent, just as Naomi did after Ruth's eloquent "where you go I will go" speech. Perhaps Ruth has that effect on people because she speaks the truth in love. And does so humbly, eloquently.

With that, our scene fades to black, leaving the air charged with possibilities.

A Jug of Wine, a Loaf of Bread—and Thou

After a few hours of laboring under a hot sun, Boaz's workers are ready for some chow.

> At mealtime Boaz said to her, "Come over here." *Ruth 2:14*

The workers will be returning to the field after they eat, so we can assume this is "the lunch break" (MSG). Boaz is sharing their meal, but they're not dining at his house. Not covered in soil, sweat, and barley. Instead, they're seated cross-legged around a common pot of food and are using pieces of flatbread to scoop out their portions.[37] No chairs, no table, just a rug to sit on.

Boaz invites Ruth to dine with them. "Come, eat with us" (CEV), he says, though the KJV is far more appealing: "Come thou hither."

She's been standing to the side, uncertain if she is permitted to join them and not wanting to make assumptions. At once Boaz "welcomes her to the intimate circle of their noon meal."[38] It's really bigger than that; he wants her to feel part of the community as a whole. His level of empathy and compassion for her plight is off the chart, especially since "Hebrew men normally had little to do with women in public, much less with a foreign woman."[39]

His mother, Rahab the harlot from Jericho, deserves some of the credit for her son's sensitivity. When Boaz was a boy, he must have seen how people treated his foreign mother. Heard the snide comments, recognized the judgment in their eyes. Yet, as it says in James, "was not even Rahab the prostitute considered righteous for what she did?"[40] You betcha. Because of that experience with his mother, Boaz has no doubt gone out of his way to make outsiders feel like insiders.

When a Moabite widow showed up in his field this morning, our hero knew exactly what to do. Now it's time to help her take the next step.

"Have some bread and dip it in the wine vinegar." *Ruth 2:14*

This bread is closer to a grain cake, and the vinegar is "wine or strong drink turned sour."[41] Sounds awful, I know. But the dark wine vinegar isn't at all intoxicating and has an agreeable sweet-and-sour taste.[42] More like salad dressing. Balsamic vinaigrette. All the best restaurants serve it.

What they're eating isn't the point. "These are not mere dining instructions. Boaz wants to introduce Ruth to Bethlehem society, starting with his own workers."[43]

Take a careful look at how our redeemer-to-be includes her. Come to the table. Take a piece of bread. Dip it in the wine. That's right: communion.

Sharing bread and wine, as Jesus did when he celebrated the Passover with his disciples[44] at what we now call the Last Supper, was a custom that stretched back to antiquity. It is the way of God's people, and Ruth is about to learn how it's done.

When she sat down with the harvesters,... *Ruth 2:14*

That's the first step for all of us. To come to the table. To sit down together and admit our shared spiritual hunger. For followers of Christ, the bread and the cup are great levelers. We're not rich or poor or famous or anonymous. We're just people. Sinners with the same need, seeking God's forgiveness through the same Savior.

"So Ruth sat down beside the workers" (NCV). A gleaner, a foreigner, a woman made welcome at her lord's table. A splendid picture of what's to come.

…he offered her some roasted grain. *Ruth 2:14*

Common fare in Bethlehem. Ripe grain is roasted over a fire, then rubbed free of the husks.[45] What's *not* common is how Ruth receives this food: from Boaz's own hand. Whether he "reached" (KJV) or "heaped up for her" (NRSV) or merely "passed" (MSG) the grain to Ruth, Boaz did the serving—"an exceptional act for any man, especially an older, wealthy one."[46]

I couldn't quite tell from here. Did his hand brush hers? Did Ruth blush when she took the grain? Maddening to be so close and not catch every detail. But we *can* see how near they are to each other. And how truly hungry Ruth is as she enjoys bite after bite without worrying about this man watching her eat.

So much for daintily nibbling at a salad on the first date.

She ate all she wanted and had some left over. *Ruth 2:14*

How like Boaz to serve her "more than she can possibly eat,"[47] following the example of Almighty God, who "is able to do immeasurably more than all we ask or imagine."[48]

What to do with the leftovers? Take them home to share with Naomi. Unfortunately, there's not a to-go box in the place, nor can the cook wrap the grain in tinfoil and shape it like a swan. (You've eaten at that restaurant, right?) Ruth apparently finds something to hold the rest of her dinner, because we'll see it again later.

Meanwhile, time to return to the barley field.

As she got up to glean,… *Ruth 2:15*

She's the first to stand, honoring his kindness to her. A slight bow, a warm smile, and Ruth is headed "back to work" (NLT) ahead of the others.

Shall we follow her? Or stay and see why Boaz has insisted the rest of them tarry a moment?

Right.

An Extra Measure

> …Boaz gave orders to his men, "Even if she gathers among
> the sheaves, don't embarrass her." *Ruth 2:15*

His strong, authoritative voice has returned. When Boaz speaks with Ruth, we see his gentle side. With his men, we see the war hero, hinted at when he was described as a "man of standing."

Remember, gleaners are allowed to pick up only the trampled or overlooked grain that falls by the wayside. They aren't supposed to gather "around the piles of cut grain" (NCV). Seems these men usually had the task of setting gleaners straight. Boaz is telling his harvesters to say nothing to Ruth if she gleans among the sheaves, unaware of the laws of the land. His tone grows firmer still: "do not insult her" (NASB) or "reproach her" (NRSV). And whatever happens, "don't tell her to go away" (NCV). Especially not that.

Then a spark brightens his eyes, as if he's thought of something else he might do. Something even more generous.

> "Rather, pull out some stalks for her from the bundles
> and leave them for her to pick up, and don't rebuke her."
> *Ruth 2:16*

Look at him rubbing his hands together! He's already anticipating Ruth's bounty by day's end. "Better yet, pull some of the good stuff out" (MSG), he tells the men, then issues a second warning not to belittle her.

When his men begin to disperse, we step back into the bright afternoon sunlight and find Ruth laboring away, humming to herself as she gleans. Is she aware of what Boaz is up to, working behind the scenes to make her life easier?

No more than we're aware of the wonderful things God is doing on our behalf right now.

Sometimes at the end of a hard day, we find ourselves making a mental list of all the things that went wrong: the car battery that died; the dry cleaning that wasn't ready; a coworker who strolled in an hour late; the school project that was due yesterday.

What if instead we listed all the things that went *right:* the clean shirt discovered in the back of the closet; the fresh groceries waiting in the kitchen cabinet, thanks to hubby's late-night trip to the store; the friend willing to take over your carpool duties when you called in a panic; the stranger who let you take the last parking space and drove on, looking for another; the teenager at the post office who said your ten-year-old purse was cool; the bowl of soup served hot, fragrant, and delicious by a friendly waiter.

Wait, you're thinking. *That list could go on and on.*

Exactly. Learning to be thankful for the many blessings that come our way makes it easier to weather the occasional hassles. And if we can fully grasp that God is "over all and through all and in all,"[49] that every aspect of our lives concerns him, that the God who watched over Ruth in Bethlehem is the same God who watches over us—then the joy of the Lord will be a reality in our lives and not simply words on a page.

Ruth worked with her hands and trusted with her heart.

Please, Lord, help us do the same.

> So Ruth gleaned in the field until evening. Then she threshed
> the barley she had gathered, and it amounted to about an ephah.
> *Ruth 2:17*

After laboring from dawn to dusk, she also has to thresh the barley? Right. And it's no easy task. It requires beating the grain with a curved stick, a wooden hammer, or a large stone, then separating the husks from the kernels so they're easier to carry.[50]

How much is Ruth taking home? A bunch. "Nearly a full sack of barley!" (MSG). The measurement given here, an "ephah," amounts to thirteen quarts *or* twenty quarts *or* forty-two quarts, depending on which reference you choose.

That means it's enough to feed Naomi and Ruth for one week *or* two weeks *or* a full month.

While the scholars sort that out, I'll have whatever she's having. Food that doubles and quadruples like that would come in very handy between paydays.

The actual amount of grain doesn't matter. Suffice it to say, it was an enormous quantity.

One woman's hard work and one man's generous provision accomplished much this day. Ruth and her mother-in-law will not starve after all. Blow the trumpets, and bang the drums. "The great reversal has begun!"[51]

Ruth In Real Life: MICHELLE

"I don't know what I did to win his heart! How did I ever deserve this sweet man, who loves God and loves me so faithfully?"

Ruth In Real Life: HEATHER

"My Boaz came into my life unexpectedly. I was broken, hurting, and angry with God. This younger man (scandalous!) reached out to me, helped me heal, and always pointed me to Christ. He never tried to change me and always made me feel important. He volunteered at church, fed the homeless…an amazing man. Christ used him to rescue me. He loves me completely, believes in me, makes me feel beautiful, sexy, smart. He makes me laugh and is my constant encourager. I never knew love like this existed. I want to shout from the mountaintops how amazing God is for giving me this man."

Seven

Well, Bless His Strong and Wealthy Self

The good news? Ruth has more than thirty pounds of threshed barley to take home. The bad news? Ruth has more than thirty pounds of threshed barley to take home.

> She carried it back to town,... *Ruth 2:18*

After her long day of labor, Ruth has "gathered up her gleanings" (MSG) and is headed for Naomi's house on foot with the grain slung over her shoulder. As pastor Iain Duguid describes it, "The bag she brought home was the size of a colossal bag of dog food!"[1] Right, and without a grocery cart. Not that you could roll one of those down a Bethlehem street.

Our girl "took it up" (ASV) and "carried the grain" (NCV). Some impressive upper-body strength there. Much as we'd like to help, we can only follow Ruth home as the setting sun disappears from view. A young boy with pebbles in his hands and mischief in his eyes darts in and out of her path until he's called home to dinner and casts his stones aside.

There's Naomi, waiting in the open doorway with a look of wonder on her face. Her daughter-in-law went away empty-handed, but the Lord has brought her back full.

> ...and her mother-in-law saw how much she had gathered. *Ruth 2:18*

Ruth carries the barley inside and eases the sack to the floor with a grateful sigh. As we look about the house, it's evident Naomi's been working hard too. The spider webs are gone, the storage niches in the walls are empty of debris, and the low, broad platform used for sleeping and for sharing meals is swept clean.

Naomi bends to smooth her hand across the sack of grain. "So much," she breathes, the flickering light from the oil lamp illuminating her features.

Her daughter-in-law smiles and reaches inside her tunic. "I saved something for you."

> Ruth also brought out and gave her what she had left over
> after she had eaten enough. *Ruth 2:18*

The moment Ruth presents Naomi with the remains of her lunch, her famished mother-in-law tears into the grain cakes, barely pausing to murmur her thanks. Ruth touches her shoulder, affection in her eyes. The word *love* doesn't appear until the closing verses of Ruth, yet that tender emotion permeates every scene.

The moment she swallows the last bite, Naomi flaps her hand in the direction of the barley.

> Her mother-in-law asked her, "Where did you glean today?
> Where did you work?" *Ruth 2:19*

Naomi is so excited she repeats herself. "Where did you gather all this grain today?" (NLT) she wants to know. She's not suspicious, only curious. After all, it's a *lot* of barley for one day's work. And she's been waiting since dawn for news.

Before Ruth can respond, Naomi blurts out a praise report.

> "Blessed be the man who took notice of you!" *Ruth 2:19*

How like Naomi not to applaud hardworking Ruth. Instead she honors the unnamed benefactor: "Bless whoever it was who took such good care of you!" (MSG). Nicely put, though let's hang on to the word "notice" in the NIV, echoing Ruth's earlier statement about Boaz's noticing a foreigner.

Kinda surprising no one stopped by Naomi's house that afternoon to tell her where Ruth landed. Naomi clearly doesn't know, since in the Hebrew text she omits both the man's name and the Lord's in her impromptu burst of enthusiasm: "Blessed be whoever noticed you!" (NCV).

HE'S THE ONE

> Then Ruth told her mother-in-law about the one at whose place she had been working. *Ruth 2:19*

Check out how Ruth skips over any mention of the field where she gleaned. Or the quality of the barley. Or the names of the other farmworkers. Or how long they took for lunch. Instead she tells Naomi about "the one." The man. The lord of the harvest.

> "The name of the man I worked with today is Boaz," she said. *Ruth 2:19*

Not the man she worked *for;* the man she worked *with.* To her way of thinking, the two of them are already laboring toward the same end. And it's true that Ruth wasn't working for Boaz; she was collecting grain for herself and for Naomi, period. Boaz got nothing out of the deal except the pleasure of her company and the satisfaction of his generosity.

Clever girl, saving his name for last. The most important bit of information that Naomi has been waiting to hear comes in a dramatic reveal: "The man with whom I worked today? His name is Boaz" (MSG).

Makes me wanna shout, "Ta-da!" Which is, in essence, what Naomi does.

> "The LORD bless him!" Naomi said to her daughter-in-law. *Ruth 2:20*

Another exclamation—"Why, GOD bless that man!" (MSG)—with the Lord's name included. This is the tipping point for Naomi, the moment when everything changes. No more whining, bitterness, sorrow, or self-pity. Her faith in the Almighty is fully restored. The Lord guided her daughter-in-law to their kinsman-redeemer's field, and Boaz sent Ruth back home with an undeniable blessing.

Naomi doubts no longer. She sees. She believes.

Though we're called to "live by faith, not by sight,"[2] at times God does something visible and practical to grow and strengthen our faith. Have you seen his generosity in action, sis? A sudden windfall that made your finances stretch further, or a job offer that came when you needed it most, or an unexpected blessing that could only be God's doing?

That's definitely how things are working at Naomi's house tonight. Just listen to the woman gush!

> "He has not stopped showing his kindness to the living and
> the dead." *Ruth 2:20*

Wait a second, Naomi. Which "he" do you mean? God? Or Boaz?

A delectable—and perhaps intentional—ambiguity. Both the Lord *and* the landowner are treating these women with compassion, honoring their deceased husbands in the process, and demonstrating a generous measure of *hesed*, "the word for love that goes above and beyond the call of duty."[3]

"God has not stopped showing his kindness…"

"Boaz has not stopped showing his kindness…"

True in both cases, wouldn't you agree?

You'll remember Naomi once said to her daughters-in-law, "May the LORD show kindness to you."[4] Now that her prayer has been answered, no wonder she's excited. Naomi, who once felt forsaken, knows the truth: "GOD hasn't quite walked out on us after all!" (MSG). Neither has Boaz.

The lines in Naomi's face have all but vanished. Glowing with renewed faith, she has thrilling news for Ruth.

ALL IN THE FAMILY

> She added, "That man is our close relative; he is one of our
> kinsman-redeemers." *Ruth 2:20*

What is it about the poetic term *kinsman-redeemer* that so warms our hearts? The weight of it tells us this is no ordinary role. By using that phrase Naomi is telling Ruth that this landowner she has just met is not only someone who will "take care of us" (NCV); he also has "the right to redeem us" (AMP), meaning he can rescue them from financial or physical ruin and bring them back into the fold.

And he's family—a kinsman, a clan member, a close relative—who stands ready to deliver and protect and who makes certain no one in their family circle is ever "lonely or destitute,"[5] which certainly describes our two widows. Easy to see why Naomi is elated to have Ruth gleaning in the field of their kinsman-redeemer! She knows Boaz will soon see their plight and take action.

In the time of our story, a kinsman-redeemer handled all sorts of clan business, from assisting in lawsuits to avenging a murder.[6] Most families today are so scattered geographically or so distant emotionally that we may have trouble picturing any of our male relatives stepping into such a role—paying off our mortgages, helping a loved one get out of prison, seeing to our daily needs.

If you're thinking, *I want someone like that in my life,* that's exactly what God is up to with the book of Ruth. He's showing us all the things a kinsman-redeemer does so we'll long for that kind of protection and provision, which the Lord alone can handle. Even Boaz, a real pro in the redemption and restoration business, gives us only a tiny glimpse of how much our heavenly Father desires to redeem and restore us through Jesus, our Kinsman-Redeemer, who came "to redeem us from all wickedness and to purify for himself a people that are his very own, eager to do what is good."[7]

The redemption is his work. The purifying is his work. And our eagerness to leave our Bad Girl selves behind comes from him too.

As we watch our lives in Christ unfold, as we hear ourselves saying no to things we used to say yes to, it's almost like learning a foreign language. With constant use this new language becomes second nature. We don't have to think, *What's the Spanish word for* water? We just say it: *agua.* In the same way, we don't have to think, *How should I behave in this situation?* We do or say as the Spirit leads and are amazed to discover we did something good and right.

The tricky part for me is remembering to give God all the glory and keep none for myself. That's why "we have this treasure in jars of clay to show that this all-surpassing power is from God and not from us."[8] Boaz took no credit for his kindness, nor did Ruth. Even Naomi, who at first blessed the landowner, praised God when she learned the man's name. We can follow her fine example, giving God the credit for "every good and perfect gift."[9]

GO, GO, *GO'EL*

Naomi's words still hang in the air, like dust rising from a freshly swept floor: "That man, Ruth, is one of our circle of covenant redeemers, a close relative of ours!" (MSG).

Stunned by the news, Ruth abruptly sits down on the stone platform as if all the wind has been knocked out of her. She stood in this man's field the entire day, yet Boaz never mentioned he was "near of kin" (KJV). Why, she must be wondering, didn't he tell her?

I can think of several possible reasons. Bet you can too.

Maybe Boaz wanted his generosity to be seen as heartfelt—which it was—rather than as mere duty or expectation. Could be he preferred to meet this newcomer on an even footing without family entanglements getting in the way. Or, rather than having the other gleaners and harvesters treat her differently because she's related to him, Boaz may have hoped they'd accept Ruth on her own merits, as he does.

Of course, we can't know what Boaz was thinking, but it's a tad more apparent what Naomi has on her mind as she spills the beans about this kinsman. Ruth is decidedly part of the family now: "our" close relative, "our" kinsman-redeemer. And Boaz is in a position to help them both. Yes, they have a roof over their heads and grain at their feet, but they have no real source of long-term income. What will happen when the harvest season ends in a few weeks?

Naomi knows Boaz can redeem the situation, because she knows how real estate in Israel works. God provided each tribe a portion of the Promised Land, which was never to be sold outside the tribe. If dire circumstances forced a family to sell its property, "a wealthier kinsman could redeem it"[10]—that is, buy the land so that the family received the money and the land stayed in the tribe. That redeemer is called a *go'el,* a term from Israelite family law[11] that appears in the book of Ruth twenty times.

At the moment Naomi is worried about financial salvation, not spiritual redemption. Short-term stuff, not long-term. But as you and I know, "Yahweh himself is the quintessential *go'el,* the compassionate Redeemer,"[12] who saves us from ourselves—a far greater redemption.

When we're worn out, stressed out, and wrung out, if we can stop the spin cycle long enough to cry to God for help, we'll find he always comes to our rescue. Always. By calling out his name, asking for his help, and listening to his counsel, we're given the strength and direction we need to press on.

That's how it is for Naomi and Ruth: "They remembered that God was their Rock, that God Most High was their Redeemer,"[13] and that Boaz was his earthly servant, ready to come to their rescue. Boaz is no longer simply a wealthy man with a sterling reputation. He's their kinsman-redeemer. He's their *go'el.*

Stick with the Sisters

Then Ruth the Moabitess said,... *Ruth 2:21*

Wow, that came out of nowhere. Is "the Moabitess" really necessary? Ruth is living in Israel now, and Naomi is claiming her as a true family member. Feels like a step backward to bring up her old life.

Rahab would understand. The writers of the New Testament insist on calling her "Rahab the prostitute"[14] and "the harlot Rahab"[15] as though the world's oldest profession is part of her name. In her case it's a badge of glory. Who she *was* makes who she *became* by God's grace all the more impressive.

Those among us who are FBGs—Former Bad Girls—often claim "Amazing Grace" as our song. "A wretch like me"? Couldn't have put it better. "I once was lost"? Boy, was I ever. "But now am found"? Thank you, Jesus. "Was blind"? As the proverbial bat. "But now I see"? I do, Lord, I do!

Even if you're a Good Girl, you may be nodding your head. *Yes, Liz, I get it too.*

Absolutely, dear sister. However good or bad others may perceive us to be, we're all lost without the Lord. We all need his amazing, unchanging grace.

So it is with Ruth the Moabitess. References to her old stamping ground appear in Scripture when we need to be reminded that she no longer calls Moab home. She's a new woman, God's woman. Maybe her foreignness is emphasized here because it makes the attention Boaz paid her all the more breathtaking.

> "He even said to me,…" *Ruth 2:21*

Love that word "even." In spite of her Moabite background, in spite of her poverty, in spite of her travel-worn clothing, Boaz chatted with Ruth personally. An unspoken question hovers over this scene: "Could God be behind it?"[16] It's like the Samaritan woman meeting Jesus at the well and then going back to town and saying with a measure of awe, "Could this be the Christ?"[17]

Yes and yes. When God is on the move, he invariably leaves footprints.

Here's what Ruth recalls Boaz saying.

> "…'Stay with my workers until they finish harvesting all
> my grain.'" *Ruth 2:21*

Not quite, Ruth. Boaz asked you to stay close to the young *women*,[18] not "keep fast by my young men," as the KJV puts it. Either Ruth's memory is faulty, or she doesn't fully grasp the language, which is understandable. As a newcomer to Israel, she'd have found the basic vocabulary similar but the dialects distinct. Like a native of Boston trying to sort out what someone from Mobile, Alabama, is saying, and vice versa. Same words, different sounds.

Naomi quickly realizes what Boaz told Ruth and why. She knows how foreign women can be mistreated, knows the dangers involved. Judging by the expression on Naomi's face, she's feeling guilty right now for not warning Ruth before she left the house this morning.

Time to make amends.

> Naomi said to Ruth her daughter-in-law, "It will be good for
> you, my daughter, to go with his girls,…" *Ruth 2:22*

"My daughter" is a reminder that Naomi plays a dual role in Ruth's life: mother-in-law *and* mother. She sits beside Ruth, patting her arm before she continues. We've not seen this protective, nurturing, caring side of Naomi before. Nice, eh? God is doing a mighty work in both women's lives by gently yet firmly directing their steps.

"It is better," Naomi tells Ruth, "for you to continue working with his women workers" (NCV). Boaz isn't their owner, but he is their overseer, charged with looking out for them. "You'll be safe in the company of his young women" (MSG), Naomi promises.

She's already seeing how the next two months of harvest might play out. Naomi not only wants Ruth near the other girls; she also wants Ruth close to Boaz. In a single day he's already heaped an ephah's worth of blessings on her daughter-in-law's shoulders. Think what he might do come harvest's end!

To make certain Ruth doesn't stray from his side, Naomi offers the same explanation as Boaz did earlier.

> "…because in someone else's field you might be harmed."
> *Ruth 2:22*

No need to run through all the other meanings of the word—"molested" (AMP), "harassed" (NLT), "bothered" (NRSV), and so on—though one version describes the danger in no uncertain terms: "being raped in some stranger's field" (MSG). No, no. We don't want that. Not for Ruth, not for anyone. If Naomi means to frighten her daughter-in-law into sticking close to Boaz, this will do it.

She's not simply protecting Ruth from violence; Naomi is also setting her apart for Boaz. Though Ruth is a widow and therefore not a virgin, she has not borne a child. Her womb is untried. So, like Sarah and Rebekah before her, Ruth is being kept pure "for an as yet unknown purpose, perhaps even to bear a child of destiny."[19]

Ooh, I like the sound of *that*.

> So Ruth stayed close to the servant girls of Boaz to glean
> until the barley and wheat harvests were finished. *Ruth 2:23*

Each crop took three to four weeks to harvest, so we'll flip the calendar pages from late April to early June. Obedient young woman that Ruth is, "she kept fast by the maidens of Boaz" (KJV) right through "early summer" (NLT).

Here's what I miss: no courtship scenes with Boaz and Ruth. No Friday nights gazing at the stars over Bethlehem, no long walks across the Judean hills, no picnics in the olive grove beyond the town gate.

Ruth cleaved and gleaned. That's what we know for sure.

And one more very important thing: she loved, honored, and served the Lord by loving, honoring, and serving Naomi.

MOTHER-IN-LOVE

Sometimes the month of May is one big blur. With Mother's Day and awards banquets and spring concerts and final exams and prom nights and graduations (and, where I live, the Kentucky Derby), those weeks all mush together until suddenly it's June, and we're staring summer right in the face.

That's how this May is for Ruth. *Whoosh.* The barley harvest flows into the wheat harvest as day flows into night. While you and I zoom forward in time to grab an iced chai latte in air-conditioned comfort, Ruth gleans until the cows come home and sometimes later than that.

At the end of each day, a familiar face greets Ruth at the door.

And she lived with her mother-in-law. *Ruth 2:23*

For some stand-up comics, that'd be a punch line. You can almost hear the audience groaning. "She lives with her *mother-in-law*?"

Right or wrong, when it comes to m-i-ls, it's always open season. "My mother-in-law is well balanced," the old joke goes. "She has a chip on *both* shoulders." Or another classic: "How many mothers-in-law does it take to change a light bulb? One. She holds it in place and waits for the world to revolve around her." (Rim shot here.)

Years of hearing horror stories about overbearing, condescending, hyper-controlling mothers-in-law can make a bride-to-be leery about meeting her fiancé's mom. In my case I was engaged to an only child who'd waited thirty-four years to marry. Really, do I need to say anything else? The pressure was *on*.

I was in my early thirties, established in my career, and comfortable in my skin, but I was still a nervous wreck when the time came to meet the woman who'd come first in Bill's life for three decades. What if she didn't like me? What if she convinced Bill that I wasn't the woman for him? What if we had nothing in common? What if we were alone in a room for five minutes and had nothing to say to each other? What if... What if... *What if??*

Then I met Mary Lee Higgs. She had majored in English in college. So had I. She loves to read. Me too, me too. She adores her son. Right there with her. She has a delightful sense of humor. I am more than willing to amuse.

But in the early days of my marriage, I was so worried about staking my claim on my man, about having Bill all to myself, about raising our kids our way (okay, *my* kids *my* way), I barely cracked open the door of my heart to my mother-in-law. Sure, I said and did all the right stuff. I smiled; I hugged; I gave her nice gifts. But anxiety—the kind you can't name or explain or put your finger on—kept me from building a nest for her in my heart, though she certainly deserved it.

Then I began studying the book of Ruth, never imagining what God had in store. When I compared the loving-kindness Ruth showed her mother-in-law with my own pitiful efforts, I was totally ashamed and utterly convicted. Something had to change, and that something was me.

So I called Mary Lee just to say hello. She may not remember that brief phone call, but I do. My hand was shaking as I punched in the numbers. Usually I phoned her about family business—"Who's bringing what for Thanksgiving?"—but this was a *real* call with no agenda. Actually, a *huge* agenda from God's perspective.

The moment I heard Mary Lee's voice on the other end of the line, an overwhelming sense of joy washed over me. I mean *instantly!* Whatever fears I'd harbored—of rejection, of losing her as I'd lost my own mother, of not measuring up—were gone. Nothing was left but love.

The next time I saw her, I wrapped my arms around her cute little self and gave her my first true hug. Even now I have tears in my eyes as I remember that embrace. I look for every opportunity to spend time with her and am saddened when my writing or speaking schedule keeps us apart.

I shared the impact of Ruth's story on my life with a close friend, who confessed that she needed to love her mother-in-law more intentionally too. When I started teaching Ruth from the platform, more women came forward to admit the same need. If you have a mother-in-love and are already following Ruth's example, well done, my sister. Show us the way. If you're like the rest of us, with room for improvement, then this study of Ruth might be especially meaningful for you.

Don't have a mother-in-law? Ruth is still a model of devotion for any relationship. Just be ready for a gentle (or not-so-gentle) nudge from the Holy Spirit. Ruth's sacrificial love sets a high bar, though it's nothing you and the Lord together can't handle.

TAKE A DEEP BREATH

The closing line of this chapter in the book of Ruth is all about catching our breath before we wade into "the rapid and dramatic unfolding of events"[20] soon to come.

The whole harvest season is summed up with the words "all this time she lived with Naomi" (CEV). No mention of Boaz or his foreman or the Bethlehem women we met at the town gate. Just Ruth returning to Naomi's house day after day. *Shubh. Shubh.*

Even so, change is in the air. With the last of the spring wheat harvested and gleaned and the fields reduced to stubble and turning brown beneath the hot summer sun, Naomi and Ruth are preparing to enter a new season of their lives.

If you're thinking it's all smooth sailing from here…well, what kind of story would *that* be?

Ruth In Real Life: BONNIE

"I have always loved my mother-in-law, but for years we saw each other only on holidays with a house full of children and grandchildren all vying for attention. It wasn't until I read the story of Ruth and Naomi and began to grasp the depth of their love that I realized I needed to share that with my Naomi in a letter, telling her all that was in my heart, including my gratitude for her and for the son she raised. As simple and unpolished as that letter was, to this day she still tells me it was one of the most precious gifts she has received."

Eight

Your Mission, Should
You Choose to Accept It

This chapter won't self-destruct in five seconds, but our story is about to kick into overdrive.

One day Naomi her mother-in-law said to her, "My daughter, should I not try to find a home for you, where you will be well provided for?" *Ruth 3:1*

Most translations use some basic intro like "and" or "then." But the NIV is spot on with "one day" since everything in the third chapter of Ruth literally takes place within twenty-four hours.

It's as though the translators are winking at us and signaling, "Don't miss this!"

One day. We got it.

It also suggests some time has passed, though we don't need a clock to know that. Naomi is a changed woman. Her features are relaxed, her mood is mellow, and her tone is as pleasant as her name.

The real change? Naomi is thinking about someone other than herself. She's thinking about the young woman who has lived under her roof for many months, even years—first in Moab, then in Bethlehem. Even better, Naomi is thinking about how Ruth "may prosper" (AMP). She wants her daughter-in-law to have more than she has now. Freedom. A husband. A better life.

Even if it means Naomi will have less. No one to care for her. No one to live with her.

Naomi's willingness to let go of Ruth is so huge it can only be *hesed.*

Warren Wiersbe sums up Naomi's transformation like this: "God used Ruth to turn Naomi's bitterness into gratitude, her unbelief into faith, and her despair into hope."[1] Yes on all counts. Now it's Naomi's turn to be used by God in Ruth's life. There's something so right about that. A sense of balance and fairness that life doesn't always deliver, but God definitely does.

I love the way Naomi says "my daughter" now. As if she means it. As if she'd given birth to her. *My Ruth.*

While we watch from a quiet corner of the house, Naomi combs Ruth's hair in long, even strokes, taking her time. Morning sunlight streams through the open doorway, along with sounds of the village stirring to life. No gleaning in the field of Boaz this day. The wheat is fully harvested. Only the winnowing remains.

Naomi's question still hangs in the air: "My dear daughter, isn't it about time I arranged a good home for you so you can have a happy life?" (MSG). Months ago in Moab I might have suspected Naomi had an ulterior motive—to send her daughter-in-law packing.

But that was the old Naomi.

Our new-and-improved model is surely recalling the blessing she once spoke over Ruth: "May the LORD grant that...you will find rest in the home of another husband."[2] Though it's Naomi's parental duty to serve as matchmaker, I think she revels in this God-ordained assignment. You can tell by the light in her eyes and the lilt in her voice that she's been waiting for the perfect time.

Honey, this is it.

> "Is not Boaz, with whose servant girls you have been, a kinsman of ours?" *Ruth 3:2*

Naomi is ever so coy. Ruth's been hanging with the girls for weeks and knows all about the family connections with Boaz, though it's nice to hear Naomi again say "our kinsman" (NASB).

You *know* Naomi's had her eye on Boaz ever since Ruth returned from her first day of gleaning. Obviously his wealth and strength have appeal. His trustworthiness and godliness, even more. But it's his role as kinsman-redeemer that makes him Bachelor Number One.

Enough with the small talk. "Time to make our move" (MSG).

> "Tonight he will be winnowing barley on the threshing floor."
> *Ruth 3:2*

Something about the way Naomi says the word "tonight" makes me shiver with anticipation. It's meant to. This whole chapter is shrouded "in the dark dress of mystery and intrigue."[3]

In the KJV this sentence begins with a literal translation of the Hebrew: "Behold."

Too right. Open your eyes, Ruth. Boaz is ripe for harvest.

IT'S A TOSSUP

Field laborers plow, sow, reap, and gather, but the master alone winnows. Another shiver as I think of John the Baptist describing the Lord: "His winnowing fork is in his hand, and he will clear his threshing floor, gathering his wheat into the barn and burning up the chaff with unquenchable fire."[4] Eating our Wheaties won't cut it, girlfriend. Gotta know and love the One with the winnowing fork to survive *that* harvest.

"Threshing" and "winnowing" are common terms in Scripture but uncommon to those of us who didn't major in agriculture (where I grew up, we affectionately call them "aggies"). Let's look at how the process works.

After cattle or oxen trample the sheaves, loosening the grain[5]—that's the threshing part—the master tosses the grain into the evening breeze, using a winnowing fork with five or seven tines.[6] Wind scatters the lighter chaff while the valuable grain falls at the master's feet. (Ooh, like Ruth! Sorry, getting ahead of myself.) The kernels are sifted for stones and debris, the straw is collected as fodder for the animals, and the chaff is used for fuel.[7]

Though it sounds like all work and no play, winnowing is "the festive, joyous climax of the harvest,"[8] with plenty of drinking and feasting, as well as the observance of certain, um, fertility rites.

The threshing floor is party central. Picture a smooth circular area made from "exposed bedrock or hard, stamped earth,"[9] some fifty feet in diameter. It's out in the open on elevated ground,[10] exposed to the prevailing winds. The town's communal threshing floor is very much a public place, with people buying and selling goods of all sorts there during the hours it's not in use for winnowing.[11]

Threshing the spring crops is such a big deal the town elders are usually on hand to oversee things.[12] Landowners remain too, guarding their property, since thieves lurk about at harvest time.[13] That's why Naomi is certain Boaz will be there, sleeping on the threshing floor, keeping watch over his grain by night.

Naomi sits across from her daughter-in-law now, the comb abandoned, her expression intent as she takes Ruth's hands in hers.

PLAYING DRESS-UP

"Wash and perfume yourself, and put on your best clothes."
Ruth 3:3

Ruth pulls back, a startled look on her face. In ancient Israel bathing wasn't an everyday thing. Maybe not even a weekly thing. (I know. *Eeew.*) And anointing the body was even less common,[14] reserved for special occasions.

Remember your first date? You started getting ready the second you got home from school. Longest. Shower. Ever. Perfume sprayed from head to toe. Five different outfits tried on before you found the right one.

That's what is about to happen in Bethlehem.

With no Estée Lauder counter in sight, Ruth will need fragrant oils made from imported plants.[15] An expensive investment on Naomi's part, but this *is* her idea. She wants to present Ruth to her potential bridegroom freshly bathed and sweetly scented—not at all like the gleaner he met in the field, sweating beneath the noonday sun in her dusty tunic.

"Clean and neat" is the way Matthew Henry put it, "but not the attire of a harlot."[16] Ruth is far too virtuous for such shenanigans. Instead, her changed appearance will "signal to Boaz both her availability and her serious intentions."[17]

Long before I met the Lord—or my husband—a man who'd broken my heart reappeared at my door one evening. I almost didn't recognize him, he looked so altered. No torn jeans, no faded T-shirt, no scruffy beard. Instead he was closely shaven and dressed in a tailored sports coat as if he were applying for a job. I soon learned he'd come with a proposal—unfortunately, not the kind that leads to marriage. Though in the end I declined, I was willing to hear him out simply because he'd taken such care with his appearance, as Ruth will tonight.

Never underestimate the power of a shower.

As for clothing, some translations make it sound as if Ruth is reaching for a prom gown: "get all dressed up" (MSG) "in your nicest clothes" (NLT). But most commentators think Naomi's talking about a "heavy mantle"[18] or some kind of "big outer garment"[19] meant to ward off the chilly night air and conceal Ruth's identity. Elsewhere in the Old Testament, the same Hebrew word is translated simply "clothes"[20] or "cloak."[21]

No silken gown trimmed in gold thread, then.

Bummer. I was hoping for a peasant-to-princess scene, weren't you? With Cinderella's fairy godmother singing "Bibbidi-Bobbidi-Boo."

But Ruth will be dressed in something finer than any costly gown. The Lord has clothed her "with garments of salvation" and arrayed her "in a robe of righteousness."[22] She's been cleansed and made new. The fragrance of life clings to her skin.

Were God not behind this, Naomi would never send her daughter-in-law on so dangerous an assignment.

THE GIRL IS FLOORED

"Then go down to the threshing floor,…" Ruth 3:3

Hearing those words, Ruth is positively ashen. We are too. Go *there*?

'Fraid so. When Naomi says, "Get thee down to the floor" (KJV), it's not a suggestion. She's telling Ruth to go "to a very public place and take a very public risk."[23]

Naomi is no fool. She knows sexual encounters often take place on the threshing floor at night.[24] But that's definitely *not* the outcome Naomi has in mind. She simply wants Ruth to have a chance to speak with Boaz away from home. Still feels risky, though. Must be why Naomi wants Ruth to bide her time and wait "until the party is well under way" (MSG).

> "…but don't let him know you are there until he has finished
> eating and drinking." *Ruth 3:3*

It's true that a man who's happily fed is more likely to listen. (That's not a sexist comment; it's twenty-five years of marital experience.) I think Naomi is more concerned about the *other* men at the threshing floor. She wants them wined, dined, and toddling off to their pallets before Ruth ventures forth.

Hate to bring this up, but "do not make yourself known to the man" (NRSV) sometimes means "to know sexually."[25] *Yikes*. We'll soon discover this whole passage of Scripture is filled with "erotic double entendres."[26] They're just *there*, beloved. In the Hebrew language, from the beginning. No getting around it.

All these innuendos will eventually serve a purpose, and a God-honoring one at that. Blush, if you must, but let's keep going.

> "When he lies down, note the place where he is lying." *Ruth 3:4*

Maybe this is meant to be suggestive, but it sounds more like common sense to me. "Watch him," Naomi says, "so you will know where he lies down to sleep" (NCV). Please, Ruth, do take note, since "no amount of darkness would hide the embarrassment of approaching the wrong man!"[27]

Imagine having to talk your way out of that one. "Oh! Sorry, sir. I thought you were Bo… I mean…er, someone else. My name? Um…Orpah."

Naomi barrels on with her daring plan.

> "Then go and uncover his feet…" *Ruth 3:4*

Ruth just got that deer-in-the-headlights look.

How I wish Naomi meant "the place of his feet" or, as we often say it, "the foot of his bed."[28] A mere location, nothing more, with Ruth there as a "humble petitioner seeking his protection."[29]

Unfortunately, Naomi is stating very clearly, "When he is asleep, lift the cover" (CEV). Sure. Got it. Approach a sleeping man on a dark threshing floor and whip back the blanket, exposing his feet. How presumptuous would *that* be?

Never mind the possibility that Naomi doesn't mean his feet and is referring to another part of a man's anatomy altogether. A few commentators go there, but we don't have to, especially since none of the fourteen translations I used had any word other than "feet."

Alas, it's harder to ignore *this* interpretation of the verse: "take your clothes off at the place by his feet."[30] Hold it. You mean Ruth doesn't uncover Boaz—she uncovers *herself*? The argument goes that when Ruth later tells Boaz, "Spread the corner of your garment over me," it's because she disrobed.[31] Another commentator thought her desire to be covered "is given meaning precisely because she is naked."[32]

Oh please.

It's a sexy scene, all right, but it's *not* a sex scene! Since Ruth is wearing a cloak, she might have removed that, but nothing untoward happens. That's the real story, the one that matters.

If two dozen scholars put forth the notion of a bare-it-all Ruth, we'd have to seriously consider it. But that's not the case. It's a dubious reading at best. Most scholars go with the traditional, literal interpretation of Ruth's uncovering Boaz's feet, period.

Naomi is asking her daughter-in-law to be brave, not brazen. Well, except for the next bit. Definitely brazen.

"…and lie down." *Ruth 3:4*

As it happens, "lie down" can also be translated "lie with."[33] And not only is the phrase "lay thee down" (KJV) highly suggestive, but so is the action. A fully dressed woman lying next to a partially unclothed man "was far from customary or accepted practice."[34]

Why does the Word use such ambiguous, sexually charged language, cranking up the tension not only for Ruth and Boaz but also for the reader, for us?[35] To make it clear this couple's faith is being tested.

TESTING, TESTING: ONE, TWO, THREE

Ruth and Boaz have both openly declared their devotion to God, calling upon his power. Ruth said, "May the LORD deal with me…,"[36] and Boaz said, "May the LORD repay you…"[37] They love, honor, and serve God with every breath they take and every move they make. But when they're tossed together in this "crucible of moral choice,"[38] when they're ground like grain and sifted like wheat, will they emerge with their honor intact and their vows unbroken? *That's* the big question and the point of all these sexual innuendos.

Like Ruth, we constantly have our beliefs tested by the culture we live in. Do we sleep with someone because we can or wait until marriage because we should? Do we abort a baby because the law permits us to or carry the child because love compels us to? Do we choose a same-sex partner because we have the right or resist that path because God's Word calls it wrong?

It comes down to this: do we please ourselves or please the Lord? The apostle Paul reminds us, "Those controlled by the sinful nature cannot please God."[39] Not a verse most of us underline. We know our sinful natures all too well.

The psalmist poses the question, "If you, O LORD, kept a record of sins, O Lord, who could stand?"[40] The answer is painfully obvious, yet on its heels comes hope: "But with you there is forgiveness; therefore you are feared,"[41] meaning "revered," "worshiped," and "obeyed." It's like Moses saying to the people, "God has come to test you, so that the fear of God will be with you to keep you from sinning."[42]

Thank you, thank you, thank you, Lord.

As Ruth prepares her heart and her body for this ultimate test at the threshing floor, we are drawn into her spiritual dilemma, knowing what's at stake. When she lies down next to a man who has the power to redeem her or to reject her, will the two of them take the high road or the low? Will the spirit reign or the flesh? Or will we discover, as John Piper said, "what sexuality becomes when it runs like a deep and mighty river between the high banks of righteousness"?[43]

Her mother-in-law is confident of the outcome and says so.

"He will tell you what to do." *Ruth 3:4*

How can Naomi be sure of his response? Has she spoken with Boaz? Given him a heads-up? Or does she think that Ruth's appearance on the threshing floor won't surprise him, that he'll understand at once what's expected of him?

Heaven forbid if Boaz should misread Ruth's bold actions and take advantage of the situation! After all, she's hardly a maid. No man in Bethlehem would come to her defense.

Except this man. And Naomi knows it. In fact, is banking on it.

Is our mostly good Naomi behaving like a Slightly Bad Girl here? Growing impatient, running ahead of God, forcing others to risk everything while she waits safely at home? Or is she working in tandem with the Lord, responding to his leading and urging her daughter-in-law to do the same?

Maybe this will lead to our answer: suppose the "he" in "he will tell you what to do" is the Lord himself.

Ooh. I love that distinct possibility. If God is at the heart of this plan, and he is going to lead Ruth every step of the way, then no wonder Naomi has "a kind of feverishness about her desire for 'God's will' to be done."[44]

Looks like her daughter-in-law has caught that fever too.

TRUST AND OBEY

"I will do whatever you say," Ruth answered. *Ruth 3:5*

What?! No concerns, no protests? Not this girl.

Ruth assures her mother-in-law, "All that you tell me I will do" (NRSV). I'm not sure I've said those words to another human being in my entire life! Have *you* ever made such a promise? "If you say so, I'll do it, just as you've told me" (MSG). Gotta trust somebody a ton to make that kind of commitment.

We've heard Ruth speak this way before, on the road to Bethlehem: "Your people will be my people."[45] Yup. Same tone of voice, same conviction we're seeing and hearing now. Her chin is lifted, and her gaze is steady. She's obedient, but she's not subservient. Tonight's actions may be wholly unfamiliar to her, yet she's willing to go forward, with "no sign of desperation, anxiety, codependency, or lust."[46]

Easy to see why Ruth has remained a role model for women through the ages. Courage, faith, determination, hope, righteousness, and sacrificial love—she's the complete package, having every quality a woman of God needs to go the distance.

Even so, I suspect at least three questions are pressing on Ruth's heart: *Do I trust Naomi? Do I trust Boaz? Above all, do I trust God?*

To the first question, yes. Though Ruth's love forged their mother-daughter bond, Naomi has definitely come through for her since their arrival in Bethlehem. The fact that she's making arrangements to secure Ruth's future tells us what we need to know: Naomi can be trusted.

To the second question, yes again. "Naomi and Ruth are confident right from the beginning in the nobility of Boaz's heart,"[47] and nothing he's said or done since then has shaken their good opinion of him. Boaz too can be trusted.

To the third question, yes, yes, yes. God is utterly trustworthy. Just ask Ruth's great-grandson, David: "Those who know your name will trust in you, for you, LORD, have never forsaken those who seek you."[48] Ruth knows she won't travel alone this night; God will be with her on the threshing floor. She may be tested, but she won't fail.

For now, Ruth must get on with Naomi's to-do list, starting with that bath.

Both women head for the cistern, clay water jars balanced on their heads. Neighbors call out greetings, shielding their eyes from the morning sun and studying the two smiling widows, who seem to share some secret.

WHEN ALL IS SAID AND DONE

> So she went down to the threshing floor and did everything
> her mother-in-law told her to do. *Ruth 3:6*

That's it? End of story?

No, end of scene. These storytellers really knew what they were doing, leaving the audience on tenterhooks. While the stage crew prepares to lower the curtain and raise the house lights, the narrator sums up the action to come, telling us everything and nothing at the same time.

Naturally, Ruth will "put her mother-in-law's plan into action" (MSG). She's a woman of her word. I bet it wasn't long until "Naomi's plan became Ruth's plan."[49] That's how it works with a good idea. It soon becomes *your* idea, especially if you have to do the heavy lifting.

Interesting that Naomi's family position, rather than her name, is used in this verse. I'm thinking it's a reminder of her authority over her daughter-in-law as the two women go forth, "enacting time-honored roles."[50] We've heard no mention of Mahlon or Elimelech or that unfortunate season in Moab. The days of mourning are over. It's all about the future now.

Their steps sure, Naomi and Ruth pass through the town gate, glancing downhill at the threshing floor crowded with men and beasts. For the moment.

Ruth In Real Life: CHRISTIE

"My Boaz is shy, but still waters truly do run deep. He waited for me and waited for the vows before God and man before he asked for all of me. My Boaz bows his heart before God daily. While he may not be the type to do the dishes every night or bring me flowers just because, he honors me daily with his integrity, love, and encouragement. A listening ear he has in full measure. And, a friend to accompany me through life he most definitely is. I am my beloved's and he is mine."

Nine

Good Night, Sweetheart

he sun has long set. Ruth slips out the door, wrapped in a warm cloak, her freshly scrubbed face shining brighter than the moon. A sweet, heady fragrance trails after her. Though the Bible doesn't describe her scent, ancient perfumes were usually made from olive or almond oil, fixed with milk, honey, or salt, and scented with "nard and saffron, calamus and cinnamon...myrrh and aloes and all the finest spices."[1] Sounds like a nice addition to Donna Karan's Be Delicious collection, no?

At this late hour the narrow lanes between the houses are deserted except for a few laborers hurrying home to their beds, too weary to look up. Ruth heads east, downhill and downwind from the village.[2] Even in the dark the threshing floor is easily found. The sound of male laughter rises like chaff on the night wind.

Having drawn as close as she dares, Ruth pauses, her gaze fixed on the scene before us. The threshing floor is pitch dark, with no lanterns burning lest the wheat catch fire and the harvest be lost. We see nothing more than vague shapes moving around the piles of grain and pick up only snippets of conversation.

One voice in particular stands out. A deep baritone, burnished over time.

Ruth closes her eyes. In prayer? In fear? In delight? She alone knows her heart.

Now we must wait until the men settle down for the night. One Aramaic translation has Ruth tarry "until Boaz starts 'snoring.'"[3] Oh yes, we all get that.

The main thing needed is a happy hombre. And he certainly qualifies.

> When Boaz had finished eating and drinking and was in
> good spirits,... *Ruth 3:7*

Apparently he's had "a good time, eating and drinking his fill" (MSG), leaving him in a "contented mood" (NRSV). No need to fret over his drinking, though. Boaz isn't described here as inebriated, and "the book's general picture of him makes it unlikely."[4]

Finally it's bedtime for Boaz.

> ...he went over to lie down at the far end of the grain pile.
> *Ruth 3:7*

An auspicious start, him landing "at the end of the heap" (NRSV) rather than in the middle of things. A heavy blanket of exhaustion falls across the threshing floor. The beasts have been driven elsewhere for the night, and the lords of the harvest sleep like dead men, their winnowing forks abandoned.

Victor Hugo, best known for writing *Les Misérables,* also crafted a work of poetry called *"Boöz Endormi,"* or "Boaz Slept." Check out his description of our hero:

> Overcome with weariness, he kept
> To the same rough quarters as before:
> All day had seen him on the threshing floor
> And now, by sacks of wheat, tired Boaz slept.[5]

Hmm. That wait-until-he-snores idea has merit. How else to know if Boaz is truly asleep?

SOFTLY AND TENDERLY

While we watch from the sidelines, Ruth steps onto the broad circular floor. She lifts the hem of her ankle-length tunic lest it catch on the tines of his winnowing fork, then inches closer and bends over his sleeping form.

Boaz is stretched out on his side, using his upper arm as a pillow. His features are slack, his breathing shallow and even. Well and truly asleep, then. How trusting he is, nodding off in this public place where anything might happen.

Our heroine is preparing to join him—an even greater act of trust.

Ruth approached quietly,... *Ruth 3:7*

She moved toward him "softly" (KJV), "stealthily" (NRSV), "secretly" (NASB). We get it: the girl's not making a sound. Of course, she still has to play footsie with the man. That's the part that makes me nervous.

...[she] uncovered his feet and lay down. *Ruth 3:7*

Bless Ruth, she's following Naomi's instructions to the letter. Is he stirring? Not yet, it seems. If this is meant to be an "active invitation to intimacy,"[6] as one scholar suggests, it's not working. Boaz is still out like a light. Meanwhile, the way Matthew Henry saw it, Ruth "kept awake, waiting for an opportunity to tell her errand."[7]

Oh, Reverend Henry. Her "errand"? I think our sister has much more planned than that.

Meanwhile, Boaz has only one thing to say: *ZZZZZZZZZ*

In the middle of the night... *Ruth 3:8*

I'm seldom asleep before one o'clock in the morning, but in ancient times people went to bed with the sun. For them, the middle of the night was in fact midnight—"a time of momentous events,"[8] when ladders came down from heaven and prison doors flew open. "And it came to pass at midnight" (KJV) prepares audience and reader alike as we near the "tension-packed danger point in this story."[9]

There's already plenty of drama here on the threshing floor. Boaz's feet are showing. Ruth's apprehension is growing. And the snores and grunts of his fellow landowners are getting louder by the minute...

Oh!

SURPRISE, SURPRISE

...something startled the man,... Ruth 3:8

When "Boaz suddenly woke up" (NLT), Ruth jumped a little too. What startled him exactly? An angelic nudge? The sound of her soft breathing? The warmth of her body? Maybe it was just his uncovered feet grown cold.

Truth is, he's not merely awake; "the man was afraid" (KJV). Since the fear of demons was widespread in the ancient Near East, some scholars believe Boaz might have decided the figure next to him was "a night demon."[10] I'm not buying it, unless the ugly little dude wears perfume.

However frightened Boaz may be, he's intrepid enough to look.

...and he turned... Ruth 3:8

Make that "bent forward" (NASB), "sat up" (MSG), or "rolled over" (NCV).

I dunno. Sounds more like Fido than Boaz.

In the Hebrew text we get a clearer picture: "the man trembled,"[11] and not from the cold. June nights in Bethlehem hover around seventy degrees. Our strong Boaz is "frightened"[12] by what he sees.

...and [he] discovered a woman lying at his feet. Ruth 3:8

He's not only "shocked" (CEV) and "surprised" (NLT); he's now "fully alert!"[13] The man's wide-eyed expression is proof. Boaz looks rather like Jacob must have on the morning after his wedding to Rachel when "behold, it was Leah!"[14]

Notice that the names Boaz and Ruth don't appear in this verse. Just "man" and "woman," as if the storyteller is shielding their identities for propriety's sake. Or emphasizing their genders and the potential scandal that would erupt if they were discovered.

We can only guess what thoughts are running through Boaz's sleep-drugged mind. *What have I done? What does she want?* Finally he speaks, his voice low and strained.

"Who are you?" he asked. *Ruth 3:9*

The first time he saw Ruth, Boaz questioned his foreman, "Whose young woman is that?"[15] This time he speaks to her directly, using the feminine pronoun.[16] It's dark but not *that* dark. Boaz knows she's a she.

Lots of possibilities why he doesn't recognize Ruth: the unusual hour, the unexpected location, the unfamiliar perfume, the darkness, the cloak she's wearing. Confusion fills his eyes. *Who? Why?*

Ruth's expression mirrors his, for a different reason entirely. Naomi promised her, "He will tell you what to do." But that's not happening. Boaz has offered her no direction, no assistance. Only a question, and a profound one at that, asking her not merely to identify herself but also to define herself. "Who art thou?" (KJV).

She could slip away without a word, leaving him to wrestle with his night demons.

But role models don't run.

Keeping her voice low, she meets his troubled gaze and speaks the truth without apology.

I'M ALL YOURS

"I am your servant Ruth," she said. *Ruth 3:9*

Notice she doesn't call herself Ruth the Moabitess!

The older translations are closer to the Hebrew order of things: "I" first, used for emphasis, then her name, and then her role. "I am Ruth thine handmaid" (KJV). She belongs to Boaz and wants to make her intentions known. He has nothing to fear. She is there to serve him, not seduce him.

By sharing her name, Ruth also demonstrates how much she trusts Boaz. In ancient Israel, knowing someone's name gave you the power to control him or her.[17] Doubly so, I'd say, if you add the word "servant," as Ruth has.

Should she wait for him to respond? Probably. But that's not our Ruth.

Instead, she presses on with a bold proposal. Her unique way of describing marriage doesn't appear in Scripture before her story and only once after. Nor do we have any record of Naomi telling Ruth what to say.

He will tell you what to do.

I believe with all my heart that the Lord himself breathed the following words into Ruth and then gave her the courage to speak them:

"Spread the corner of your garment over me,..." *Ruth 3:9*

Every syllable astounds me. The beauty, the imagery, the poetry.

And, yes, the audacity. She's asking him to do *what*? Of all the loaded language in this chapter, her shocking request takes the prize.

From the first word we're on alert. "Spread"? *Eeek.* Yet it's in every translation from the KJV of 1611 to the NIV of 2011. We're immediately relieved when we realize it's a garment she's asking him to spread over her. Whether called a "skirt" (KJV), a "cloak" (NRSV), or a "covering" (NASB), it's a mere piece of fabric and perfectly innocent.

Since Boaz is currently wearing said covering, Ruth is *not* asking him to take it off. She needs only "the edge" (CEV) or "the corner" (NLT) as a pledge of betrothal, with one goal in mind: "a commitment to marriage, not a single night of passion."[18]

Here's what I love: Ruth is proposing to Boaz, not the other way around! And she's not asking him. No, girlfriend, she's telling him gently but firmly, "Marry me."

Sometimes the Hebrew word for "covering" is translated "wing" (AMP), found in Boaz's earlier blessing: "May you be richly rewarded by the LORD, the God of Israel, under whose wings you have come to take refuge."[19]

Ruth has done her part, Boaz. Time for you to wing it on the Lord's behalf.

BACK IN THE DAY

When writers tell us, "Spreading out a garment or a cloak symbolized contracting a marriage,"[20] we assume that custom goes way back to...well, way back. As Tevye would say in *Fiddler on the Roof,* "Tradition!"

But such customs had to start somewhere. They weren't always a tradition. In the time of Ruth, "for a woman to propose to a man, or a younger person to an elder, or a field worker to a field owner"[21] ran completely against the cultural norm. Such things were simply not done. Yet Ruth did all three.

As for a man spreading his garment over a woman to symbolize marriage, Ruth seems to have broken new ground. Before her time, we find no mention of such a thing in Scripture. Since then, history bears witness to all the ways this symbolic act has been woven into wedding ceremonies. For example, in medieval Jewish wedding ceremonies, "the groom took off his prayer shawl and covered his bride as a symbol of his willingness to tenderly cover her with protection, provision, and love."[22] And there's a marriage custom "still attested among Arabs whereby a man symbolically took a wife by throwing a garment-corner over her."[23]

I believe Ruth started something. Or rather, God started something with Ruth.

We find this imagery one other place, in the book of Ezekiel, where God himself is doing the covering: "When I looked at you and saw that you were old enough for love, I spread the corner of my garment over you and covered your nakedness. I gave you my solemn oath and entered into a covenant with you, declares the Sovereign LORD, and you became mine."[24] Once again God uses that beautiful wording to convey deep truth.

Scripture never ceases to amaze me. Sometimes it comforts, other times it convicts, and every now and again it stirs to life a painful memory, long buried, that desperately requires his healing touch. When I read the above passage in Ezekiel while working on this book, I was suddenly swept back to my freshman year of college, and tears filled my eyes.

That first year on my own was not a good one. I would do *anything* to be accepted by a sea of strangers in a place that felt nothing like home. When one of the cutest guys on campus invited me to stop by his dorm one Friday night, I was too flattered to consider his motives. Freshly bathed and scented like our Ruth, I showed up at nine, figuring the two of us would sit around and talk, maybe go out for pizza, watch a little television.

It was soon clear what he had in mind. To say the least, pizza was not on the menu. I didn't encourage him, but, sadly, I didn't resist him either. When he finished with me, he suddenly jumped up, grabbed all my clothes, and ran into the hall, where his friends were waiting.

Then I heard them laughing.

In shock, I sat on the edge of his bed, covered in nothing but shame. How could I have been so foolish? How would I ever get home? I'd never felt so exposed. Not just my body. Everything about me.

"When I looked at you and saw that you were old enough for love…"

I was old enough. But it wasn't love.

The Lord would gladly have spread his garment of grace over me, covered my nakedness, and called me his own. But I was too stubborn then, too prideful to cry out his name.

Still, God never gave up on me. Just as he will never give up on you, my sister.

Whatever you've done, wherever you've been, whomever you've known, however you've failed, our all-knowing, all-loving God is waiting for you to stop trying to fix your life so he can fix it for you. "He heals the brokenhearted and binds up their wounds."[25] That's not an empty promise; it's a proven fact.

Years later, when I finally threw myself at his mercy, the Lord washed away my shame, dressed me in a robe of righteousness, and forgave me. For all of it. Including the things that weren't my fault yet left me smothered with guilt.

It took me a decade to discover what Ruth already knows: God is the only One who can redeem us from our past and guarantee our future.

"I gave you my solemn oath and entered into a covenant with you…"

Faithful, faithful God. He not only invites us to touch the hem of his garment; he covers us with it too.

I KNOW THAT MY REDEEMER LIVES

In Boaz we see an earthly picture of our heavenly Redeemer. Ruth clearly sees that as well and so appeals to Boaz, asking him "to give her what no law can."[26] Hope, for one thing. *Hesed*, for another.

Ruth has already asked Boaz to marry her. Now she goes a step further and says, "Redeem me."

"…since you are a kinsman-redeemer." *Ruth 3:9*

It's that phrase we cherish. Somehow "close relative" (NASB) or "next-of-kin" (NRSV) falls short, leaving out that all-important aspect of redemption. The job of these "covenant redeemers" (MSG) was to care for the unfortunate, to "stand as their supporters and advocates."[27]

Boaz is *so* the man for the job. He responds at once, with joy and conviction.

"The LORD bless you, my daughter," he replied. *Ruth 3:10*

He's been awake less than a minute, and already "God and his ways are in the center of his thoughts!"[28] Any concerns over how she might be received have just flown out of Ruth's mind now that Boaz has spoken: "GOD bless you, my dear daughter!" (MSG).

However exuberant his words appear on the page, Boaz is barely speaking above a whisper. The two must not be seen, cannot be heard. *Shhh.* They're both sitting up now, quite close but not touching. Even in this dark midnight hour, "Boaz's godliness shines."[29]

Again he calls Ruth "daughter." Her cheeks grow rosy, perhaps because he says the word with such tenderness. The phrase "my daughter" appears eight times in Ruth's story—far more than in any other book of the Bible. Naomi and Boaz both voice that endearment and to a native of Moab, no less! Just can't emphasize enough how grace-giving that is.

Boaz's positive response to Ruth's two-part request lets us know he's "flattered and inwardly pleased."[30] She has asked him to act both as *go'el*, a redeemer who can save them from certain poverty, and as *levir*, a close relative who's expected to marry his deceased brother's wife so she might bear sons to carry on their father's name.

It all sounds rather boring and unromantic. Yet underneath these laws flows a river of loving-kindness, of *hesed*. God is all about providing for "the alien, the fatherless and the widow,"[31] with faithful Boaz as his chosen instrument.

He's chosen us as well, to share his good news with the poor, to bind up the brokenhearted, to comfort those who mourn, to provide for those who grieve.[32] Whether that means ladling bowls of soup at a downtown mission, reading aloud to a person who's visually impaired, standing in line at a funeral home to offer a word of comfort, or taking a meal to a Sunday school member who has buried a loved one, these acts of love are living proof that God's *hesed* still beats in the hearts of believers today, just as it did in the heart of Ruth's kinsman-redeemer.

WISE GUY

How smart is Boaz? Very.

Having blessed the woman, he now begins singing Ruth's praises—music to any woman's ears.

> "This kindness is greater than that which you showed earlier:…"
> *Ruth 3:10*

Good thing we've been with these two from the beginning, or this sentence might leave us scratching our heads. "This kindness" means her decision to seek a husband from within Elimelech's clan, which "goes beyond the call of duty."[33] And the "earlier" kindness was her full-tilt commitment to Naomi. "You are showing even more family loyalty now than you did before" (NLT) makes the meaning clearer, and this nails it: "What a splendid expression of love!" (MSG).

High praise coming from such a man. Mr. Generous has met his match.

Don't you love when two good people find each other? You don't leave their wedding saying, "I give it six months." You leave with a smile on your face, picturing them as grandparents.

> "You have not run after the younger men, whether rich or poor."
> *Ruth 3:10*

Awww, Boaz. Beneath your Superman suit beats the heart of someone who's sensitive about his age. We can't be certain how many years older than Ruth he is, but he probably belongs in "her father-in-law's generation."[34] So, yeah, older. Maybe even lots older. This isn't your typical fresh-out-of-high-school couple.

Boaz realizes what a sacrifice Ruth is making. "You could have had your pick of any of the young men around" (MSG). Maybe so, but on this threshing floor she has eyes only for you, Boaz. It isn't passion that fuels her or a desire to be a rich man's wife. She wants to be certain Naomi will be provided for and her family property and name redeemed. That kind of *hesed* touches Boaz "more than if she had fallen in love with him."[35]

Faithfulness—to God, to family, to community—is what makes his heart beat faster. The thought of a young woman sharing his convictions is almost more joy than he can handle. But handle it he does.

> "And now, my daughter, don't be afraid." *Ruth 3:11*

Kinda funny since Boaz was the one trembling in his tunic at the start of things. He's feeling his confident self again, assuring Ruth with the tenderness of a father, "Now don't worry about a thing" (NLT). Or in classic KJV phrasing, "Fear not."

Ruth's already proven she's not afraid of the dark, not afraid of speaking her mind, and not afraid of rejection. But she *has* risked losing her reputation in Bethlehem—"a reputation she has spent all summer establishing."[36]

No worries. Boaz promises Ruth that her good name is safe with him. Not only because he is an honorable man but also because, in this time and place, cultural taboos prevent a man in Boaz's high social position from taking advantage of a woman lest he destroy her reputation and endanger his own.[37] Not that he needs such restraints imposed on him. Boaz is good because he belongs to God. And now this godly young woman may soon belong to him.

Just as the Almighty said to Israel, Boaz is eager to tell Ruth, "Fear not, for I have redeemed you; I have summoned you by name; you are mine."[38]

RUTH GETS WHAT'S COMING TO HER

Here's a statement every woman on the planet would love to hear her man say:

> "I will do for you all you ask." *Ruth 3:11*

Four centuries ago these words sounded positively poetic—"I will do to thee all that thou requirest" (KJV). Though "I'll do all you could want or ask" (MSG) works too.

What Ruth wanted, asked, and required was for Boaz to marry her and so redeem her, to which Boaz has just said, "I do." Actually he said what brides and grooms usually say now: "I will."

Here's the exciting truth: our Redeemer's vows to us are even more poetic, even more powerful. He "who gives generously to all without finding fault"[39] assures us, "Ask and you will receive, and your joy will be complete."[40]

Boaz's pledge to Ruth may be heartwarming, but the Lord's promises to us are mind blowing. He doesn't give to just one; he gives to all. He doesn't give simply what we ask for; he gives us joy, a finished work. Done and dusted.

What do you need that you haven't asked him for, dear sister?

Ask him. Yes, right now. Since "your Father knows what you need before you ask him,"[41] he won't be surprised or dismayed. He'll be ready. Just *ask*.

Meanwhile, Boaz is on a roll here, not letting Ruth get a word in edgewise as he continues to heap accolades on her head.

> "All my fellow townsmen know that you are a woman of noble character." *Ruth 3:11*

Ah, "noble." A fine word to describe young Ruth, with a lot more punch than "good." The girl's just plain impressive. Over the years people have dubbed her "a virtuous woman" (KJV), "a worthy woman" (NRSV), "a woman of excellence" (NASB), and "a woman of strength (worth, bravery, capability)" (AMP). To sum things up, she's "a real prize!" (MSG).

Ruth never toots her own horn, never draws attention to herself, yet Boaz practically crows when he tells her, "You are respected by everyone in town" (CEV). He knows Ruth will bring him honor everywhere he goes, and no one will object to his marrying this Moabitess.

If "a wife of noble character is her husband's crown,"[42] then Boaz just became king. (Can we have a coronation? Please?)

Here's something I found fascinating: in the Hebrew Bible, which puts books in a different order from our Old Testament, the book of Ruth comes right after Proverbs, which ends lauding "a wife of noble character."[43] What a perfect lead-in to Ruth's story!

In fact, the Hebrew term *eset hayil*,[44] which describes our Proverbs 31 woman, is the same term Boaz just used to honor Ruth and is the identical language that first ushered our strong and wealthy Boaz into the story. God's Word really is like hidden treasure.[45]

IN SEARCH OF A GOOD WOMAN

The writer of Proverbs 31 posed the question "Who can find a virtuous wife?"[46] Surely that wouldn't be a challenge today with a church on every corner, women's conferences every weekend, and Bible studies cranking around the clock. Surely a host of Ruths are waiting to be found. Right?

Maybe. Though I know three single guys in their early thirties—handsome, bright, educated, hardworking, and totally devoted to serving the Lord— who long to marry yet cannot find young women who share their passion for Christ and want to serve him as equal partners.

Girlfriend! Are we listening but not learning? Reading the Word without applying it to our lives? *Groan.* I don't need to look any further than my own heart for the answer. Ruth's willingness to care for her grumbling mother-in-law, her steadfastness to glean beneath a hot sun week after week, her eagerness to cleave to God no matter the cost—I have a long, *long* way to go to reach that level of sacrificial living.

There certainly are Ruths to be found. You've known a few. I have as well. But they're rare and often unnoticed, quietly doing what God has called them to do. It takes a special woman to be worthy of a Boaz. Never mind that Ruth was once a Moabite. "The purity of Ruth's soul outweighed her genealogy."[47]

Theirs is a unique love story—perhaps the most beautiful in all literature— but it doesn't fit the popular definition of a romance. These are two people who love and serve God first and others second. Whatever mutual love or affection they might feel is never mentioned in Scripture.

Boaz and Ruth are meant for each other in the deepest sense. They're both people of honor. Bold when boldness is called for yet gentle at all times. We can easily picture them doing an eHarmony commercial, telling us how they met in the barley field and quickly realized they had all twenty-nine compatibility dimensions covered.

Here on the threshing floor, Ruth must be wondering about the next step. A consultation with a wedding planner over breakfast seems like the perfect way to begin the next day. But we have a little problem. No, a big one. The fact that "Boaz nowhere symbolically covered Ruth with his garment-corner as she asked"[48] gives us a little clue.

You know when the minister says, "If any person here can show just cause or impediment why this couple may not be joined in holy matrimony, speak now or forever hold your peace"?

Don't look now, but Boaz just raised his hand...

Ruth In Real Life: PENNEY

"A week after I met my Boaz, we went to his house to watch a movie, and I was fast asleep within minutes. An hour later, when I began to stir, I heard someone talking and realized he was praying that God would keep our relationship pure! That was the moment I fell in love with him. Boaz Qualities 1 and 2: a man of prayer and a man of purity. Planning our wedding, I was very focused on being financially conservative, but he insisted we have the wedding of our dreams! Boaz Quality 3: a man who goes above and beyond to give his Ruth the desires of her heart."

Ten

Sitting Tight for Mr. Right

Our noble Ruth is about to discover the impediment that stands in the way of her marriage to Boaz.

We're from the future. We know what's coming. The hope shining in her eyes is almost more than we can bear. Please, Boaz, just tell her.

> "Although it is true that I am near of kin, there is a kinsman-redeemer nearer than I." *Ruth 3:12*

Her shoulders sink and surely her heart as well. Poor Ruth! Even the kindness in his voice and the warmth of his expression can't disguise the truth: there's "another kinsman more closely related" (NRSV) than Boaz. As the nearer relative, he is the one who should marry her, redeem her family's property, and give her a son.

Dreadful news now that Ruth has laid herself at Boaz's feet. Was she aware such a kinsman existed? Surely Naomi didn't know about another redeemer in the wings or she wouldn't have put this whole night in motion.

Unless…

Unless our wise Naomi trusted Boaz *and* the Lord, who in all things "works for the good of those who love him." I know Romans 8:28 isn't in the Old Testament, but God's truth is eternal. If ever a couple was "called according to his purpose," it's this one. Once again, Boaz demonstrates his integrity, even if it means throwing his own happiness on a burning altar.

After dropping that little bombshell, Boaz quickly lays out his plan.

"Stay here for the night,..." *Ruth 3:13*

Remember how Naomi promised, "He will tell you what to do"? If, in fact, she meant Boaz, he's finally doing his part. Boaz urges Ruth to "tarry" (KJV) or "remain" (NRSV) through the night. The literal translation is "lodging," but have no fear. He's not asking Ruth to shack up with him! This isn't Rod Stewart belting out "Stay with Me" at the Roundhouse in London. This is our godly Boaz trying to do the right thing.

I love the way one Jewish writer paraphrased it: "May you be mine by virtue of this night!"[1] Boaz is not sending her away, nor is he claiming her, but at least he's protecting her and guarding both their reputations by not allowing her to be seen or heard on the threshing floor.

This is what makes Boaz such a hero. He thinks beyond the moment.

He also must attend to Ruth's concerns. Who is this other kinsman? Is he young or old? Rich or poor? Smart or dull? Kind or cruel? Those are the things *we're* worried about.

What surely troubles Ruth? He's not Boaz. Worse, he's a stranger. Yet he has the right to claim her, which Boaz makes abundantly clear.

"...and in the morning if he wants to redeem, good; let him redeem." *Ruth 3:13*

What? Boaz, you cannot be so heartless! Do you really mean, "If he decides to take care of you, that is fine" (NCV)? Well, that is *not* fine with Ruth. Or Naomi. Or us.

Though, to be fair, Boaz doesn't look or sound like a man who's unconcerned. Quite the opposite. He bends closer, his eyes filled with compassion. "If he is willing to redeem you," Boaz says softly, "very well. Let him marry you" (NLT).

As ever, he's thinking about her welfare, about his family duties, about doing what's proper and good. He gets so many points for that. Whatever his feelings for Ruth, Boaz is determined to honor the Almighty at all costs. A fine quality in a husband; an absolute necessity in a redeemer.

ON THE OTHER HAND

"But if he is not willing,..." *Ruth 3:13*

A smile plays at the corners of his mouth as if he knows something about this other man. Might the dude *not* be willing? Boaz has planted that possibility in our minds. "If he isn't interested" (MSG), Boaz says. "If he does not wish to redeem you..." (NASB). He lets that sink in, then presses on, his voice firmer.

"...as surely as the LORD lives I will do it." *Ruth 3:13*

Now it's Ruth's turn to smile. "The eternal God"[2] surely does live! Boaz is unabashedly telling her, "I will redeem you" (NASB), "I will take care of you" (NCV), "I promise by the living God to do it myself" (CEV). Woo hoo! We know how this is going to turn out. In the Hebrew text the word "I" is emphasized. Boaz is as determined to stay with Ruth as she was to stay with Naomi.

And isn't it grand how he always brings the Lord on board? As Isaiah proclaimed, "Our Redeemer—the LORD Almighty is his name—is the Holy One of Israel."[3] God is ever on Boaz's mind. He's convinced the Lord is in charge and takes him at his word.

God is not only involved in the lives of these biblical characters, but he is also fully involved in our lives—every second, every minute, every hour, every day, every week, every month, every year. From long before we were born until after we go on to glory, the living God is doing his redeeming work: creating us in his image, then re-creating us into "the likeness of his Son."[4]

Boaz urges Ruth to trust him and invokes the Lord's name just as Ruth did when she made her pledge to Naomi. By taking an oath, which was not done lightly in Israel of old, Boaz means to dispel any lingering doubts or fears.

He's not only asking Ruth to stay. He's asking Ruth to rest, both physically and spiritually, trusting God to take care of things.

"Lie here until morning." *Ruth 3:13*

Nothing inappropriate here. Although Boaz may enjoy having Ruth close by his side, "the simple instruction steers well clear of sexual activity."[5] This is mostly about safety. He can't leave his grain unguarded on the threshing floor to escort her home. And he can't dispatch her on her own in the middle of the night. Best to keep her near until just before dawn, when she can slip away undetected and unharmed.

After their whispered exchange, a hush falls over Bethlehem's threshing floor. Ruth expected to be a betrothed woman by this dark hour. Instead, she is a lady in waiting.

> So she lay at his feet until morning,... *Ruth 3:14*

Just as she obeyed her mother-in-law, Ruth now obeys Boaz. Those of us who are naturally rebellious may chafe at her willingness to do what she's told. But it's not cowardice on Ruth's part; it's common sense. These two are her elders and residents of Bethlehem besides. They know the score and are concerned for her welfare, so Ruth wisely respects them and does their bidding. She's smart, not timid.

Boaz said nothing about lying at his feet, but that's where she's landed. Safer that way, rather than curling up like spoons in a drawer or putting her perfumed skin any closer to his than necessary. Ruth may have "stayed" (NCV), but I doubt she "slept" (MSG) as she watched for a faint gray light in the eastern sky.

Unlike the daughters of Lot, Ruth lay at a man's feet all night without breaking the Law. One commentator calls Ruth "the anti-Moabite,"[6] so chaste was her behavior, especially compared to her ancestors.

Finally dawn approaches. Ruth is ready. More than ready.

RISE AND SHINE

> ...but [she] got up before anyone could be recognized;... *Ruth 3:14*

It's still dark amid the piles of grain. We can see figures but not faces. All are asleep, save Boaz and Ruth.

Gathering her cloak around her, "she rose up before one could know another" (KJV), no doubt reluctant to leave Boaz but eager to leave the threshing floor. "She was not shy of being known to be a gleaner in the field," Matthew Henry observes. "But she would not willingly be known to be a night-walker."[7] A prostitute or thief who roams about at night? Not our Ruth.

Boaz stands as well, moistening his lips, preparing to speak. If only he'd say something romantic, like "Rise up, my love, my fair one."[8] But drawing attention to Ruth is the last thing he wants.

> ...and he said, "Don't let it be known that a woman came
> to the threshing floor." *Ruth 3:14*

The name Ruth doesn't appear in the Hebrew text. Only "woman." Boaz doesn't even whisper her name lest he be overheard. And Ruth doesn't speak at all. A low male voice at that hour might not be noticed. A higher, female voice would definitely stand out.

It's not primarily the town gossips that concern them. The real danger is, if a man is suspected of having sex with a Gentile, he cannot marry her and perform the role of *levir*.[9] No way is Boaz gonna risk losing her over a technicality or ruining her future with this other redeemer if it comes to that.

The sooner she's on her way, the better.

But, true to his nature, Boaz cannot send her home empty-handed.

Spread Your Garment

> He also said, "Bring me the shawl you are wearing and hold it
> out." *Ruth 3:15*

Whether her outer attire is called a "cape" (CEV), a "veil" (KJV), a "cloak" (NRSV), or a "mantle" (AMP), it's made of a sturdy fabric, strong enough to bear the weight of what Boaz has in mind. However, "bring" seems an odd request since she's right next to him. Perhaps he's asking her to hold it up or, better yet, to "spread it out" (NLT).

Lovely symmetry here. At midnight Ruth asked him to spread his garment for her. Now at the break of day, he's asking Ruth to spread her garment for him.

The best part is, now that the black sky is turning to gray, "Ruth and Boaz can gaze into one another's eyes for the first time."[10] We find no shame reflected in those dark brown depths, only mutual respect, fond affection, and a faith that cannot be shaken.

As Boaz turns to the bounty of grain well within reach, our dutiful Ruth spreads out her shawl.

> When she did so, he poured into it six measures of barley...
> *Ruth 3:15*

Fascinating. *Six,* not seven. Throughout the Bible seven is the number of completion. But Boaz isn't finished yet; he hasn't redeemed her. So "six scoops of barley" (NLT) it is. Basically, "a lot of grain" (CEV). After all, how much is a "measure"?

It's the kind gesture that matters, not the amount. He's given her as much as she can carry. So much, she's struggling to handle it. Struggling to hide her tears too. After all, this is barley Ruth has not gleaned or gathered or cleaned or threshed. It's a gift. Pure grace from Boaz's hand. He has yet to fill her body with a son, but he has filled her cloak with his grain, hinting at a future harvest.

As a side benefit, if anyone should stop Ruth as she leaves the threshing floor, she'll have valid proof of why she was there: breakfast cereal for Naomi.

But first she has to lug it all home.

> ...and [he] put it on her. *Ruth 3:15*

Did Boaz put the barley "on her back" (NLT), "on her shoulder" (CEV), or "on her head" (NCV)? There's so much barley, it really covers all three. I watched a woman in Jerusalem stroll through the marketplace balancing an enormous sack on her head and shoulders. Ruth is doing the same, doubled over with his blessing. She's a walking, talking example of the Lord's provision for those who are generous: "A good measure, pressed down, shaken together and running over, will be poured into your lap."[11] Except her lap is the one place Boaz could *not* put her barley, or good luck walking home.

Personally, I wish Boaz had filled a wheelbarrow, though with this hilly, rugged terrain, it's probably best if she carries it. Nice that he "assisted Ruth in positioning it."[12] It's the first time we have the slightest hint of physical contact between our virtuous duo. Boaz takes great care as he arranges the makeshift sack of grain, his hand lightly grazing her shoulder, then brushing against her arm. So tender is his touch we might think we imagined it except for the look of contentment on Ruth's face.

RETURN TO SENDER

Then he went back to town. Ruth 3:15

I thought he had to stay with his grain. Now that the sun is coming up and those night-walking thieves have vanished, maybe it's safe for Boaz to leave.

Some translate the verse "she went into the city" (KJV). So did he go, or did she go? Don't lose any sleep over this. The fact is, they both went back to Bethlehem, though you can be sure they didn't leave together. Nor were they headed to the same location. Boaz, as we'll soon learn, is bound for the town gates with important business matters to discuss. Ruth is hurrying home to an anxious mother-in-law, who probably hasn't slept a wink.

Even weighed down with her load of barley, Ruth quickly hoofs it uphill toward town, grateful for the early hour. Women will start appearing with their water jars any minute. At last Ruth steps through the door of their home and lets the cloak full of grain slide from her shoulders into a heap.

Naomi stares at the barley, gapes at the girl, then blurts out a question.

> When Ruth came to her mother-in-law, Naomi asked, "How did it go, my daughter?" Ruth 3:16

That's what most people would ask, but the literal translation of the Hebrew is "Who art thou?" (KJV). Or in the Lizzie Revised Version, "Who are you? Mrs. Boaz?"

For the third time in this story, Ruth's identity is questioned. Maybe it's because her identity keeps changing. From wife to widow. From Moabite woman to Israelite woman. From wannabe gleaner to wannabe bride.

It's a question worth asking in any century. Who are you, dear sister? What are the roles that define you? The tasks that shape your day? The titles and labels you wear? Beneath it all, who is the real you, the one only God sees?

In the same way, I think Naomi's question for Ruth goes far past the surface. Not just who are you, but also how are you, and where are you, and when will your redemption come? Change is in the wind; Naomi is sure of it. In her simple query hides a deeper one: "Art thou a bride or no? Must I give thee joy?"[13]

Naomi has waited all night to find out if their kinsman-redeemer has done his part. Ruth wastes no time spilling the beans, if not the barley.

> Then she told her everything Boaz had done for her... *Ruth 3:16*

Nice summation. No need to repeat it all for audience or reader. We were there when it happened.

It's what Ruth leaves out that I find interesting. Though she describes "all that the man had done to her" (KJV), we get no description of all that she said and did to him. No mention of her fearless proposal, no discussion of her spread-the-corner-of-your-garment invitation, no exploration of her feelings when he took his time fitting the grain across her shoulders.

Nothing about herself. Just Boaz, Boaz, Boaz.

By focusing Naomi's gaze in Boaz's direction, Ruth neatly avoids having to recount her own bold actions. She did what Naomi, the Lord, and Boaz directed her to do. No point belaboring it.

> ...and [she] added, "He gave me these six measures of barley, saying, 'Don't go back to your mother-in-law empty-handed.'"
> *Ruth 3:17*

Hold it. When did Boaz tell Ruth, "You must not go home without a gift for your mother-in-law" (NCV)? I didn't hear him say that. Did you?

Maybe he whispered those words when he placed the grain on Ruth's shoulders. Could be the storyteller included them here for more impact now that we're looking at Naomi. We can be sure Boaz made that statement; it would be entirely out of character for Ruth to lie, not even to bless her mother-in-law.

Whenever they were spoken, his words echo Naomi's earlier comment about returning to Bethlehem "empty."[14] Now her heart is full of hope, her house is full of barley, and her arms may yet be filled with grandchildren. Naomi's life is anything but empty.

The barley itself "is a sign for Naomi that Boaz is committed to both the women."[15] He won't redeem Ruth and leave Naomi to fend for herself.

This may surprise you: Ruth has spoken her last line. Though her book continues for another full chapter, her dialogue does not. From first word to last, she has affirmed her commitment to her mother-in-law. Though she did many other fine things, Ruth is most remembered for guiding another woman on her journey from misery to joy.

No wonder she's a role model for all women, for all time.

A FINAL WORD FROM NAOMI

Then Naomi said, "Wait, my daughter, until you find out what happens." *Ruth 3:18*

Impatient, fretful Naomi telling someone, "Just be patient and don't worry" (CEV) is hilarious. "Sit still" (KJV) is closer to the Hebrew, which literally means "sit down" or, as we might put it today, "sit tight."[16] Either way, sitting is involved—difficult to do when you're wound like a top. "Sit back and relax" (MSG), eh? I think Naomi really means, "Wait and see, dear girl. This will go well."

We wondered earlier if Naomi knew about this nearer kinsman-redeemer. You bet she did. This is her late husband's family. And, remember, she said of Boaz, "He is one of our kinsman-redeemers."[17] But he's not the only one. And not the nearest one.

Still, if Naomi's not worried, that's a big clue for Ruth: Boaz has it all covered.

"For the man will not rest until the matter is settled today." *Ruth 3:18*

Even as Naomi is telling Ruth to rest, she's assuring her that Boaz *won't* rest "until everything is settled today!" (CEV). That's Boaz's character, all right: he keeps his word and doesn't drag his feet. The same can be said of our Redeemer: "He who is coming will come and will not delay."[18]

Meanwhile, Naomi and Ruth can do nothing to help things along. They can't work, can't glean, and can't scheme. All they can do is sit tight.

Maybe that's the simplest definition of faith: sitting tight. Waiting without fretting. Trusting without second-guessing. Believing without demanding proof.

True confession: I am the worst when it comes to waiting. How about you, sis? Are you, like me, far better at fretting? If Naomi can learn patience, there's hope for us. Here's a word of encouragement to point us in the right direction: "be strong and take heart and wait for the LORD."[19]

Naomi's closing speech reveals how far the woman has come. "Today!" she says. And we believe her.

No pressure, Boaz, but the clock is ticking.

Ruth In Real Life: JUDY

"At first I did not have a good relationship with my mother-in-law, who lived just across the road from me. However, I never denied her access to my children, and they grew up loving her. Eventually she became milder, and so did I. She is in heaven now, and our lives are richer for having known and loved her."

Ruth In Real Life: STEPHANIE

"When I met my husband, I was a broken, damaged single mom trying to recover from the pain of divorce from an abusive man. My Boaz is the most loving, selfless man I've ever known. He was so patient with me as I healed, and he loved my daughter like his own. I could never have dreamed that such a man existed, and I am so grateful that the Lord gave him to me!"

Eleven

Our Hero Makes His Move

W hen last we stood at the town gate, a group of women welcomed home an old friend who insisted they call her "Bitter." My, how things have changed. This time it's the guys who are gathering, beginning with one fine man in particular.

Meanwhile Boaz went up to the town gate and sat there. *Ruth 4:1*

The simple word "meanwhile" is a powerful reminder that life goes on, that it doesn't begin and end with our momentary triumphs and struggles. While we're obsessed with here and now, God is focused on forever.

He doesn't make an appearance, yet we sense God's presence in the sunlit business hub of Bethlehem. As Paul wrote, "He will bring to light what is hidden in darkness and will expose the motives of men's hearts."[1]

We know Boaz's motives are pure. It's that other kinsman-redeemer we're worried about. While Naomi and Ruth sit tight, Boaz is seated too after heading "straight to the public square" (MSG), just as Naomi said he would.

Boaz looks very much at home, settled in a prominent spot from which he can easily observe who's coming and going this morning. As a wealthy landowner, he's probably a town elder, charged with maintaining peace within Bethlehem's walls.[2]

Today he has only one goal in mind: redeeming Ruth and guaranteeing her future. His expression is resolute, his gaze even, as he scans the crowded square. He must have stopped by his house en route, because he's dressed in a costly tunic edged in gold, and his head covering is neatly arranged across his shoulders. Though he is rich and powerful, Boaz wants to make certain the laws and customs of the land will protect and provide for Ruth should he not be the one to redeem her (perish the thought!).

If only that other kinsman would hurry up and get here...

Oh. Hello.

Right on Cue

When the kinsman-redeemer he had mentioned came along,...
Ruth 4:1

Would you look at this guy? Ambling past as if he has all the time in the world and no good way to spend it. Literally, he has "wandered by"[3] and at the very moment he's needed. As we've seen before in this story, the timing is too good to be anything but God's plan.

Boaz is already beckoning the man closer.

...Boaz said, "Come over here, my friend, and sit down." *Ruth 4:1*

Check out this translation from four centuries ago: "Ho, such a one!" (KJV). Hear that underlying note of derision? In Hebrew, Boaz calls the man *peloni 'almoni,* "a rhyming but meaningless phrase."[4] It's the equivalent of "Joe Schmo or John Doe."[5] Or better yet, "Mr. So-and-So."[6]

Boaz surely knows this kinsman. Has he momentarily forgotten the man's name? (Happens to me all the time. "Great to see you...um, again!") Or is the storyteller letting us see how unimportant the guy is? As a novelist I name my primary and secondary characters, but walk-ons get little more than a brief description: gray-haired man with rheumy eyes, couple in rustic clothing, coy dairymaid with dimples.

A name says, "Pay attention."

No name says, "Never mind."

Boaz commands, if not demands, this unnamed fellow's attention. "Turn aside and sit down" (AMP), he tells him.

So he went over and sat down. *Ruth 4:1*

Not exactly scintillating narrative, but it tells us that Mr. No clearly respects Boaz. The man takes a seat without raising a single question or complaint.

And he's about to have company.

ORDER IN THE COURT

Boaz took ten of the elders of the town and said, "Sit here," and they did so. *Ruth 4:2*

Has our hero been reading a stack of leadership books in his spare time? Because he is definitely running the show this morning. Boaz calls together "ten of the older leaders" (NCV)—generally the patriarchs of the various families—and informs them, "We've got some business to take care of" (MSG). The rabbis of old thought ten was the ideal number for such councils.[7] Throw in Boaz and Mr. No, and we have a sizable group forming.

Around the busy square, people start elbowing one another and nodding in this direction. It's common knowledge that Ruth has been gleaning in the fields of Boaz for many weeks, and his preferential treatment of the young Moabitess has not gone unnoticed. A rich bachelor. A poor widow. The townsfolk think they know how this is going to play out.

But you and I were at the threshing floor. We know that much is yet to be decided.

When Boaz speaks, all of Bethlehem listens.

Then he said to the kinsman-redeemer, "Naomi, who has come back from Moab, is selling the piece of land that belonged to our brother Elimelech." *Ruth 4:3*

Wait a second. "Land"? What land? Isn't this supposed to be about redeeming Ruth?

We aren't the only ones confused. Modern scholars offer any number of explanations for Boaz's unexpected foray into real estate.

Basically, their theories boil down to these two: (1) Naomi's family owns a parcel of land, which she's now forced to sell because they need the cash, or (2) Elimelech sold this land before they left for Moab, and Naomi needs to buy it back because family property can't be sold permanently. She has no money, of course, which means a kinsman needs to redeem the land on her behalf.[8]

The Lord knows what he's doing. We didn't need to hear about the land issue until this moment.

Boaz knows what he's doing too. Property first, wedding bells later. Kinda fun to watch him work the crowd in his open-air courtroom.

> "I thought I should bring the matter to your attention and suggest that you buy it in the presence of these seated here and in the presence of the elders of my people." *Ruth 4:4*

My, how formal he sounds. Smart too. Boaz could've informed his kinsman privately and then pulled in the elders to oversee the transaction once an agreement was reached. Doing it all in public forces Mr. No to decide on the spot and reveals his true character in the bargain.

I'm intrigued by that last phrase, "my people." If Mr. No is related to Boaz and Naomi, aren't these his people too? We get the idea Mr. No isn't part of Bethlehem society. Maybe he lives elsewhere in Israel or has ties to another clan. Now he has the chance to own property in this area and earn a name for himself—literally.

Boaz puts the choice before him.

> "If you will redeem it, do so. But if you will not, tell me, so I will know." *Ruth 4:4*

He sounds so casual, so matter-of-fact. "You have first redeemer rights," Boaz says to the man. "If you don't want it, tell me so I'll know where I stand" (MSG). Boaz doesn't tip his hand, doesn't look the least bit concerned. And still no mention of Ruth.

"For no one has the right to do it except you, and I am next in line." *Ruth 4:4*

Boaz makes it clear who's next at bat: "I come after you" (NRSV). If there are other potential redeemers in the wings, Boaz doesn't bother mentioning them. Their services won't be needed.

His straightforward offer produces an immediate response from Mr. No:

"I will redeem it," he said. *Ruth 4:4*

His words sound more greedy than gracious. "All right" (NLT), he tells the elders. "I'll buy it" (MSG). Mr. No is a happy camper, thinking once he's purchased this land, all he'll have to worry about is providing for Naomi, an older widow with no children.

But what about RUTH?! Sorry, don't mean to shout, but she's the elephant in the room, the obvious subject no one is talking about.

Until now.

LET'S MAKE A DEAL

Then Boaz said, "On the day you buy the land from Naomi and from Ruth the Moabitess, you acquire the dead man's widow, in order to maintain the name of the dead with his property." *Ruth 4:5*

To say "this goes well beyond the traditions of Mosaic Law"[9] is the understatement of the decade. Boaz is determined to honor Ruth's request that he serve as both *go'el* and *levir*. He's taking two separate laws and combining them into one and doing it with such conviction that not one of the town elders raises the slightest objection.

Let's do a quick review since these ancient laws can be confusing.

Redeeming family property was the job of the *go'el:* "If one of your countrymen becomes poor and sells some of his property, his nearest relative is to come and redeem what his countryman has sold."[10] Okay, we get that—be the man and buy the land.

Marrying a childless widow was the task of the *levir:* "Her husband's brother shall take her and marry her and fulfill the duty of a brother-in-law to her. The first son she bears shall carry on the name of the dead brother so that his name will not be blotted out from Israel."[11] An outrageous idea to our modern way of thinking, but, yes, we have some grasp of the concept—marry your brother-in-law to keep the family name and genes alive.

But Ruth's brother-in-law, Kilion, is dead. Elimelech's family line is kaput. Levirate law didn't require a young widow to climb up and down the family tree until she found some living male relative willing to give her a son. Only a blood brother (or their father, in a pinch) could fulfill the role of the *levir.*

That's why Ruth's midnight proposal to Boaz blew his mind. She doesn't *have* to marry him; she *chooses* to marry him. She doesn't want just anyone for a husband; she wants a righteous man who speaks the language of loving-kindness, of grace. No wonder he'll do anything within the spirit of the law to make that happen.

Smooth-tongued Boaz makes this double redemption sound like standard procedure. "Of course," he says to Mr. No, "your purchase of the land from Naomi also requires that you marry Ruth, the Moabite widow" (NLT). "Of course"? Now that's chutzpah. Eugene Peterson phrases it, "You realize, don't you..." (MSG). If Mr. No didn't realize it before, he does now.

Remember on the threshing floor when Boaz told Ruth that all his fellow townsmen considered her "a woman of noble character"?[12] Maybe that's why the men of Bethlehem are letting Boaz spin this finely woven web. If Mr. No isn't worthy of such a woman, what better way to put an end to his redemption offer than to make it seem like a bad idea?

THREE STRIKES, SHE'S OUT

Look again at how Boaz introduces Ruth to this kinsman-redeemer. First he calls her a "Moabitess." No Israelite in his right mind would welcome one of those foreign women into his bed. Then Boaz points out she's a "dead man's widow." (Didn't know there was any other kind!) Simply hearing the words "dead man" would send most guys packing. Without saying so, Boaz may be hinting that foul play was involved. And since she requires a *levir* to redeem her husband's name, the woman is definitely childless and perhaps even barren.

Were Ruth standing there, I doubt Boaz would have painted so unappealing a portrait. But since she's safely back at Naomi's house, he can say whatever he likes about the "widow of the deceased" (NASB) as long as it produces the desired result.

And it does.

> At this, the kinsman-redeemer said, "Then I cannot redeem it…"
> *Ruth 4:6*

Buying the land is a legal obligation; marrying Ruth is a moral obligation. Now we understand why this guy's not worthy of a name: he was willing to do *A* but not *B*. As quickly as he said yes, he's now scrambling to say no. "Oh, I can't do that" (MSG), he insists.

Boaz exchanges glances with the town elders while Mr. No desperately tries to make them understand: "I don't want to buy it!" (CEV). As far as Mr. No is concerned, it's all about the money. Ruth isn't even mentioned when he offers this feeble excuse:

> "…because I might endanger my own estate." *Ruth 4:6*

You see, if he were to give Ruth a son, then the property Mr. No agreed to buy would go to her child. "He'd actually be losing on the deal, then, paying for land he would never own."[13] This is why Boaz is such a good guy: he's okay with buying, then losing the land. More than okay, he's eager to do right by Ruth, whatever it costs him—not because he loves her in a romantic way, but because he loves her in a *hesed* way.

Boaz is showing the ancient world what a redeemer looks like, what happens when "love transcends law,"[14] preparing the way for a far greater Redeemer to come. Out of a sense of justice, Boaz will sacrifice some of his wealth to redeem

Ruth, to give her hope and a future. Out of a heart of mercy, Jesus would later sacrifice his life to redeem his people, giving us the very same things: hope and a future.

Somebody please shout "Amen!"

The book of Ruth isn't just a love story; it's *the* love story. It's a picture of God wooing his bride, drawing her into his embrace, and whispering words of comfort and assurance. *You're mine. You're safe. No one can take you from my side.* It's God revealing his steadfast nature through Boaz, an earthly ancestor of his beloved Son.

Like Ruth, we are poor in spirit. We have no dowry to offer our Bridegroom, nothing of worth. Yet the Lord is preparing a home for us in heaven,[15] where we'll each be given a new name.[16] That's our kinsman, Jesus. That's our Redeemer.

Mr. No can't redeem Ruth or preserve the family name because he doesn't have what it takes. He doesn't have *hesed*. And he knows it.

> "You redeem it yourself. I cannot do it." *Ruth 4:6*

Having already withdrawn his offer a second ago, Mr. No quickly steps down as kinsman-redeemer. "You can have my rights" (msg), he tells Boaz. Like Esau, who sold his birthright to Jacob for a bowl of stew, Mr. No is relinquishing his duty to another who is more worthy. Since he isn't Mahlon's brother—a true *levir*—what Mr. No is doing isn't illegal or immoral, but it's also not honorable. It's not *hesed*.

One more step and Ruth's redemption will be a done deal.

SHOE, MR. NO!

The next verse is enclosed in parentheses in some translations, like a sidebar providing helpful info about an Israelite custom that was no longer followed. It's also an indication that many years passed between the life of Ruth and the recording of her story. The audience then—and readers ever after—needed to know how real estate changed hands circa 1200 BC.

(Now in earlier times in Israel, for the redemption and transfer of property to become final, one party took off his sandal and gave it to the other. This was the method of legalizing transactions in Israel.) *Ruth 4:7*

Today we'd sign a document. Back then people kept things simple and symbolic. Why'd they use a sandal? Because when land was purchased, the buyer measured his property by walking along the boundary. Sandals became a portable title.[17]

Ah, but there's more going on than just handing over footwear. When that whole levirate marriage thing got started, a widowed woman whose brother-in-law refused to marry her had one recourse. She could go to the elders at the town gate (sound familiar?) and charge her brother-in-law with dropping the ball. If he didn't listen to reason, she'd "take off one of his sandals, spit in his face and say, 'This is what is done to the man who will not build up his brother's family line.' That man's line shall be known in Israel as The Family of the Unsandaled."[18]

The guy not only lost his sandal; he lost his family name too. *Hmm.* Kinda like Mr. No, who keeps repeating himself.

So the kinsman-redeemer said to Boaz, "Buy it yourself." And he removed his sandal. *Ruth 4:8*

Having "signed the deal by pulling off his shoe" (MSG), Mr. No disappears from the scene, limping off in disgrace, while our hero, proudly standing with both feet shod, addresses the crowd.

HER REDEEMER LIVES

Then Boaz announced to the elders and all the people, "Today you are witnesses that I have bought from Naomi all the property of Elimelech, Kilion and Mahlon." *Ruth 4:9*

He begins his short speech with "you are witnesses," and he'll end with those words too. In between, he neatly sums up the proceedings for the whole town to hear lest there be any doubt about who owns what. It's all his.

Enough about the land, Boaz. Tell us about the girl.

> "I have also acquired Ruth the Moabitess, Mahlon's widow, as my wife,…" *Ruth 4:10*

It's done, girlfriend. Ruth is redeemed! A murmur of approval swells through the crowd. Someone is already hightailing it to Naomi's house with the good news.

Boaz uses the same Hebrew word for claiming both the land and the lady—*qnh,* "to acquire"[19]—but that's just to make things legal. We can hear the difference in his voice, the warm note of affection, when he speaks of taking Ruth "to be my wife" (NRSV). He includes her homeland not only to identify her but also to honor her, showing the crowd he isn't ashamed to marry this godly Moabite woman. He doesn't care that she's foreign, that she's widowed, that she's poor. He will gladly do for her all that she asks and more than she can imagine.

Boaz really has this hero thing down.

Is he one of a kind? Or can you name lots of men with his winning combination of faith, integrity, strength, and generosity—men who'd qualify as a Boaz In Real Life?

My daughter-in-law, wise beyond her years, defines his modern counterpart like this: "A Boaz is a man of emotional and spiritual maturity who comes into your life during a period when you most need him and helps you see the worth you already possess."

By that definition, I'm grateful to say I married a Boaz.

I wasn't a Moabitess, but I was assuredly a Former Bad Girl. I wasn't a widow, but I'd left a string of dead relationships trailing behind me. And I wasn't barren, but in ten years of promiscuous living, I'd not conceived a child.

Even so, a good man said, "I will" and "I do," and he has and he does.

Can I step inside Ruth's sandals and know what she's feeling right now?

Oh yes, my dear sister, I can.

Ruth has just heard the news from a breathless friend gasping out the words in the cool interior of Naomi's house. "He did it! Boaz has redeemed your property. And you as well!"

Her heart about to burst, Ruth reaches for Naomi's hand and pulls her through the door. They are running by the time they reach the town gate. Tears of joy stream down Ruth's face, and Naomi's smile is triumphant.

I'm laughing *and* crying. You too? O happy day.

The women arrive just in time to hear Boaz affirm what will happen when Ruth bears him a son. We hear no hesitation or doubt in his voice, only a strong sense of resolve.

> "…in order to maintain the name of the dead with his property,
> so that his name will not disappear from among his family or
> from the town records." *Ruth 4:10*

It's not easy for a man to say he'll make certain that his wife's first husband is never forgotten, that his "memory and reputation" (MSG) will be kept alive. But this is what a Boaz does: he keeps his word, and he looks to the future.

My own dear Boaz never speaks of my past, never tosses my indiscretions in my face, never reminds me how generous he was to overlook that miserable decade of my life. Do I deserve such grace? Not for a minute. Am I grateful for his love? Every hour of every day of our happily married lives.

Thank you, thank you, thank you, Lord. You too, sweet Bill.

Only a Redeemer would pair a Former Bad Girl with a Truly Good Guy.

Why does the Lord do such seemingly impossible things? Because he can. And because he delights in getting the glory. Redemption always bears God's signature.

Time for Boaz to verbally bang his gavel. Though he speaks loudly enough for the whole town to hear, his warm gaze is fixed on Naomi and Ruth.

> "Today you are witnesses!" *Ruth 4:10*

Such exuberance! How appropriate that these are the last recorded words of Boaz, ringing through the centuries: "ye are witnesses this day" (KJV). Naomi said the issue would be resolved today, and indeed it has been.

> Then the elders and all those at the gate said, "We are witnesses."
> *Ruth 4:11*

With their echo of Boaz's words—the equivalent of scrawling their names at the bottom of a document—this day's transaction is complete. The elders observed, approved, and will stand by Boaz's redemption of Ruth. So will all of Bethlehem. As ministers have declared through the centuries, "What God has joined together let no man put asunder."

Are we done then? Tea and biscuits at the town gate?

Not quite. The elders have a wedding present for the happy couple. Not something wrapped in white paper or tied with a gold bow but definitely a gift.

BLESS YOU, GIRL

When Boaz beckons Ruth to his side, she does not hesitate. They look nothing like the couple on top of a wedding cake. His hair is shot with silver; her worn tunic has seen better days. But their faces shine like the sun.

One elder speaks for all, his words resounding through the crowded town square.

> "May the LORD make the woman who is coming into your home
> like Rachel and Leah, who together built up the house of Israel."
> *Ruth 4:11*

Granted, Ruth isn't mentioned by name, but the blessing the elders are bestowing on her and the two names they *do* mention boggle the mind. Ruth is no longer a Moabite; she's an Israelite. She's no longer a foreigner; she's family. She's no longer a widow; she's a wife.

And she's compared to two of the matriarchs who, with a little help from their maidservants, produced *all twelve tribes of Israel*. Oh baby. Make that "babies." When it comes to blessing a new bride in old Bethlehem, it doesn't get any better than this.

Are you thinking, *Lucky Ruth*? Beloved, this story isn't about her, not at the core. It's about our Sovereign God, who has the power to change our lives, our circumstances, our hearts. To turn wrong to right and dark to light. To restore what was lost, to redeem what was squandered, to revive what was dead and buried.

Ruth will be the first to tell you: God rocked her world. He can definitely rock yours.

We use words like "too late" and "too far gone."

God uses words like "create" and "build up."

The elders of Bethlehem are speaking life into Ruth in the same way God's Word speaks life into us today. Why do teachers and speakers and preachers go on and on about the Bible? Because "they are not just idle words for you—they are your life."[20] His holy Word fills your spirit the way food nourishes your body. Stop eating? Die physically. Stop taking in the Word? Die spiritually.

I realize you know this, sis. Maybe I just need to hear it myself. We live in a culture that makes it easy to lose an hour on Facebook and hard to find ten minutes for Bible study. Please, Lord, make us so hungry for your Word that we say with the psalmist, "How sweet are your words to my taste, sweeter than honey to my mouth!"[21]

The elders offer delicious, life-sustaining words, calling on God to bless Ruth yet acknowledging his lordship by beginning with the word "may." People lightly toss out the phrase "Lord willing," but not these guys. They know Ruth's womb will be blessed only if God so ordains it. Still, to be like Rachel and Leah means to have an empty womb one moment and a full one the next. That sounds promising.

And the fellas aren't done yet.

> "May you have standing in Ephrathah and be famous in Bethlehem." *Ruth 4:11*

Having just mentioned Rachel, now they bring up her burial place "on the way to Ephrath,"[22] another name for Bethlehem. When I taught the story of Rachel as I stood beside the hilly road leading south from Jerusalem, a flock of sheep appeared over the rise—a fitting tribute to the only shepherdess mentioned in Scripture. Though she died in childbirth, Rachel did indeed "produce children in Ephrathah" (NRSV). The elders now wish the same for Ruth to enhance Boaz's standing in his hometown. Not so he'll be famous in the sense of being a celebrity but famous as in the family name going forward.

> "Through the offspring the LORD gives you by this young
> woman,…" *Ruth 4:12*

A slight blush appears on Ruth's cheeks. She's still not addressed by name, but she takes no offense, knowing the elders are referring to her. I can barely keep from calling out, "No worries, Ruth. We're still talking about you in the twenty-first century!" But she doesn't need that assurance. Being known and loved by God is more than enough.

Boaz smiles down at her, perhaps remembering that day in the field when he asked, "Whose young woman is that?"[23] He knows the answer now: she belongs to God. And for the rest of his earthly life, she also belongs to him.

> "…may your family be like that of Perez, whom Tamar bore
> to Judah." *Ruth 4:12*

Ooh, another biblical sister! Tamar, a woman I once described as "Bad for a Good Reason." We mentioned her sordid story earlier, but you'll find the whole of it in Genesis 38. Tamar and Ruth have several things in common: both were outsiders, one Canaanite, one Moabite; both had young husbands who died abruptly; both were left childless and desperate; both approached an older man in a "socially unacceptable way";[24] and those encounters prompted the men in their lives to give them honor. Judah said of Tamar, "She is more righteous than I,"[25] and Boaz called Ruth "a woman of noble character."[26]

But their stories end differently. Tamar deliberately sought a sexual encounter, while Ruth carefully avoided it. Judah did not marry Tamar, yet Boaz intends to marry Ruth.[27]

Could be why the elders don't say, "May you be like Judah…" Instead they say, "As Tamar gave birth to Judah's son Perez, may the LORD give you many children through Ruth. May your family be great like his" (NCV). How great? Judah's clan numbered 76,500.[28] Exceedingly great. Greater than great. The largest of the twelve tribes.

Meanwhile, the townsfolk are beaming as people often do at weddings. Even when we don't know the couple well, we smile. New life is in the air. And we are witnesses.

So, how long must we wait until Boaz kisses the bride?

Ruth In Real Life: AMMIE

"Just weeks after we started dating, my future husband's first gift to me was a Bible. He told me then that he might let me down, but he knew Someone who never would. I'd attended church for years and considered myself saved, but this man showed me the real depths of our Savior in ways I'd never understood. And as for letting me down, not once has my Boaz failed me in any of the important things. Through many trials, including illnesses, moving, job changes, the loss of our home, the deaths of loved ones, and other family issues, he has been my best friend, my confidant, my cheerleader, and my love."

Twelve

Talk About Happily Ever After!

oss the birdseed, and we'll send the happy couple on their honeymoon.

> So Boaz took Ruth and she became his wife. *Ruth 4:13*

No white gown, no fitted tux, no flowers, no music, no bridesmaids. Just not how things are done here. As Boaz gazes into Ruth's dark eyes, her hands clasped in his, we'll have to imagine him pledging those time-honored words: "I, Boaz, take you, Ruth, to be my wedded wife." In truth, no spoken vows were recorded, only a brief account of the facts: "Boaz married Ruth. She became his wife" (MSG). Simple, straightforward, and admirably inexpensive.

> Then he went to her,… *Ruth 4:13*

That is to say he "had sexual relations with her" (NCV). We get the picture. Weddings may change over the centuries, but wedding nights follow a fairly predictable pattern.

In the very next breath, good news.

> …and the LORD enabled her to conceive,… *Ruth 4:13*

Many chapters ago I promised a second God incident to frame the story. This is it: another divine intervention. With the first one the Lord provided food for Ruth (and Naomi and everyone else in Israel). Now he's giving Ruth something far more satisfying: a son.

God's role isn't merely implied; it's stated clearly in every translation: "the LORD gave her conception" (KJV); "the LORD let her become pregnant" (NCV); "the Lord caused her to conceive" (AMP). This pregnancy isn't proof of Boaz's virility or Ruth's fertility. It is "GOD's gracious gift" (MSG).

Though she was married to Wimpy—well, Mahlon—for perhaps as long as ten years without bearing a child, the word *barren* never appears in the book of Ruth. God did not need to open a closed womb, as he did for Sarah,[1] Rebekah,[2] Leah,[3] Rachel,[4] Hannah,[5] and Elizabeth.[6] In Ruth's case the Lord simply blessed her union with Boaz.

The swiftness of her conception adds a touch of the miraculous. To heighten the excitement, a divinely blessed union in Scripture often foretells the birth of a hero,[7] though in Ruth's case she married one.

Our storyteller leaps ahead to delivery day.

> ...and she gave birth to a son. *Ruth 4:13*

You and I might wish Ruth had given birth first to a daughter just to see how Boaz would handle it. Graciously, I'd imagine. But a son is needed to carry on Elimelech's family name, so a son it is.

The men of Bethlehem handed out their blessings at the town gate many months ago. Now the women of Bethlehem will have the last word. You'll remember that when we first met these neighbors, Naomi did most of the talking—okay, whining. Today she's listening. Last time her daughter-in-law wasn't even mentioned. Now Ruth gets top billing.

Our girl has already built a fine nest in Boaz's sprawling home. Colorful swaths of woven fabric decorate the walls, and the stone floor is freshly swept. At the moment a roomful of women crowd around the new mother, who cannot take her eyes off the squirming bundle in her arms. Nor can her mother-in-law. Nor can we. I've not held my children nestled in the crook of my arm for ages, but it's a joy like none other, never forgotten.

We'll start with a hallelujah from the sisters.

UNTO NAOMI A CHILD IS BORN

The women said to Naomi: "Praise be to the LORD, who this day
has not left you without a kinsman-redeemer." *Ruth 4:14*

God is honored first, and rightly so. "Blessed be GOD!" (MSG), they cry out
in unison. Then Naomi is applauded, and to Matthew Henry's way of thinking,
that's only fair. "She was the match-maker."[8] Why shouldn't she get some of the
credit for putting all this in motion?

I believe it's more than that. Of our three main players, Naomi has traveled
the most ground emotionally and spiritually.

The whole time we've known Ruth and Boaz, they've been strong in character and steady in nature. Though Ruth clearly had a dramatic transformation,
turning away from the gods of Moab to worship the God of Israel, we don't
watch it unfold on the pages of Scripture.

Naomi, on the other hand, put it all out there for us: the pain, the loss, the
sorrow, the anger, the denial, the acceptance, and, finally, the redemption. For
some of us, Ruth is our heroine, but Naomi is our soul sister. The one with
issues. The one we get. The one whose journey through life looks a lot like ours.
Peaks and valleys. Not much in the middle.

Yet God walked with Naomi every step of the way. He was with her through
Wimpy and Frumpy and whiny and grumpy, loving her not in spite of her
weaknesses but because of them. In his own words, "my power is made perfect
in weakness."[9] God takes us as we are, even as he takes us where we need to go.

When hubby and I reach any given destination, the female voice of our GPS
system announces, "You have arrived." I always laugh. First, because she sounds
so happy about it. And, second, because I know better. Spiritually speaking,
we're not there yet. God is still working on us.

But on this day, in this house in Bethlehem, Naomi is rightly celebrating
how far she's traveled.

To her credit, Ruth doesn't appear the least bit miffed when the women
focus on Naomi, saying, "Today he has given you a grandson to take care of
you" (CEV). Once again, "today" makes an appearance. A powerful word, it

brings us into the present and reminds us to be grateful. "This is the day the LORD has made,"[10] we often sing. Wouldn't it be grand if we really did "rejoice" and were "glad," behaving as if each day were a gift from God with our name on the tag?

This certainly is Naomi's day. As Boaz redeemed Ruth months ago, so this newborn babe now redeems Naomi. By law, the instant he was born, the child inherited the property that once belonged to Naomi's husband, Elimelech, and then to her son Mahlon. That means he can care for Naomi in her old age, something children in ancient Israel were expected to do—providing food, shelter, legal protection, and a proper burial.[11] We won't dwell on that last bit. But when the day comes, Naomi need not be afraid.

At the start of our journey together, I floated the scholarly notion that female storytellers were the first to share Ruth's account. Perhaps that troupe began with these very women who publicly rejoiced at the birth of Naomi's infant redeemer.[12]

"May he become famous throughout Israel!" *Ruth 4:14*

In the same way the elders blessed the father, now the women bless the son, crowing, "May his name be renowned in Israel!" (NRSV). I would never wish fame on my children, but a favorable reputation? Absolutely. "A good name is more desirable than great riches,"[13] and that's what these women want for the child.

Then they remind Naomi of what this grandson will mean for her future.

"He will renew your life and sustain you in your old age."
Ruth 4:15

Almost sounds like some kind of snake oil peddled on the Internet, promising to "restore your youth" (NLT) and "make you young again!" (MSG). Except what's being restored isn't Naomi's once-dewy complexion or thick, bouncy hair; it's her reason for getting up in the morning. What better motivator than a long-awaited grandchild?

"He will give you new life" (NCV), the women assure her. Literally, he'll "bring back,"[14] which is the same Hebrew verb as the one spoken by Naomi when she arrived in Bethlehem: "the LORD has brought me back empty."[15]

God has definitely brought Naomi back—but to fullness, to vibrancy, to life!

And Ruth's *hesed* paved the way.

A LOVE LIKE NO OTHER

"For your daughter-in-law, who loves you..." Ruth 4:15

Like Naomi, I hit the jackpot with my daughter-in-law, Beth. She not only tells me she loves me; she also shows me on a regular basis.

For our first Christmas together, she gave me an estate in the Highlands of Scotland. It's a small property, to be sure—ten square feet—but I have the official paperwork and the title to go with it. (Feel free to call me Lady Elizabeth.)

When I unwrapped the glossy packet with its handsome certificate and red embossed seal, I had tears in my eyes and a huge lump in my throat. Not because I owned a tiny plot of land in bonny Lochaber, but because the Lord—and my discerning son—brought into my life thoughtful, generous Beth, who knows me so well and showers me with undeserved affection.

Naomi must feel the same. We can tell by the look of gratitude on her face that she is in complete agreement with her neighbors when they make a startling comparison, describing Ruth's regard for her.

"...and who is better to you than seven sons,..." Ruth 4:15

Wow.

Since seven is the number of perfection and sons were the sole measure of a woman's value in ancient Israelite society, they could not have heaped greater praise on Ruth. "She's worth more to you than seven sons!" (MSG). We're talking a seriously over-the-top compliment, "the ultimate tribute."[16]

It's not her ability to give birth—whether one son or seven—that has earned their respect. It's Ruth's love for Naomi. This translation gets to the heart of it: "she loves you more than seven sons of your own would love you" (CEV).

These women know *hesed* when they see it. They recognize loyalty and compassion and loving-kindness. They're applauding Ruth for her deep commitment to Naomi, her lengthy trek from Moab, her weeks of gleaning, her willingness to marry an older man, her eagerness to bear an heir for Naomi's family, her hours of labor to bring this redeemer into the world, and, above all, her faith in the God of Israel. Those are seven solid reasons; we could probably come up with seventy more.

Remember, they're praising a former Moabitess, considering her "of more value to Israel than seven of its finest sons."[17] You can't see me jumping up and down, girlfriend, but I am! God is making a big statement here about the worth of women and how much he cherishes those of us who feel less than lovable, less than valuable. Whatever our story, we have a future with God and are worthy to be included in his family.

Meanwhile, Ruth just stepped into the lineage of Christ, bearing the future grandfather of King David. More jumping for joy.

"...has given him birth." *Ruth 4:15*

As the women remind Naomi, "she has given birth to your grandson" (NCV). Of course, the child doesn't have one drop of Naomi's blood. For her to have a grandson, God had to make a new way, create a new lineage, and he used a foreigner—a Gentile—to accomplish his will.

GRAFTED IN

Many women who traveled with me to Israel brought home a necklace with a design featuring a menorah at the top, then the Magen David, or "shield of David," at the center, and at the bottom the fish symbol used by early Christians—the Greek word for "fish," *ichthus,* serving as an acronym for "Yeshua, Messiah, Son of God, Savior." These three Jewish and Christian symbols are forged into a single design that goes back to the second century and is commonly called "Grafted In."

The name comes from a message Paul gave the young church in Rome. "I am talking to you Gentiles,"[18] he began, reminding them, "you, though a wild olive shoot, have been grafted in among the others and now share in the nourishing sap from the olive root."[19] The olive root is Israel—in this story, our Boaz. And the wild olive shoot represents Gentiles—here, our Ruth. She's not simply married to the man; she is grafted in with his people.

Tamar was grafted in with the birth of Perez.

Rahab was grafted in with the birth of Boaz.

And Ruth was grafted in with the birth of this baby boy.

All three women are listed in the genealogy of Jesus at the start of the New Testament, making it clear that Gentiles are part of God's plan. Those of us not counted among the descendants of Jacob—God's "chosen people"[20]—have been grafted in, such that we too are called "a chosen people, a royal priesthood, a holy nation, a people belonging to God."[21] Breathtaking, isn't it?

Easy to see why this birth is so much more than just "Hooray, a son!" For all who love the God of Israel, it's further assurance of our place in his kingdom.

One of the highlights of our time in Jerusalem was celebrating *Shabbat*—the Sabbath—with a bright, young Jewish couple who invited us into their home to partake in traditional foods, prayers, and songs. "We're not putting on a show," they assured us. "This is how our family enters into *Shabbat*. Welcome."

I brushed away tears of joy most of the evening. We *did* feel welcome. Included. Grafted in. Like Tamar, like Rahab, like Ruth. Like family. "I will be a Father to you, and you will be my sons and daughters, says the Lord Almighty."[22] Whatever our birth or adopted family experience, we have a perfect Father and a ton of siblings who share our faith and our future.

Let's face it: to call the body of Christ "one big happy family" might be a stretch. Not there yet. But you can definitely call us "one family," as Paul does: "There is one body and one Spirit—just as you were called to one hope when you were called—one Lord, one faith, one baptism; one God and Father of all."[23]

GRANNY NAOMI

When I autograph children's books for grandmothers to keep and share, it's fun to write out the special names their grandchildren have bestowed on them—names like Nana, GiGi, Memaw, and Grandma Kitty for a woman whose grandchildren remember her as the one with a cat.

You can be sure whatever this boy chooses to call Naomi, it will be the sweetest word she'll ever hear.

> Then Naomi took the child, laid him in her lap and cared for him.
> *Ruth 4:16*

Another famine has ended as this child satisfies "the hunger in Naomi's soul that could not be filled with food alone."[24] After bringing Naomi back empty, God has filled her arms to overflowing.

Holding her grandson, Naomi "became nurse unto it" (KJV)—but not *that* kind of nursing. When my Irish friend, Stuart, moved to the United States, he soon learned the difference. Sitting near a woman with a fussy infant, he kindly offered, "Can I nurse yer baby?" Needless to say, she didn't hand over the child!

Naomi simply "held him in her arms, cuddling him, cooing over him, waiting on him hand and foot" (MSG). Oh yes, we've seen grandmothers in action.

When our son was born, my mother-in-law beamed as she entered my hospital room, then promptly lifted Matthew right out of my arms. I was momentarily bereft, having waited thirty-three years to give birth to that dear boy. But Mary Lee had waited far longer to become a grandmother, enduring endless rounds of photos and stories from friends who'd already had several grandkids. Finally it was her turn. No wonder she wanted to hold him, just as Naomi is holding her grandson now.

> The women living there said, "Naomi has a son." *Ruth 4:17*

Look at that expression on her face! Pure bliss. Ask a mother to describe her child, and you'll hear the good and the bad, the joys and the challenges. Ask a grandmother to describe her grandchildren? Nothing but perfection.

Truth is, "this boy was born for Naomi" (NCV).

It's only fitting that this is our closing scene. The story opened with Naomi, then we met Ruth, and then Boaz. They disappear from view in reverse: Boaz first, then Ruth, and finally Naomi. Lovely poetic symmetry.

As for the women of Bethlehem, they hang around long enough to perform one final duty.

Oh Boy!

And they named him Obed. *Ruth 4:17*

Wait a second. "The neighborhood women named him" (CEV)? Not the boy's mother or father? Not even Naomi? That's right. The same women who were there when Naomi renamed herself "Bitter" have now named her grandson. You won't find another example in the Old Testament of the townsfolk naming a child.

I love the community feel of it, the shared responsibility. Not unlike when a child is brought before a congregation for their blessing. In our church we respond as one, saying, "With God's help we will so order our lives after the example of Christ, that this child, surrounded by steadfast love, may be established in the faith, and confirmed and strengthened in the way that leads to life eternal."[25] When I speak those words from my perch in the choir loft, I feel the weight of that promise settling across my shoulders. If we want the next generation to know God, it's never too soon to begin showing them God's love.

That's what the women of Bethlehem are doing here: speaking a blessing over this child.

"Obed," eh? Not a name we often hear in the nursery. His name means "one who works/serves."[26] Since we know he'll be caring for Naomi in her old age, it's proper that Obed's loving gift of service be reflected in his name.

Closing Credits

Alas, our time here is ending. We feel the pull of the present as the scene before us starts to fade. The storyteller pauses for dramatic effect before revealing the identity of the next generation. And the next.

He was the father of Jesse, the father of David. *Ruth 4:17*

The audience of old might have gasped, cheered, applauded, or, at the very least, smiled and nodded to one another. *David. Of course. We knew this was coming.*

We're smiling too, knowing that from his line will come the Messiah. As John Piper noted, "This simple little story opens out like a stream into an ocean of hope."[27] If a Moabitess can be the great-grandmother of the king of Israel, what blessing might God have in store for us and for those we love?

Before going forward with Obed's lineage, the storyteller steps backward to Perez, just as the men of Bethlehem did earlier.

> This, then, is the family line of Perez: Perez was the father of Hezron, Hezron the father of Ram, Ram the father of Amminadab, Amminadab the father of Nahshon, Nahshon the father of Salmon, Salmon the father of Boaz, Boaz the father of Obed, Obed the father of Jesse, and Jesse the father of David. *Ruth 4:18–22*

Remember what the rabbis said about ten men? That's what we have here. Nice number. David appears last, the most significant position. And Boaz is seventh, a spot reserved for an ancestor of special importance.[28] No mention of Elimelech or Mahlon, though. Legally, Obed redeemed that family's inheritance. But spiritually and biologically, he's the son of Boaz.

Compared to our two redeemers, Boaz and Obed, the other men in this story are less impressive. Elimelech leaves the Promised Land, then dies. His sons marry Moabite women, then the sons die too. The harvesters are to be avoided by Ruth lest they abuse her. The nearer kinsman withdraws his offer of redemption. The elders are virtuous yet remain unnamed.

But all ten generations in the lineage of David are carefully identified, one by one, demonstrating God's power to restore his people. As Phineas Camp Headley wrote a century and a half ago, "So did the family of Elimelech on the border of extinction, emerge from gloom into splendor which shines onward through all the lineage of David."[29]

The day will come when another baby will be born in this town called Bethlehem. Two blind men will cry out to him, "Have mercy on us, Son of David!"[30] And crowds will one day follow him, shouting, "Hosanna to the Son of David!"[31]

His Beloved One

It's only right that the very last word of the book of Ruth is "David," a man after God's own heart,[32] a man whose name means "beloved."[33] That's what God calls us too: "my beloved and longed-for brethren, my joy and crown, so stand fast in the Lord, beloved."[34] Twice in one verse!

Love is the heart and soul of this story, just as it is in every story about God. Ruth's love for Naomi was evidence of God's *hesed* at work, followed by Boaz's love for God, which empowered him to redeem Ruth, which assured Naomi that God had never stopped loving her. Love definitely made their world go 'round.

Whenever we have trouble loving one another, it's usually because we've forgotten how much God loves us. If we go back to the Source, if we fill our hearts and minds with his Word, then his loving-kindness will naturally—no, supernaturally—pour out of us and into the lives of others. As his Word assures us, "If we love one another, God lives in us and his love is made complete in us."[35]

Love the Lord, love one another. That's how Ruth walked out her faith.

Time for us to do the same, my sister, walking step by step until the day we meet our Kinsman-Redeemer face to face.

Ruth In Real Life: JANET

"It was because of my husband's love that I finally understood God's love for me. My Boaz regarded me as beautiful, talented, and able to do anything I set my mind to. I realized God loved me the way my husband did—but better."

Have You Got It?

ere's the question I've been longing to ask you since page one: Are you ready to trust God with your whole heart? With your whole life? With everything?

Maybe you still feel like an outsider when it comes to matters of faith. Perhaps you read this book because someone gave it to you, or because your book club picked it, or because you found it in the library and were intrigued by the title. If so, I hope you've discovered among these pages a nugget of truth, more valuable than gold: "Brothers and sisters, God loves you, and we know he has chosen you."[1]

Will you respond to his love, to his calling?

As Boaz would say, will you do so "today"?

Maybe you're a believer who has lost her way for a season. Still living among God's people, yet feeling hurt, ashamed, or unsure of God's love. If so, here's the good news you've been waiting to hear: "the God of all grace, who called you to his eternal glory in Christ, after you have suffered a little while, will himself restore you and make you strong, firm and steadfast."[2]

Will you welcome God back into your life?

As Naomi would say, will you "return"?

Wherever you may be in your spiritual walk, the Lord is with you, beloved. Right here, right now. He knows your every thought and hears your unspoken words. Though I'm the one asking the question, he's the One waiting for your answer.

Will you trust him to forgive your past, handle your present, and provide for your future?

He is more than ready, more than willing, and way more than able to do all that for you and more. As the Bible assures us, "God is our refuge and strength, an ever-present help in trouble."[3]

I'm praying for you as I write these words, hoping that right now, as you read them, you can boldly say with Ruth, "Your God is my God."

If so, you've got it, girl. Now and forever.

Discussion Questions

If your book club will be chatting about *The Girl's Still Got It* in a single session, here's a brief list of questions to kick-start your discussion. Or you might use them to enhance your personal takeaway once you've finished reading the book.

1. In *Seasons of Friendship,* Marjory Zoet Bankson wrote, "The Book of Ruth introduces another view of God who is more feminine and relational: nurturing, protective, and creative."[1] In what ways does God nurture Ruth's faith? When is his protection of Naomi apparent? And how does God show his creative nature through Boaz's actions?

2. Our story begins with a funeral as Naomi and her daughters-in-law bury Mahlon and Kilion. Do you feel more sympathy for Naomi or for Ruth at this point in the narrative, and why? How might such a tragic loss affect your faith?

3. Add up all that Ruth is leaving behind in Moab. Then consider her future in Israel, "with its dark, forbidding hills, its alien faces, its unknown trials."[2] What qualities does Ruth possess that would empower her to make such a move? Of those characteristics, which one do you admire most, and why?

4. For my Scottish historical novel *Here Burns My Candle,* inspired by the first chapter of Ruth, I chose the title from Shakespeare's *The Third Part of King Henry VI:* "Here burns my candle out; ay, here it dies." In what ways does the old Ruth die? Now consider the words of Sinclair Ferguson: "It is a gospel secret that death is the way to life."[3] How might you apply that truth to Ruth's spiritual journey? And to your own?

5. When Naomi and Ruth arrive in Bethlehem, the whole town is stirred, yet it's the women who do the talking. When they exclaim, "Can this be Naomi?" what are they really asking, do you think? Sometimes we find it hard to show compassion to people who are suffering the consequences of their poor choices. Why might that be so? Practically speaking, how can we do a better job of loving one another rather than judging one another?

6. In chapter 5 I describe my friend Evelyn helping a woman in need by hiding canned goods in a Dumpster. What unique expressions of generosity have you observed? When you've been on the receiving end of someone else's largess, how have you responded outwardly? And how did you feel inwardly? In what ways does Ruth's humble gratitude for Boaz's kind treatment speak to you?

7. Victorian writer Phineas Camp Headley believed Ruth was "endowed with every virtue and charm that render a woman attractive."[4] If you've always imagined Ruth as beautiful, why might that be the case? We may champion inner beauty, yet most women secretly (or not so secretly!) long to be more physically attractive. What steps can we take to focus more on our internal rather than our external selves? What direction might Proverbs 31:30 offer us: "Charm is deceptive, and beauty is fleeting; but a woman who fears the LORD is to be praised"?

8. Why does the eighteenth-century hymn "Amazing Grace" still touch us so deeply? Think through the lyrics—or look them up in a hymnal or on the Internet—and choose one line that resonates with you, then explain why. Which line from the hymn might have spoken most powerfully to Naomi? And to Ruth?

9. Ruth told her mother-in-law, "I will do whatever you say." Have you ever made such a promise to another person? If not, what might have stopped you? If so, when, where, how, and why did you commit to follow another's lead? What was the outcome? We read in 2 John 1:6, "And this is love: that we walk in obedience to his commands." How is obedience to God an expression of our love for him?

10. Boaz made an equally open-ended promise to Ruth when he said, "I will do for you all you ask." Our Redeemer makes the same astound-

ing offer to us, as recorded in Matthew 7:7: "Ask and it will be given to you; seek and you will find; knock and the door will be opened to you." Why are we often hesitant to ask, seek, and knock? If you need something that only God can provide, take a moment to write out your request, keeping in mind his assurance about giving, finding, and opening.

11. At the close of each chapter of *The Girl's Still Got It,* one or more "Ruth In Real Life" stories appear. Look through them and pick a favorite. Why are those words particularly meaningful to you? If you have neither a Naomi nor a Boaz in your life right now, how might these real-life stories apply to other relationships that are important to you?

12. The most vital relationship we'll ever have is with our Redeemer. What new truths have you discovered about the Lord after spending time with Naomi, Ruth, and Boaz? And what changes will you make in your life because of what you've learned?

Study Guide

This longer guide is designed with Bible study groups in mind. Whether you meet for two sessions, twelve sessions, or anything in between, this guide and *The Girl's Still Got It* companion DVD are meant to enrich your Bible study experience.

At its heart a book is a conversation between friends. Throughout these pages I've shared my discoveries about Naomi, Ruth, and Boaz, adding a few bits from my own life. Now it's your turn, dear sister, to take what you've learned and let it impact your world.

That's the ultimate goal of Bible study—not only filling our heads with knowledge and our hearts with understanding, but also equipping our hands to put God's Word into action, empowered and led by the Holy Spirit.

As we travel together from Moab to Bethlehem, we'll look for practical, personal ways to apply the truths we've gleaned from the book of Ruth. You'll need a place to write your answers—a notebook, a computer, whatever works—and the willingness to explore both Scripture and your own heart at a deeper level.

If you're ready, then here we go. Make that *grow*.

Before We Dive In
Which Girl's Still Got It?

Read "Before We Dive In" (pages 1–8).

1. On page 1 of *The Girl's Still Got It,* you'll find a description of what "it" means to me: "Value. Significance. Vibrancy. Worth."

a. What words would *you* use to describe "it" in this context?

b. Name an older woman you know who's still got it. What has she taught you by example?

c. Now think of a younger woman who's already got it. What can you learn from her?

d. Without a doubt, you've got it too! What vital, meaningful truth might another woman learn from you?

2. Throughout the writing process I kept a small sign on my desk, reminding me of this goal for our study: "to more fully grasp God's sovereignty and loving-kindness so we can learn to trust him with every aspect of our lives."

a. Does trusting God come easily for you, or is it a struggle? Why might that be the case?

b. What would trusting God look like to you in a difficult real-life situation—when a job ends unexpectedly, a loved one is critically ill, or a relationship falls apart?

c. How might the following verses encourage you to trust the Lord even in hard times: Psalm 9:10; Psalm 37:5–6; Proverbs 3:5–6; Isaiah 26:4?

3. When it comes to applying biblical truth to our lives, it often helps to break things down into bite-size pieces.

a. Can you trust God with your past? Think of a specific instance—whether it happened ten years or ten days ago—that you still feel guilty about. Are you willing to lay it down, emotionally and spiritually, and accept the truth that you are forgiven completely? What assurance does Psalm 34:5 offer you?

b. Can you trust God with your present? Put into words what's weighing on your mind right now, some problem that seems overwhelming. What will it take for you to release that concern into God's able hands? How might the promise found in Psalm 55:22 help you?

c. Can you trust God to provide for your future? Consider what you're most worried about as you look toward the coming months and years. Is it health concerns? Finances? Job worries? Independence (or the loss of it)? Now turn to Psalm 37:25. What comfort do you find in those words?

Chapter 1
Off to a Rocky Start

Read chapter 1 (pages 9–25).

1. As we unpack the opening verses of the book of Ruth, one fact becomes clear: Naomi and Ruth endured a heap of heartache in Moab. The tragedies they faced are still with us today. Nearly one billion people worldwide suffer from the scarcity of food.[1] In the United States alone, two and a half million loved ones die each year.[2] And infertility is a painful reality for one in ten couples.[3]

a. What's the most traumatic event you've weathered during the last six months, and what made that experience especially difficult for you?

b. Where did you turn for support, compassion, and a listening ear? How were your needs met?

c. What hope do the following verses offer those who suffer: Job 36:15; Psalm 22:24; Psalm 33:18–19; Psalm 119:50?

2. On page 12 you'll find the statement, "If I'm going to suffer, at least let it be for a good reason. Make that a God reason." Let's consider what those reasons might be.

a. Read Romans 5:3–4, and you'll see the passage begins with rejoicing and ends with hope, yet it's those challenging steps in the middle that strengthen our faith. Describe a time you've seen this progression in action, either in your own life or in the life of another believer. Is hope a sufficient goal for you?

b. Read Ecclesiastes 7:14 and Romans 8:28. How do you reconcile these two truths: that God oversees our bad times, yet "works for the good"?

c. What good have you seen come from the recent difficulty in your life? If you've yet to see any positive outcome, what can you do to keep from losing heart?

d. How has God revealed himself to you during this challenging time?

3. Naomi and Ruth may not have grasped the concept of a heavenly future, but we can.

a. According to the oft-quoted John 3:16, God *loved* and God *gave*. What one thing must we do to have eternal life?

b. John 5:24, 6:40, and 10:28 describe how we can be assured of eternal life. Read those verses, then restate them in your own words. What might happen if you shared this truth with a friend or family member who has yet to cross over "from death to life"?

c. For Elimelech and his sons, death had the final word. According to 2 Corinthians 5:1, what does our future hold?

Read Ruth 1:1–5 once more. What's the most memorable truth you've learned from this passage?

Chapter 2
Coming or Going?

Read chapter 2 (pages 27–42).

1. As Proverbs 25:25 tells us, "Like cold water to a weary soul is good news from a distant land." No question, Naomi's soul was parched, and the report of God's provision in faraway Judah was definitely welcome.

a. Read the much-loved parable recorded in Luke 15:11–20, then find three or four ways in which the prodigal son's story parallels Naomi's experience of moving to a distant country.

b. When you read my challenge "You and I need to leave the Moabs of our own making," what situation in your life came to mind? Is it an unhealthy relationship? A shameful activity? A bad habit? What steps might you take to leave your Moab? Are you ready to do so? Whom could you enlist to help you, and when will you take that first step?

c. "God's grace transcends our rebellion," wrote pastor Iain Duguid.[4] How would you define God's grace? What further insights on grace do the following verses offer: John 1:16–17; Romans 3:22–24; 2 Corinthians 9:8; Ephesians 2:8–9?

d. How does the gift of grace empower us to "follow...revere...obey... serve...and hold fast," as Deuteronomy 13:4 commands?

2. The Hebrew verb *shubh* appears twelve times in the first chapter of Ruth. Clearly the Lord wanted to be sure we don't miss the message!

a. Write down the various ways this Hebrew word is translated in Ruth 1:6, 7, 8, 10, 11, 12, 15 (twice), 16, 21, 22 (twice), and note in which direction each instance is pointing. To Bethlehem or to Moab? To the true God or to false gods?

b. What is God saying to you with this repeated call to "return"? Might you find your answer in Joshua 24:14–15?

3. Naomi sent stiff-necked Orpah back to her people and to her gods, never to be heard from again. "For sure, there is no Book of Orpah."[5]

a. Since the scholars have yet to pinpoint the meaning of her name, why do you think she's traditionally known as "the Stiff-Necked One"?

b. What does Deuteronomy 10:16 tell us about being stiff-necked? Now take a moment to read the surrounding verses, Deuteronomy 10:12–22, to get the bigger picture. What does God require of his people so they aren't like Orpah, returning to worship false gods?

c. Not a word in God's Word is wasted, even when characters come and go in a few verses. What have you gleaned from Orpah's small but significant role in this narrative?

Read Ruth 1:6–14 once more. What's the most memorable truth you've learned from this passage?

2 -18   384 chapters

Chapter 8   56 = 180-183 · ch 3 - 4

A Wow of a Vow

Read chapter 3, pages 43–53.

1. Abraham was commanded by God, "Leave your country, your people."[6] No such heavenly calling is recorded in the book of Ruth, yet she too leaves her country and her people after making seven powerful vows, the last one involving the Lord himself.

   a. To whom in your life could you gladly say, "Where you go I will go"? What might compel you to do so? Love? Duty? Compassion? Faith? Now read Matthew 4:18–22. Why did these four men follow Jesus? How does their example challenge you?

   b. Despite Naomi's bitterness, Ruth assures her, "Where you stay I will stay." Think of a time when you shared a room with someone—whether for a week at a convention or for a semester at college—and it didn't go well. What did you learn about yourself in the process? When it comes to living beneath the same roof with others, what counsel do Proverbs 16:7 and Romans 12:18 provide?

   c. Ruth takes her commitment a step further, telling Naomi, "Your people will be my people." The biblical account doesn't describe Ruth's family or any other Moabites, but she definitely had people she intended to bid farewell. What does Jesus require of his followers, as recorded in Matthew 10:37–39? And in Luke 18:29–30, what does Jesus promise those who leave behind loved ones for God's sake?

2. Then comes Ruth's biggest leap of faith when she pledges to Naomi, "Your God my God," just as in the New Testament, believers turned away "from idols to serve the living and true God."[7]

   a. Naomi grew up knowing the God of Israel, while Ruth, raised among a pagan people, committed her life to God as an adult. In what ways might *when* and *how* we meet the Lord shape our relationship with him?

b. Scripture doesn't reveal the steps that led Ruth to embrace Naomi's God, but clearly something happened. Read Deuteronomy 6:6–9, noting those things that Naomi might have done to share her faith with Ruth. Which of those ancient methods might you incorporate in your life today? And what are some new, twenty-first-century ways to share your faith with others?

3. Ruth's promise to be buried beside Naomi might strike us as macabre, but in that culture it was a demonstration of *hesed*, of loving-kindness.

a. The Bible doesn't shrink away from discussing death. Read the following passages, and note what each one has to say about death for those who live for God: Romans 4:25; John 5:24; 2 Corinthians 4:10; Revelation 2:10.

b. Ruth calls upon the Lord to deal with her severely if she breaks her promise to Naomi. In the Old Testament, Ruth's is the first of a dozen oaths with nearly identical wording. Saul,[8] Jonathan,[9] and David[10] are among those who gave God permission to punish them if they failed to honor their vows. Why do you think they made such bold statements? Was it courage? Chutzpah? Or something else entirely? In what situation could you imagine saying such a thing (without trembling in your boots!)?

Read Ruth 1:14–18 once more. What's the most memorable truth you've learned from this passage?

Chapter 4
Throw Out the Welcome Mat

Read chapter 4 (pages 55–64).

1. You gotta respect Naomi for her honesty, however bitter her attitude. As Larry Crabb wrote in *Shattered Dreams*, "She stood before her

community, admitting who she was rather than pretending to be who she should have been."[11]

a. How do the words of Job in Job 10:1 and of Jeremiah in Lamentations 3:5 capture the essence of our bitter Naomi's experience?

b. Is it better to tell people what you're really thinking and feeling or tell them what they want to hear? Why do we often please and appease others? What approach would most honor God, do you think?

c. How do you respond to friends when they whine or complain? Is there a verse or passage you might share with them, hoping to improve their attitude? Or is it best simply to listen, and if so, why?

2. Here's the big question for Naomi, as John Piper saw it: "Can I trust and love the God who has dealt me this painful hand in life?"[12]

a. If you're going through a difficult time right now, how would you answer that question? What do Psalm 13:5 and Psalm 143:8 tell us about the source of trust and love?

b. If you're currently in a pleasant season, are you willing to embrace hardship if it comes from God's hand? What do Acts 9:16, Philippians 1:29, and 1 Peter 3:14 tell us about suffering for Christ? How do you reconcile that with the "be good, be blessed, be happy" message we often hear in Christian circles?

c. God gives life, and he takes it away, and Naomi knows that very well. What does Deuteronomy 32:39 say about that truth? And what would it take for you to embrace the conclusion stated in Job 1:21?

3. While Naomi whines, Ruth waits to be introduced to the women of Bethlehem, demonstrating not only her devotion but also a large measure of patience.

a. Which of the following verses do you think most aptly describes Ruth, and why: Proverbs 19:11; Proverbs 25:15; Ecclesiastes 7:8?

b. When you read Naomi's bitter words, "I went away full, but the LORD has brought me back empty," spoken with Ruth by her side, what was your response? If you've ever been snubbed in a similar manner, how did you handle it then? And how might you handle it now, in light of Ruth's example?

c. As homecomings go, how would you rate this scene on a scale of 1 (miserable) to 10 (marvelous), and why? What might Naomi have done to improve her homecoming experience?

Read Ruth 1:19–22 once more. What's the most memorable truth you've learned from this passage?

Chapter 5
Out Standing in Her Field

Read chapter 5 (pages 65–76).

1. One of the ways Ruth handles life's challenges is common to many of us: she immerses herself in work.

   a. Elizabeth Ruth Obbard wrote, "Work is the way she makes her love visible."[13] How might your own efforts as a working woman—paid or unpaid, in or out of your home—make your love visible to others? Who is watching, and how have they specifically recognized your labors?

   b. Read Psalm 90:17 and Proverbs 31:17 as you picture Ruth gleaning in the field. What truth do you find in these verses that speaks to Ruth's situation? And how might that truth address your current situation?

2. Contemporary commentator Gillian Rowell reminds us, "The circumstances of the women have improved considerably, and this is not through their calculations but through the providence of God."[14]

   a. What does the word "providence" mean to you? Write out your own definition, shaped by the wisdom you find in these verses: Psalm 66:5; Psalm 147:5; Lamentations 3:37; Romans 11:36.

   b. God is often described as omniscient, omnipotent, and omnipresent. Look up all three words in a dictionary, and jot down the meanings. Which word do you find the most comforting? If you find any of them discomforting, why might that be the case?

c. Now read Psalm 139:1–18. Choose a verse in that beloved passage that exemplifies each *omni-* word, then note how God demonstrated those elements of his character in Ruth's or in Naomi's life.

3. The arrival of Naomi and Ruth in Bethlehem at harvest time is a fitting irony. They came back empty-handed to discover that Naomi's homeland was full and that Ruth's task would be to glean in those rich fields.

a. Jesus used a harvest analogy to teach his disciples. Read Matthew 9:35–38. What harvest is Jesus referring to? Whom does he have in mind to work the fields? And how will that be accomplished? What ripe fields do you see around you? In keeping with Jesus's teaching, what's the next step you should take?

b. Then in 2 Corinthians 9:10–11 we find Paul using a harvest theme to encourage generosity and gratitude. According to the passage, who supplies not only the seed but also the harvest? And what's the point of being fed, of being blessed? What prompts you to be generous? And how can you be sure God gets the glory rather than you?

Read Ruth 2:1–7 once more. What's the most memorable truth you've learned from this passage?

Chapter 6
A Different Kind of Dinner Date

Read chapter 6 (pages 77–91).

1. Professor Katharine Doob Sakenfeld neatly sums up our hero: "Boaz is at once the upright citizen, the helpful relative, and the unmarried land owner."[15]

a. Of these three roles that Boaz plays in the lives of Naomi and Ruth, is one more important than the others, or are all three of equal value? Why do you say that?

b. How does the Lord Jesus fulfill similar roles in your life—as a citizen of heaven, as your helpful brother, and as your bridegroom who is preparing a place for you?

2. Boaz generously provides for Ruth with no apparent expectation of any return on his investment.
   a. The command found in Deuteronomy 15:11 may account in part for Boaz's kindness. So might Proverbs 11:25. How would you explain his motivation?
   b. Think of a time when you made a contribution prompted by guilt. Perhaps another time when you made a donation with a tax advantage in mind. Or maybe you gave to a cause that brought you some attention or recognition. Contrast those experiences with an instance in which you gave without anyone knowing about it. Why does Matthew 6:3–4 encourage us to be both generous and anonymous?

3. As a writer of many psalms, David repeatedly turned to the vivid imagery of a bird gathering its chicks under its wings to describe how God nurtures and protects his own. David's great-grandfather Boaz reached for the same word picture when he spoke this blessing over Ruth: "May you be richly rewarded by the LORD, the God of Israel, under whose wings you have come to take refuge."
   a. Read the following verses in the book of Psalms, then choose one, and describe how it comforts or encourages you: 17:8; 36:7; 57:1; 61:4; 63:7.
   b. What aspect of being beneath his wings most appeals to you? Is it the closeness? The assurance of protection? The physical warmth? The sense of being hidden from view? The peacefulness? How is that essential need for intimacy currently being met in your life? If it isn't, what's an appropriate and meaningful way for that longing to be satisfied? And how might you put that in motion?

Read Ruth 2:8–17 once more. What's the most memorable truth you've learned from this passage?

Chapter 7
Well, Bless His Strong and Wealthy Self

Read chapter 7 (pages 93–104).

1. When Ruth returns home that first evening with her arms full of grain, an elated Naomi presses her daughter-in-law for the usual who, what, when, and where details.

    a. Eighteenth-century commentator Matthew Henry wrote, "It is a good question for us to ask ourselves in the close of every day, *Where have I gleaned to-day?* What improvements have I made in knowledge and grace?"[16] How might you put his good suggestion into practice each evening? And what might the benefits be?

    b. Arriving in Bethlehem exhausted, starving, and alone, Naomi and Ruth were famished at many levels. Make a shopping list, as it were, of all the things, practical and spiritual, these newcomers needed. Boaz was able to fill their stomachs with healthy food. What does the Lord provide those who hunger and thirst, according to the following verses: Psalm 34:8; Matthew 5:6; John 4:14?

2. The Hebrew word *hesed* plays a pivotal role in the book of Ruth. According to Katharine Doob Sakenfeld, what separates *hesed* from a random act of kindness is that the action must be "essential to the survival or basic well-being of the recipient" and must be something that "only the person doing the act of *hesed* is in a position to provide."[17]

    a. With those two criteria of *hesed* in mind, how does Ruth qualify as showing Naomi *hesed*? And what about Boaz in regard to Naomi and Ruth?

    b. Again, using the above definition of *hesed*, who in your life might benefit from your unique way of expressing loving-kindness, mercy, and grace? If you sense the Lord nudging you to act, how and when might you do so?

3. Redemption resounds not only throughout the book of Ruth; it also was a favorite theme of the prophet Isaiah.

   a. Each of the following verses offers further insight into our Redeemer. Jot down what you learn from reading Isaiah 44:6, 44:24, and 48:17.

   b. Job 19:25—beautifully set to music by Handel—provides additional clues to who our Redeemer is. How do you know, absolutely, that your Redeemer lives? On the days when doubts threaten to undermine your beliefs, how do you bolster your faith?

   c. Naomi and Ruth require a kinsman-redeemer to serve as *go'el,* securing the family property, and to act as *levir,* preserving the family name. Since Boaz is a type of Christ, giving us a glimpse of the Kinsman-Redeemer to come, in what ways does Jesus secure your inheritance? And how does he preserve your name? See if the following verses help you answer those key questions: Acts 3:25; Galatians 4:7; Titus 3:4–7; 1 Peter 1:3–5; Revelation 2:17.

Read Ruth 2:18–23 once more. What's the most memorable truth you've learned from this passage?

Chapter 8
Your Mission, Should You Choose to Accept It

Read chapter 8 (pages 105–115).

1. Any trace of our whiny, bitter Naomi is gone. Now she's a mother-in-law on a mission, determined to provide for Ruth just as Ruth has so lovingly provided for her.

   a. In light of this close relationship, Louise Pettibone Smith wrote, "Ruth and Naomi stand in the Hebrew scriptures beside David and Jonathan."[18] Read 1 Samuel 18:3–4 and 19:1–6 to get a sense of their brotherly bond. In what ways does their commitment to each other mirror that of Naomi and Ruth?

b. Do you have a deep, loving relationship with another woman in your family? If your connection with her was less than promising at first and has developed and grown over the years, what brought about those changes? And if you've always been there for each other, how have you continued to nurture your close friendship?

2. Ruth's preparation for her midnight rendezvous with Boaz involves three vital rituals—bathing, anointing, and dressing—echoed in the New Testament.

a. Our Kinsman-Redeemer wants us spiritually clean. Read John 13:5–8 and Ephesians 5:25–27. In each passage who is being washed? By whom? Using what substance? And what is the outcome? How might you experience his daily cleansing in a spiritual sense?

b. Like Ruth, we are also anointed with perfume. Read 2 Corinthians 1:21–22. As with the washing, who does the anointing? To what end? According to 2 Corinthians 2:15–16, what is the purpose of our fragrant aroma? And how are you made equal to the task of bearing his scent?

c. Now we're ready to get dressed. How does Galatians 3:26–27 describe this process? What further clarification about this holy attire does Luke 24:49 add? Once again, who dresses us, and why?

3. When Naomi assures Ruth, "He will tell you what to do," we're reminded of Saul's conversion on the road to Damascus, when the Lord told him to go into the city "and you will be told what you must do."[19]

a. For the outcome of that story read Acts 9:10–12, 17. Who told Saul what to do? And who told *him* what to do? What advantages do you see to this God-ordained method of communication? How did it benefit Ananias? And how did it help Saul?

b. In chapter 8 I mentioned the possibility that Ruth will be told what to do, not by Boaz, but by the Lord himself. Might God be speaking through Naomi in this scene? What makes you say that? If you've ever had a sense of the Holy Spirit leading you as you spoke to someone, what convinced you it was the Lord's words and not your own?

c. Whoever tells Ruth what she must do, her next move requires great courage, as she embarks on "a sacred journey, a ritual descent into darkness and danger."[20] What's the scariest, holiest thing you've ever done? How did you find the strength to go forward? And what was the result of your obedience?

Read Ruth 3:1–6 once more. What's the most memorable truth you've learned from this passage?

Chapter 9
Good Night, Sweetheart

Read chapter 9 (pages 117–130).

1. It's not by chance that Ruth and Boaz meet at midnight. Throughout the Bible we find dramatic scenes unfolding at that dark hour.

a. You'll find two very different examples in Exodus 11:4–7 and Acts 16:25–31. In both situations God reveals his mighty power. Why at midnight, do you think? And why is that time ideal for Ruth to wake Boaz?

b. Scripture repeatedly tells us that God shines in such settings, turning darkness into light. How might 2 Samuel 22:29 and Job 12:22 demonstrate that truth? And how does Psalm 112:4 suit our hero, Boaz?

c. Ruth not only seems unafraid of the dark; she's also not hesitant to share her name and her heart's desire. As Marsha Pravder Mirkin saw it, "Ruth answers with the profound knowledge of a woman who knows exactly who she is."[21] Read Ruth 3:9, then note all the things she reveals about herself—not just the words she speaks, but the likely emotions and convictions behind them—as she asks Boaz to marry her.

2. In *A Conspicuous Love,* Steve Zeisler wrote of Ruth's proposal, "Such a request fit Boaz exactly, since he lived his life as an instrument of God's blessing."[22]

   a. Boaz may seem too good to be true, yet there are generous men all around us, quietly blessing others in God's name. See how many such men you can list, if not by name, then by description—godly, giving men of all ages, married or single, who've crossed your path. What instruction does 1 Timothy 6:17–19 offer those with means? And how might that truth apply to you?

   b. Boaz could have rejected Ruth's proposal, ruined her reputation, and ravished her body. Of course, he does none of those things. Instead he tells her, "Don't be afraid." Look at the following instances where that same message appears, then note who is speaking and why the listener need not fear: Genesis 15:1; Genesis 21:17; Genesis 26:24; Joshua 8:1; Judges 6:23. How does reading these heavenly assurances from centuries ago ease your fears today?

3. Boaz isn't the only man in Bethlehem who has noticed Ruth, though it's not her youth or beauty they praise; it's her noble character.

   a. Matthew Henry wrote of Ruth, "The less she proclaimed her own goodness the more did her neighbours take notice of it."[23] How do we sometimes proclaim our own goodness—online, in print, or in person? Is that a temptation for you? Or do you find it easy to avoid the miry pit of self-promotion? What do the following verses from Proverbs teach us about humility: 11:2; 15:33; 22:4?

   b. Most of us don't live in a town of two hundred people, so it's unlikely all our neighbors know us well enough to comment on our character. Choose a smaller circle instead: all the people in your class, or all the people at your job, or all the people in your Bible study. Would they see you as a woman of noble character? How might God, who knows you completely, describe you?

Read Ruth 3:7–11 once more. What's the most memorable truth you've learned from this passage?

Chapter 10
Sitting Tight for Mr. Right

Read chapter 10 (pages 131–140).

1. This chapter is all about waiting. In a story—even a true story like this one—waiting builds suspense. But in real life, waiting is a challenge.

   a. Boaz asks Ruth to wait until morning. Naomi asks Ruth to wait until Boaz settles the matter. In what area of life are you waiting right now? How can others assist you in the process? Are you willing to rest in God's sovereignty while you wait?

   b. In Psalm 38:15, David wrote with confidence, "I wait for you, O LORD; you will answer, O Lord my God." Clearly, God keeps us waiting for some good purpose. What qualities might waiting build into our character? See if Psalm 130:5 and Isaiah 26:8 offer some direction.

2. While they're stretched out on the threshing floor, Boaz and Ruth must also wait in another sense, to "avoid not only sin, but scandal."[24] (I've often said Boaz and Ruth belong on a poster for True Love Waits!)

   a. If you're in a situation where you can't flee temptation yet have to resist it, what can you do mentally, emotionally, spiritually, and physically to make the time pass without giving in?

   b. Psalm 37:7–8 offers sage advice for when we're in a bind. According to this passage, what are the two things we *should* do and the three things we *should not* do? Which of these will you try first the next time your patience is sorely tested?

3. As the third chapter of Ruth comes to a close, a sixteenth-century proverb seems tailor-made for our well-dressed heroine: "Silence is a woman's best garment."

   a. When you learned that Ruth has no recorded dialogue beyond her morning-after scene, were you surprised? Disappointed? Why might it not be necessary for us to hear from her again?

b. If the first words of biblical characters tell us something about them, perhaps their last words do too. What's the last thing Ruth says? And Naomi? What significance might you glean from their closing comments?

c. According to 1 Peter 3:3–4, what makes a woman truly beautiful in God's eyes? For those of us who are anything but "gentle and quiet" in nature, how we can honor the Lord and the truth of these verses while still being the women he created us to be?

Read Ruth 3:12–18 once more. What's the most memorable truth you've learned from this passage?

Chapter 11
Our Hero Makes His Move

Read chapter 11 (pages 141–155).

1. Finally, the moment we've been waiting for. Will Mr. No redeem Ruth, or will it be Mr. Right? Even knowing how the story ends, we're eager to watch it play out.

a. A nineteenth-century commentator suggested, "The name of the kinsman was either unknown or purposely concealed."[25] Considering that Boaz is aware of the other kinsman's existence, which scenario seems most likely to you, and why? By not addressing the man by name, what is Boaz communicating to him? And to the ten elders? And to all the citizens of Bethlehem within earshot? Why is it important that they see who Mr. No is...and who he is not?

b. Since in the Bible the word *name* can also refer to one's reputation, what else might this man's lack of a name tell us about him? A good name is not easily obtained and can be quickly lost. What counsel does Proverbs 3:3–4 offer when it comes to keeping our good names?

2. One writer believes Mr. No "is a foil, allowing Boaz to shine even more brightly."[26] Let's test that theory.

   a. Write down as many descriptive words for Mr. No as you can come up with. Then next to each one write the opposite meaning—Unknown/Renowned, Indecisive/Decisive, etc. Take a look at the list on the right. Do those words in fact describe Boaz? Consider how the following verses from Proverbs might help us understand these two very different kinsmen: 10:7; 11:28; 12:23.

   b. Does Naomi seem overly concerned about this other kinsman-redeemer? What makes you say that? As to Ruth, does anything indicate she is worried? What might their responses teach us about trusting God?

3. As we thunder toward the finish line, we have a sense that all of Bethlehem is rooting for this "man of standing" and this "woman of noble character." But it will not be enough for them to marry and for Boaz to buy Naomi's land. That only redeems the family property. It will take a child to redeem the family name.

   a. How do the elders invoke God's favor on this couple? Should wedding ceremonies today include a prayer or blessing concerning future children? Why or why not?

   b. Women today may not have town elders to bless their wombs, but Rebekah and Hannah show us another way. In Genesis 25:21–22, who speaks to God on Rebekah's behalf? Yes, and who else? How did the Lord respond? In 1 Samuel 1:10–11, how does Hannah address the issue of childbearing? Then in 1 Samuel 1:17–20, who else chimes in? And how does the Lord respond? What hope do their stories offer modern couples who long to have offspring?

Read Ruth 4:1–12 once more. What's the most memorable truth you've learned from this passage?

Chapter 12

Talk About Happily Ever After!

Read chapter 12 (pages 157–167).

1. Contemporary opinions about Ruth are all over the map. Some say she's too perfect, too compliant. Others see her as radical and a risk-taker. Some think she fits the stereotypical mold for women—that is, we're only of value if we marry and have children. Others see her as a supreme role model of faithfulness to God.

   a. Back in the 1950s, Edith Deen described Ruth as "modest, meek, courteous, loyal, responsible."[27] Are all five qualities still held in high esteem in today's culture? Should they be? Why or why not?

   b. In many ways Psalm 113 parallels Ruth's life. Read all nine verses, then pick three that seem especially suited to her story, and explain why.

2. Our story ends with Naomi holding the future in her arms. We are reminded again of her bitter words, "the LORD has brought me back empty," even as we rejoice over God's willingness to restore what was lost.

   a. Of all the times we might expect Naomi to speak, this would be a major one. Maybe her heart is simply too full. If you've held a new-born in your arms, what was that experience like for you? What thoughts come to mind when you consider that the overwhelming love you felt for that little one pales in comparison to the love God feels for you?

   b. Think of all the ways Obed redeemed Naomi just by being born. Now think of all the ways Jesus redeemed us by dying on the cross. How does Ephesians 1:7–10 bring the truth of that redemption alive for you? (If time permits, read all of Ephesians 1 for a fuller glimpse of the Big Picture.)

3. Our storyteller winds things up with a quick review of who's who. While a listing of "so-and-so is the father of" may not make the most inspiring reading for us, ancient listeners had tears of joy in their eyes by the time the storyteller reached the last word: "David," their beloved king.

   a. We have even more reason to be moved, knowing whose name appears in the first sentence of the New Testament: "Jesus Christ the son of David." How far back can you trace your ancestry? Few of us could name our great-great-great-grandparents, let alone all the names stretching back for a thousand years. When you look at the sea of names in Matthew 1:1–16, what strikes you about that detailed listing? How might it build up your faith?

   b. There is a far longer list of names that will be revealed someday. David is the first to mention "the book of life" in Psalm 69:28, and Paul makes reference to it in Philippians 4:3. You'll find a more complete description of the Lamb's Book of Life in Revelation 21:27. How can you be certain your name appears there? What hope does John 10:27–30 offer?

Read Ruth 4:13–22 once more. What's the most memorable truth you've learned from this passage?

Before We Go
Have You Got It?

Read "Before We Go" (pages 169–170).

Wherever you may be spiritually right now, you can be sure the Lord wants to deepen your relationship with him.

   a. One of the ways we demonstrate our love for him is through trusting his Word. Ruth's great-grandson certainly did! What assurances about God's Word do you find in the following verses from Psalms: 12:6; 119:89; 138:2?

b. Another way we express our love for God is by obeying the prompting of the Holy Spirit. How do Paul's words in Romans 15:13 and Titus 3:4–7 help you understand the Spirit's role more clearly?

c. In closing, write out your commitment to God in words as simple and heartfelt as Ruth's pledge to Naomi: "Where you go I will go, and where you stay I will stay. Your people will be my people and your God my God." What would you like to say to the Lord who loves you?

GREAT READS RE: RUTH

Want to dig even deeper into the book of Ruth? Of a hundred published resources I turned to, here are my Top Ten:

1. Robert L. Hubbard Jr., *The Book of Ruth*, in *The New International Commentary on the Old Testament*, 1988.
2. Katharine Doob Sakenfeld, *Ruth: Interpretation; A Bible Commentary for Teaching and Preaching*, 1999.
3. Marjory Zoet Bankson, *Seasons of Friendship: Naomi and Ruth as a Model for Relationship*, 2005.
4. Sinclair B. Ferguson, *Faithful God: An Exposition of the Book of Ruth*, 2005.
5. Iain M. Duguid, *Esther and Ruth*, in *Reformed Expository Commentary*, 2005.
6. Kirsten Nielsen, *Ruth: A Commentary*, 1997.
7. Ellen van Wolde, *Ruth and Naomi*, 1998.
8. Carol M. Bechtel, *Above and Beyond: Hearing God's Call in Jonah and Ruth*, 2007.
9. Frederic W. Bush, *Ruth, Esther*, vol. 9 of *Word Biblical Commentary*, 1996.
10. Elizabeth Ruth Obbard, *Ruth and Naomi: A Story of Friendship, Growth and Change*, 2003.

As for learning how people lived during the time of Naomi, Ruth, and Boaz, these two books were especially helpful:

1. Ralph Gower, *The New Manners and Customs of Bible Times*, 1987.
2. Howard F. Vos, *Nelson's New Illustrated Bible Manners and Customs: How the People of the Bible Really Lived*, 1999.

NOTES

Before We Dive In

1. Proverbs 19:21, NLT
2. David Atkinson, *The Message of Ruth: The Wings of Refuge* (Leicester, UK: InterVarsity, 1991), 14.
3. Louisa M. R. Stead, "'Tis So Sweet to Trust in Jesus," in *Then Sings My Soul: 150 of the World's Greatest Hymn Stories* (Nashville: Thomas Nelson, 2003), 210.
4. Robert L. Hubbard Jr., *The Book of Ruth,* in *The New International Commentary on the Old Testament* (Grand Rapids: Eerdmans, 1988), 2.
5. H. V. Morton, *Women of the Bible* (New York: Dodd, Mead, 1941), 76.
6. Ruth 4:14
7. Sinclair B. Ferguson, *Faithful God: An Exposition of the Book of Ruth* (Bridgend, UK: Bryntirion, 2005), 67.
8. Katharine Doob Sakenfeld, *Ruth: Interpretation; A Bible Commentary for Teaching and Preaching* (Louisville, KY: Westminster John Knox, 1999), 5.
9. Hubbard, *The Book of Ruth,* 23.
10. Walter C. Kaiser Jr. and Duane A. Garrett, eds., *NIV Archaeological Study Bible: An Illustrated Walk Through Biblical History and Culture* (Grand Rapids: Zondervan, 2005), 386.
11. Joan D. Chittister, *The Story of Ruth: Twelve Moments in Every Woman's Life* (Grand Rapids: Eerdmans, 2000), 1.
12. Edward F. Campbell Jr., *Ruth,* vol. 7 of *The Anchor Bible* (New York: Doubleday, 1975), 18.
13. F. B. Huey, "Ruth," in *The Expositor's Bible Commentary* (Grand Rapids: Zondervan, 1992), 3:511.
14. Campbell, *Ruth,* 20.
15. "Origin of the Bible," www.truth net.org/Bible-Origins/4_How _was_Bible_written/index.htm.
16. Sakenfeld, *Ruth,* 5.
17. Hubbard, *The Book of Ruth,* 24.
18. Exodus 15:21
19. Judges 5:12
20. Luke 1:46
21. Richard Bauckham, *Gospel Women: Studies of the Named Women in the Gospels* (Grand Rapids: Eerdmans, 2002), 3.
22. Hebrews 12:2
23. Rose Sallberg Kam, *Their Stories, Our Stories: Women of the Bible* (New York: Continuum, 1995), 115.
24. Proverbs 14:1

25. Proverbs 11:16; 6:24

26. Hubbard, *The Book of Ruth*, 24.

27. Hubbard, *The Book of Ruth*, 24.

28. Nehama Aschkenasy, "Language as Female Empowerment in Ruth," in *Reading Ruth: Contemporary Women Reclaim a Sacred Story*, ed. Judith A. Kates and Gail Twersky Reimer (New York: Ballantine, 1994), 113.

29. John 4:1–42

30. Mark 5:25–34

31. Acts 16:16–19

32. Phyllis A. Bird, *Missing Persons and Mistaken Identities: Women and Gender in Ancient Israel* (Minneapolis: Augsburg Fortress, 1997), 65.

33. Kirsten Nielsen, *Ruth: A Commentary*, Old Testament Library (Louisville, KY: Westminster John Knox, 1997), 5.

34. Sakenfeld, *Ruth*, 27.

Chapter 1

1. James M. Freeman, *Manners and Customs of the Bible* (New Kensington, PA: Whitaker, 1996), 441.

2. Freeman, *Manners and Customs*, 44.

3. Ralph Gower, *The New Manners and Customs of Bible Times* (Chicago: Moody, 1987), 12.

4. Freeman, *Manners and Customs*, 184.

5. Numbers 19:16

6. Joan D. Chittister, *The Story of Ruth: Twelve Moments in Every Woman's Life* (Grand Rapids: Eerdmans, 2000), 1.

7. E. W. Bullinger, "Ruth," in *The Companion Bible (Condensed)*, commentary on Ruth 1:1, www.companionbiblecondensed.com/OT/Ruth.pdf, 361.

8. Gillian M. Rowell, "Ruth," in *The IVP Women's Bible Commentary* (Downers Grove, IL: InterVarsity, 2002), 147.

9. Robert L. Hubbard Jr., *The Book of Ruth*, in *The New International Commentary on the Old Testament* (Grand Rapids: Eerdmans, 1988), 84.

10. Judges 21:25

11. Judges 2:19

12. Iain M. Duguid, *Esther and Ruth*, in *Reformed Expository Commentary* (Phillipsburg, NJ: P and R, 2005), 131.

13. Sinclair B. Ferguson, *Faithful God: An Exposition of the Book of Ruth* (Bridgend, UK: Bryntirion, 2005), 28.

14. Judges 2:11; 3:7; 3:12; 6:1; 10:6; 13:1

15. Judges 2:12

16. Psalm 105:16

17. Psalm 105:19

18. Gien Karssen, *Her Name Is Woman* (Colorado Springs, CO: NavPress, 1977), 2:109.

19. Katharine Doob Sakenfeld, *Ruth: Interpretation; A Bible Commentary for Teaching and Preaching* (Louisville, KY: Westminster John Knox, 1999), 18.

20. Exodus 3:8

21. Kirsten Nielsen, *Ruth: A Commentary,* Old Testament Library (Louisville, KY: Westminster John Knox, 1997), 18.

22. Warren W. Wiersbe, *Be Committed (Ruth and Esther): Doing God's Will Whatever the Cost* (Colorado Springs, CO: Chariot Victor, 1993), 15.

23. Ellen van Wolde, *Ruth and Naomi* (Macon, GA: Smyth and Helwys, 1998), 7.

24. Philippians 3:19

25. Edward D. Grohman, "Moab," in *The Interpreter's Dictionary of the Bible,* ed. George Arthur Buttrick (New York: Abingdon, 1962), 3:409.

26. Numbers 26:3

27. Elizabeth Ruth Obbard, *Ruth and Naomi: A Story of Friendship, Growth and Change* (Cincinnati: Saint Anthony Messenger, 2003), 5.

28. John H. Walton, Victor H. Matthews, and Mark W. Chavalas, *The IVP Bible Background Commentary: Old Testament* (Downers Grove, IL: InterVarsity, 2000), 277.

29. Luke 15:13

30. Jeremiah 48:29

31. Jeremiah 48:7

32. Jeremiah 48:42

33. Luke 17:32

34. Genesis 19:26

35. Genesis 19:32

36. Genesis 19:37

37. Numbers 25:1–2

38. Numbers 25:3

39. Deuteronomy 23:3–4

40. Rowell, "Ruth," 147.

41. 2 Kings 23:13

42. Alfred J. Hoerth, Gerald L. Mattingly, Edwin M. Yamauchi, eds., *Peoples of the Old Testament World* (Grand Rapids: Baker, 1998), 330.

43. Rowell, "Ruth," 146.

44. Romans 8:17

45. Walter C. Kaiser Jr. and Duane A. Garrett, eds., *NIV Archaeological Study Bible: An Illustrated Walk Through Biblical History and Culture* (Grand Rapids: Zondervan, 2005), 388.

46. Hubbard, *The Book of Ruth,* 88.

47. Ann Spangler and Jean E. Syswerda, *Women of the Bible: A One-Year Devotional Study of Women in Scripture* (Grand Rapids: Zondervan, 1999), 128.

48. Julie-Allyson Ieron, *Names of Women of the Bible* (Chicago: Moody, 1998), 105.

49. Hubbard, *The Book of Ruth,* 88.

50. Dietrich Gruen, ed., *Who's Who in the Bible: An Illustrated Biographical Dictionary* (Lincolnwood, IL: Publications International, 1997), 391.

51. Nielsen, *Ruth: A Commentary,* 42.

52. Kaiser and Garrett, *NIV Archaeological Study Bible,* 28.

53. Ferguson, *Faithful God,* 28.

54. Gruen, *Who's Who in the Bible,* 349.

55. Nielsen, *Ruth: A Commentary,* 42.

56. Ferguson, *Faithful God,* 28.

57. Nielsen, *Ruth: A Commentary,* 42.

58. Gruen, *Who's Who in the Bible,* 102.

59. Virginia Stem Owens, *Daughters of Eve: Seeing Ourselves in Women of the Bible* (Colorado Springs, CO: NavPress, 1995), 42.

60. Marsha Pravder Mirkin, *The Women Who Danced by the Sea: Finding Ourselves in the Stories of Our Biblical Foremothers* (Rhinebeck, NY: Monkfish Book, 2004), 164.

61. Marjory Zoet Bankson, *Seasons of Friendship: Naomi and Ruth as a Model for Relationship,* rev. ed. (Minneapolis: Augsburg Fortress, 2005), 31.

62. Hubbard, *The Book of Ruth,* 91.

63. Rowell, "Ruth," 148.

64. 1 Samuel 17:12

65. Kathy Collard Miller, *Women of the Bible: God's Word for the Biblically-Inept* (Lancaster, PA: Starburst, 1999), 198.

66. J. Vernon McGee, *Ruth* (Nashville: Thomas Nelson, 1991), 18.

67. Psalm 139:16

68. Hayyim Schauss, "Ancient Jewish Marriage," My Jewish Learning, www.myjewishlearning.com /life/Relationships/Spouses_and _Partners/About_Marriage /Ancient_Jewish_Marriage .shtml.

69. Rowell, "Ruth," 148.

70. James L. Crenshaw, *Story and Faith: A Guide to the Old Testament* (New York: Macmillan, 1986), 335.

71. Bankson, *Seasons of Friendship,* 18.

72. Carol M. Bechtel, *Above and Beyond: Hearing God's Call in Jonah and Ruth* (Louisville, KY: Presbyterian Women, Presbyterian Church [USA], 2007), 37.

73. Carol Meyers, gen. ed., *Women in Scripture: A Dictionary of Named and Unnamed Women in the Hebrew Bible, the Apocryphal/ Deuterocanonical Books, and the New Testament* (New York: Houghton Mifflin, 2000), 146.

74. Herbert Lockyer, *All the Women of the Bible* (Grand Rapids: Zondervan, 1967), 144.

75. Bechtel, *Above and Beyond,* 35.

76. van Wolde, *Ruth and Naomi,* 8.

77. Genesis 16:3

78. Genesis 30:1–3

79. Genesis 30:9

80. Elizabeth George, *Women Who Loved God: A Devotional Walk with the Women of the Bible* (Eugene, OR: Harvest House, 1999), May 19.

81. Lois C. Dubin, "Fullness and Emptiness, Fertility and Loss," in *Reading Ruth: Contemporary Women Reclaim a Sacred Story,* ed. Judith A. Kates and Gail Twersky Reimer (New York: Ballantine, 1994), 132.

82. van Wolde, *Ruth and Naomi,* 10.

83. Gower, *New Manners and Customs,* 71.

84. Freeman, *Manners and Customs,* 131.

85. Psalm 73:26

86. John 3:16

87. Walton, Matthews, and Chavalas, *The IVP Bible Background Commentary,* 603.

88. Gower, *New Manners and Customs,* 70.

89. Job 7:9

90. Freeman, *Manners and Customs,* 44.

91. Frances Vander Velde, *Women of the Bible* (Grand Rapids: Kregel, 1985), 104.

92. Matthew Henry, *Matthew Henry's Commentary on the Whole Bible* (Peabody, MA: Hendrickson, 1991), 2:199.

Chapter 2

1. Ralph Gower, *The New Manners and Customs of Bible Times* (Chicago: Moody, 1987), 14.

2. Katharine Doob Sakenfeld, *Ruth: Interpretation; A Bible Commentary for Teaching and Preaching* (Louisville, KY: Westminster John Knox, 1999), 22.

3. Psalm 105:40

4. Ruth 1:6, NKJV

5. John 6:35

6. John 6:33

7. Sinclair B. Ferguson, *Faithful God: An Exposition of the Book of Ruth* (Bridgend, UK: Bryntirion, 2005), 25.

8. Phineas Camp Headley, *Women of the Bible* (Buffalo, NY: Miller, Orton and Mulligan, 1854), 128.

9. Nelson Beecher Keyes, *Story of the Bible World in Map, Word and Picture* (New York: C. S. Hammond, 1959), 125.

10. Edith Deen, *All the Women of the Bible* (New York: Harper and Row, 1955), 84.

11. Headley, *Women of the Bible,* 132.

12. Gower, *New Manners and Customs,* 240.

13. Deuteronomy 13:4

14. James M. Freeman, *Manners and Customs of the Bible* (New Kensington, PA: Whitaker, 1996), 416.

15. Anson F. Rainey and R. Steven Notley, *The Sacred Bridge: Carta's Atlas of the Biblical World* (Jerusalem: Carta, 2005), 129–30.

16. 2 Corinthians 11:26

17. Harold J. Ockenga, *Women Who Made Bible History* (Grand Rapids: Zondervan, 1962), 83.

18. Harold S. Paisley, *This Ruth* (Glastonbury, CT: Olive, 1995), 32.

19. F. C. Cook, ed., *Exodus to Esther,* vol. 2 of *Barnes Notes* (Grand Rapids: Baker, 1998), 473.

20. Robert L. Hubbard Jr., *The Book of Ruth,* in *The New International Commentary on the Old Testament* (Grand Rapids: Eerdmans, 1988), 103.

21. Kirsten Nielsen, *Ruth: A Commentary,* Old Testament Library (Louisville, KY: Westminster John Knox, 1997), 46.

22. Hubbard, *The Book of Ruth,* 104.

23. Sakenfeld, *Ruth,* 24.

24. Diana Hagee, *Ruth: The Romance of Redemption* (Nashville: Thomas Nelson, 2005), 30.

25. Dee Brestin, *A Woman's Journey Through Ruth: 8 Lessons on Love Exclusively for Women* (Colorado Springs, CO: Cook, 1998), 35.

26. Frederic W. Bush, *Ruth, Esther,* vol. 9 of *Word Biblical Commentary* (Nashville: Thomas Nelson, 1996), 76.

27. Gillian M. Rowell, "Ruth," in *The IVP Women's Bible Commentary* (Downers Grove, IL: InterVarsity, 2002), 148.

28. Michael S. Moore, "Ruth," in *Joshua, Judges, Ruth,* vol. 5 of *New International Biblical Commentary* (Peabody, MA: Hendrickson, 2000), 318.

29. Lamentations 1:2

30. Moore, "Ruth," 318.

31. Deuteronomy 3:24

32. Job 19:21

33. Ferguson, *Faithful God,* 37.

34. 2 Corinthians 1:3–4

35. Joshua 1:5

36. Linda H. Hollies, *On Their Way to Wonderful: A Journey with Naomi and Ruth* (Cleveland: Pilgrim Press, 2004), 24.

37. Sylvia Charles, *Women in the Word* (South Plainfield, NJ: Bridge, 1984), 73.

38. Paisley, *This Ruth,* 37.

39. Henry T. Sell, *Studies of Famous Bible Women* (New York: Revell, 1925), 47.

40. Ferguson, *Faithful God,* 38.

41. Hubbard, *The Book of Ruth,* 73.

42. Hollies, *On Their Way to Wonderful,* 14.

Chapter 3

1. Elizabeth Ruth Obbard, *Ruth and Naomi: A Story of Friendship, Growth and Change* (Cincinnati: Saint Anthony Messenger, 2003), 25.

2. Robert L. Hubbard Jr., *The Book of Ruth,* in *The New International Commentary on the Old Testament* (Grand Rapids: Eerdmans, 1988), 115.

3. Genesis 2:24, NRSV

4. Michael S. Moore, "Ruth," in *Joshua, Judges, Ruth,* vol. 5 of *New International Biblical Commentary* (Peabody, MA: Hendrickson, 2000), 321.

5. Exodus 34:17

6. Gillian M. Rowell, "Ruth," in *The IVP Women's Bible Commentary* (Downers Grove, IL: InterVarsity, 2002), 148.

7. Matthew 28:19, NCV

8. Carolyn Custis James, *The Gospel of Ruth: Loving God Enough to Break the Rules* (Grand Rapids: Zondervan, 2008), 48.

9. Psalm 33:11
10. George Matheson, *The Representative Women of the Bible* (London: Hodder and Stoughton, 1908), 193.
11. Marjory Zoet Bankson, *Seasons of Friendship: Naomi and Ruth as a Model for Relationship,* rev. ed. (Minneapolis: Augsburg Fortress, 2005), 51.
12. Margaret E. Sangster, *The Women of the Bible* (New York: Christian Herald, 1911), 127.
13. Carol Meyers, gen. ed., *Women in Scripture: A Dictionary of Named and Unnamed Women in the Hebrew Bible, the Apocryphal/Deuterocanonical Books, and the New Testament* (New York: Houghton Mifflin, 2000), 146.
14. Harold S. Paisley, *This Ruth* (Glastonbury, CT: Olive, 1995), 38.
15. Ruth Haley Barton, *Ruth: Relationships That Bring Life* (Colorado Springs, CO: Shaw Books, 2001), 9.
16. "Pocahontas," American History Quotes, http://americanhistory quotes.com/pocahontas.htm.
17. Matthew Henry, *Matthew Henry's Commentary on the Whole Bible* (Peabody, MA: Hendrickson, 1991), 2:202.
18. 1 John 4:11
19. Sinclair B. Ferguson, *Faithful God: An Exposition of the Book of Ruth* (Bridgend, UK: Bryntirion, 2005), 26.
20. Psalm 37:5–6
21. Leviticus 26:12
22. Sylvia Charles, *Women in the Word* (South Plainfield, NJ: Bridge, 1984), 74.
23. Iain M. Duguid, *Esther and Ruth,* in *Reformed Expository Commentary* (Phillipsburg, NJ: P and R, 2005), 152.
24. William Mackintosh Mackay, *Bible Types of Modern Women* (New York: George H. Doran, 1922), 238.
25. Katharine Doob Sakenfeld, *Ruth: Interpretation; A Bible Commentary for Teaching and Preaching* (Louisville, KY: Westminster John Knox, 1999), 33.
26. Duguid, *Esther and Ruth,* 142–43.
27. Genesis 23:20
28. John H. Walton, Victor H. Matthews, and Mark W. Chavalas, *The IVP Bible Background Commentary: Old Testament* (Downers Grove, IL: InterVarsity, 2000), 278.
29. Hubbard, *The Book of Ruth,* 119.
30. Henry, *Matthew Henry's Commentary,* 2:202.
31. John Piper, *A Sweet and Bitter Providence: Sex, Race, and the Sovereignty of God* (Wheaton, IL: Crossway, 2010), 34.
32. T. J. Wray, *Good Girls, Bad Girls: The Enduring Lessons of Twelve Women of the Old Testament* (Lanham, MD: Rowman and Littlefield, 2008), 75.

33. H. V. Morton, *Women of the Bible* (New York: Dodd, Mead, 1941), 79.

34. Duguid, *Esther and Ruth,* 136.

35. Nehama Aschkenasy, "Language as Female Empowerment in Ruth," in *Reading Ruth: Contemporary Women Reclaim a Sacred Story,* ed. Judith A. Kates and Gail Twersky Reimer (New York: Ballantine, 1994), 116.

36. Walter Wangerin Jr., *Naomi and Her Daughters: A Novel* (Grand Rapids: Zondervan, 2010), 172.

37. Julie-Allyson Ieron, *Names of Women of the Bible* (Chicago: Moody, 1998), 115.

38. Frederic W. Bush, *Ruth, Esther,* vol. 9 of *Word Biblical Commentary* (Nashville: Thomas Nelson, 1996), 87.

39. Hubbard, *The Book of Ruth,* 121.

40. Hubbard, *The Book of Ruth,* 121.

41. Sakenfeld, *Ruth,* 35.

Chapter 4

1. Marjory Zoet Bankson, *Seasons of Friendship: Naomi and Ruth as a Model for Relationship,* rev. ed. (Minneapolis: Augsburg Fortress, 2005), 43.

2. Ralph Gower, *The New Manners and Customs of Bible Times* (Chicago: Moody, 1987), 135.

3. Carol M. Bechtel, *Above and Beyond: Hearing God's Call in Jonah and Ruth* (Louisville, KY: Presbyterian Women, Presbyterian Church [USA], 2007), 35.

4. Alice Ogden Bellis, *Helpmates, Harlots, and Heroes* (Louisville, KY: Westminster John Knox, 1994), 211.

5. John H. Walton, Victor H. Matthews, and Mark W. Chavalas, *The IVP Bible Background Commentary: Old Testament* (Downers Grove, IL: InterVarsity, 2000), 277.

6. Edith Deen, *All the Women of the Bible* (New York: Harper and Row, 1955), 84.

7. Walton, Matthews, and Chavalas, *IVP Bible Background Commentary,* 278.

8. Elizabeth Ruth Obbard, *Ruth and Naomi: A Story of Friendship, Growth and Change* (Cincinnati: Saint Anthony Messenger, 2003), 5.

9. Gower, *New Manners and Customs,* 33.

10. Anna Trimiew, *Bible Almanac: Discover the Wonders of the Bible* (Lincolnwood, IL: Publications International, 1997), 131–32.

11. Walter C. Kaiser Jr. and Duane A. Garrett, eds., *NIV Archaeological Study Bible: An Illustrated Walk Through Biblical History and Culture* (Grand Rapids: Zondervan, 2005), 392.

12. Nelson Beecher Keyes, *Story of the Bible World in Map, Word and Picture* (New York: C. S. Hammond, 1959), 35.

13. Frederic W. Bush, *Ruth, Esther,* vol. 9 of *Word Biblical Commen-*

tary (Nashville: Thomas Nelson, 1996), 91.

14. Michael S. Moore, "Ruth," in *Joshua, Judges, Ruth,* vol. 5 of *New International Biblical Commentary* (Peabody, MA: Hendrickson, 2000), 369.

15. Bush, *Ruth, Esther,* 91.

16. Robert L. Hubbard Jr., *The Book of Ruth,* in *The New International Commentary on the Old Testament* (Grand Rapids: Eerdmans, 1988), 124.

17. Matthew Henry, *Matthew Henry's Commentary on the Whole Bible* (Peabody, MA: Hendrickson, 1991), 2:203.

18. Lydia Brownback, *Legacy of Faith: From Women of the Bible to Women of Today* (Phillipsburg, NJ: P and R, 2002), 107.

19. Iain M. Duguid, *Esther and Ruth,* in *Reformed Expository Commentary* (Phillipsburg, NJ: P and R, 2005), 155.

20. Margaret E. Sangster, *The Women of the Bible* (New York: Christian Herald, 1911), 126.

21. Walter Wangerin Jr., *Naomi and Her Daughters: A Novel* (Grand Rapids: Zondervan, 2010), 194.

22. Harold J. Ockenga, *Women Who Made Bible History* (Grand Rapids: Zondervan, 1962), 79.

23. Exodus 15:23–24

24. Gillian M. Rowell, "Ruth," in *The IVP Women's Bible Commentary* (Downers Grove, IL: InterVarsity, 2002), 149.

25. Elizabeth George, *Women Who Loved God: A Devotional Walk with the Women of the Bible* (Eugene, OR: Harvest House, 1999), May 21.

26. Hubbard, *The Book of Ruth,* 122.

27. Sinclair B. Ferguson, *Faithful God: An Exposition of the Book of Ruth* (Bridgend, UK: Bryntirion, 2005), 42.

28. Duguid, *Esther and Ruth,* 142.

29. 1 Peter 4:19

30. Lois C. Dubin, "Fullness and Emptiness, Fertility and Loss," in *Reading Ruth: Contemporary Women Reclaim a Sacred Story,* ed. Judith A. Kates and Gail Twersky Reimer (New York: Ballantine, 1994), 136.

31. Henry, *Matthew Henry's Commentary,* 2:203.

32. Dubin, "Fullness and Emptiness," 135.

33. Hubbard, *The Book of Ruth,* 126.

34. John Piper, *A Sweet and Bitter Providence: Sex, Race, and the Sovereignty of God* (Wheaton, IL: Crossway, 2010), 58.

35. Ferguson, *Faithful God,* 53.

36. Obbard, *Ruth and Naomi,* 31.

37. Phineas Camp Headley, *Women of the Bible* (Buffalo, NY: Miller, Orton and Mulligan, 1854), 129.

Chapter 5

1. Ellen van Wolde, *Ruth and Naomi* (Macon, GA: Smyth and Helwys, 1998), 31.

2. Katharine Doob Sakenfeld, *Ruth: Interpretation; A Bible Commentary for Teaching and Preaching* (Louisville, KY: Westminster John Knox, 1999), 37.

3. 1 Samuel 9:1

4. 1 Kings 11:28

5. 1 Samuel 16:18

6. Carol M. Bechtel, *Above and Beyond: Hearing God's Call in Jonah and Ruth* (Louisville, KY: Presbyterian Women, Presbyterian Church [USA], 2007), 41.

7. Matthew Henry, *Matthew Henry's Commentary on the Whole Bible* (Peabody, MA: Hendrickson, 1991), 2:204.

8. Gien Karssen, *Her Name Is Woman* (Colorado Springs, CO: NavPress, 1977), 2:132.

9. Kirsten Nielsen, *Ruth: A Commentary,* Old Testament Library (Louisville, KY: Westminster John Knox, 1997), 54.

10. Joshua 2:11

11. Robert L. Hubbard Jr., *The Book of Ruth,* in *The New International Commentary on the Old Testament* (Grand Rapids: Eerdmans, 1988), 136.

12. George Matheson, *The Representative Women of the Bible* (London: Hodder and Stoughton, 1908), 195.

13. Leviticus 23:22

14. Deuteronomy 24:19

15. Virginia Stem Owens, *Daughters of Eve: Seeing Ourselves in Women of the Bible* (Colorado Springs, CO: NavPress, 1995), 43.

16. Matheson, *Representative Women of the Bible,* 195.

17. Ruth 1:8

18. Genesis 39:21

19. Iain M. Duguid, *Esther and Ruth,* in *Reformed Expository Commentary* (Phillipsburg, NJ: P and R, 2005), 157.

20. Matheson, *Representative Women of the Bible,* 196.

21. John H. Walton, Victor H. Matthews, and Mark W. Chavalas, *The IVP Bible Background Commentary: Old Testament* (Downers Grove, IL: InterVarsity, 2000), 277.

22. Ralph Gower, *The New Manners and Customs of Bible Times* (Chicago: Moody, 1987), 17.

23. Hubbard, *The Book of Ruth,* 138.

24. Walton, Matthews, and Chavalas, *IVP Bible Background Commentary,* 278.

25. Walter C. Kaiser Jr. and Duane A. Garrett, eds., *NIV Archaeological Study Bible: An Illustrated Walk Through Biblical History and Culture* (Grand Rapids: Zondervan, 2005), 388.

26. Galatians 6:9

27. Miki Raver, *Listen to Her Voice: Women of the Hebrew Bible* (San Francisco: Chronicle, 1998), 149.

28. Exodus 34:22

29. Marjory Zoet Bankson, *Seasons of Friendship: Naomi and Ruth as a Model for Relationship*, rev. ed. (Minneapolis: Augsburg Fortress, 2005), 18.

30. Matthew 6:1

31. 1 Peter 5:6

32. Michael S. Moore, "Ruth," in *Joshua, Judges, Ruth*, vol. 5 of *New International Biblical Commentary* (Peabody, MA: Hendrickson, 2000), 329.

33. Gillian M. Rowell, "Ruth," in *The IVP Women's Bible Commentary* (Downers Grove, IL: InterVarsity, 2002), 149.

34. Sinclair B. Ferguson, *Faithful God: An Exposition of the Book of Ruth* (Bridgend, UK: Bryntirion, 2005), 59.

35. Ephesians 5:25

36. John Piper, *A Sweet and Bitter Providence: Sex, Race, and the Sovereignty of God* (Wheaton, IL: Crossway, 2010), 60.

37. Kaiser and Garrett, *NIV Archaeological Study Bible*, 389.

38. Matheson, *Representative Women of the Bible*, 196.

39. Matthew 20:8

40. Hubbard, *The Book of Ruth*, 146.

41. Thomas Hood, "Ruth," English Verse.com, www.englishverse.com/poems/ruth.

42. Bechtel, *Above and Beyond*, 41.

43. F. C. Cook, ed., *Exodus to Esther*, vol. 2 of *Barnes Notes* (Grand Rapids: Baker, 1998), 475.

44. Moore, "Ruth," 330.

Chapter 6

1. Michael S. Moore, "Ruth," in *Joshua, Judges, Ruth*, vol. 5 of *New International Biblical Commentary* (Peabody, MA: Hendrickson, 2000), 332.

2. Moore, "Ruth," 332.

3. F. C. Cook, ed., *Exodus to Esther*, vol. 2 of *Barnes Notes* (Grand Rapids: Baker, 1998), 475.

4. Gillian M. Rowell, "Ruth," in *The IVP Women's Bible Commentary* (Downers Grove, IL: InterVarsity, 2002), 149.

5. Psalm 12:7

6. Genesis 24:18

7. John 4:7

8. John 4:9

9. 1 Samuel 25:23

10. 1 Kings 1:31

11. Isaiah 45:23

12. Moore, "Ruth," 334.

13. Marjory Zoet Bankson, *Seasons of Friendship: Naomi and Ruth as a Model for Relationship*, rev. ed. (Minneapolis: Augsburg Fortress, 2005), 71.

14. Moore, "Ruth," 356.

15. Bankson, *Seasons of Friendship*, 71.

16. Edith Deen, *All the Women of the Bible* (New York: Harper and Row, 1955), 82.

17. Phineas Camp Headley, *Women of the Bible* (Buffalo, NY: Miller, Orton and Mulligan, 1854), 135.

18. Genesis 1:27

19. Isaiah 43:7

20. Revelation 4:11

21. Matthew Henry, *Matthew Henry's Commentary on the Whole Bible* (Peabody, MA: Hendrickson, 1991), 2:212.
22. Proverbs 31:30
23. H. V. Morton, *Women of the Bible* (New York: Dodd, Mead, 1941), 78.
24. Moore, "Ruth," 334–35.
25. Genesis 2:24, NRSV
26. Genesis 12:1
27. Robert Alter, *The Art of Biblical Narrative* (New York: Basic Books, 1981), 59.
28. Matthew 5:12
29. Moore, "Ruth," 335.
30. Psalm 34:2
31. Robert L. Hubbard Jr., *The Book of Ruth,* in *The New International Commentary on the Old Testament* (Grand Rapids: Eerdmans, 1988), 167.
32. Psalm 91:4
33. Bankson, *Seasons of Friendship,* 73.
34. Hubbard, *The Book of Ruth,* 169.
35. Hubbard, *The Book of Ruth,* 187.
36. Hubbard, *The Book of Ruth,* 169.
37. Ralph Gower, *The New Manners and Customs of Bible Times* (Chicago: Moody, 1987), 54.
38. Frederic W. Bush, *Ruth, Esther,* vol. 9 of *Word Biblical Commentary* (Nashville: Thomas Nelson, 1996), 128.
39. Gien Karssen, *Her Name Is Woman* (Colorado Springs, CO: NavPress, 1977), 2:127.
40. James 2:25
41. James M. Freeman, *Manners and Customs of the Bible* (New Kensington, PA: Whitaker, 1996), 128.
42. Freeman, *Manners and Customs,* 128.
43. Moore, "Ruth," 339.
44. Matthew 26:26–28
45. Louise Pettibone Smith, "Ruth," in *The Interpreter's Bible* (Nashville: Abingdon, 1953), 2:843.
46. Virginia Stem Owens, *Daughters of Eve: Seeing Ourselves in Women of the Bible* (Colorado Springs, CO: NavPress, 1995), 44.
47. Katharine Doob Sakenfeld, *Ruth: Interpretation; A Bible Commentary for Teaching and Preaching* (Louisville, KY: Westminster John Knox, 1999), 45.
48. Ephesians 3:20
49. Ephesians 4:6
50. Hubbard, *The Book of Ruth,* 179.
51. Sinclair B. Ferguson, *Faithful God: An Exposition of the Book of Ruth* (Bridgend, UK: Bryntirion, 2005), 63.

Chapter 7

1. Iain M. Duguid, *Esther and Ruth,* in *Reformed Expository Commentary* (Phillipsburg, NJ: P and R, 2005), 161.
2. 2 Corinthians 5:7
3. Carol M. Bechtel, *Above and Beyond: Hearing God's Call in Jonah and Ruth* (Louisville, KY: Presbyterian Women, Presbyterian Church [USA], 2007), 43.

4. Ruth 1:8
5. Joyce G. Baldwin, "Ruth," in *The New Bible Commentary Revised,* ed. Donald Guthrie and J. Alec Motyer (Grand Rapids: Eerdmans, 1970), 278.
6. John H. Walton, Victor H. Matthews, and Mark W. Chavalas, *The IVP Bible Background Commentary: Old Testament* (Downers Grove, IL: InterVarsity, 2000), 279.
7. Titus 2:14
8. 2 Corinthians 4:7
9. James 1:17
10. Marjory Zoet Bankson, *Seasons of Friendship: Naomi and Ruth as a Model for Relationship,* rev. ed. (Minneapolis: Augsburg Fortress, 2005), 78.
11. Robert L. Hubbard Jr., *The Book of Ruth,* in *The New International Commentary on the Old Testament* (Grand Rapids: Eerdmans, 1988), 188.
12. Michael S. Moore, "Ruth," in *Joshua, Judges, Ruth,* vol. 5 of *New International Biblical Commentary* (Peabody, MA: Hendrickson, 2000), 345.
13. Psalm 78:35
14. James 2:25
15. Hebrews 11:31, KJV
16. Hubbard, *The Book of Ruth,* 190.
17. John 4:29
18. Ruth 2:8–9
19. Hubbard, *The Book of Ruth,* 192.
20. Katharine Doob Sakenfeld, *Ruth: Interpretation; A Bible Commentary for Teaching and Preaching* (Louisville, KY: Westminster John Knox, 1999), 50.

Chapter 8

1. Warren W. Wiersbe, *Be Committed (Ruth and Esther): Doing God's Will Whatever the Cost* (Colorado Springs, CO: Chariot Victor, 1993), 38.
2. Ruth 1:9
3. Robert L. Hubbard Jr., *The Book of Ruth,* in *The New International Commentary on the Old Testament* (Grand Rapids: Eerdmans, 1988), 195.
4. Matthew 3:12
5. Walter C. Kaiser Jr. and Duane A. Garrett, eds., *NIV Archaeological Study Bible: An Illustrated Walk Through Biblical History and Culture* (Grand Rapids: Zondervan, 2005), 388.
6. Howard F. Vos, *Nelson's New Illustrated Bible Manners and Customs: How the People of the Bible Really Lived* (Nashville: Thomas Nelson, 1999), 141.
7. Hubbard, *The Book of Ruth,* 200.
8. Hubbard, *The Book of Ruth,* 200.
9. Hubbard, *The Book of Ruth,* 200.
10. James M. Freeman, *Manners and Customs of the Bible* (New Kensington, PA: Whitaker, 1996), 59.
11. Michael S. Moore, "Ruth," in *Joshua, Judges, Ruth,* vol. 5 of *New International Biblical Commentary* (Peabody, MA: Hendrickson, 2000), 348.

12. Kaiser and Garrett, *NIV Archaeological Study Bible,* 608.

13. Kaiser and Garrett, *NIV Archaeological Study Bible,* 391.

14. Katharine Doob Sakenfeld, *Ruth: Interpretation; A Bible Commentary for Teaching and Preaching* (Louisville, KY: Westminster John Knox, 1999), 54.

15. John H. Walton, Victor H. Matthews, and Mark W. Chavalas, *The IVP Bible Background Commentary: Old Testament* (Downers Grove, IL: InterVarsity, 2000), 279.

16. Matthew Henry, *Matthew Henry's Commentary on the Whole Bible* (Peabody, MA: Hendrickson, 1991), 2:209.

17. Kaiser and Garrett, *NIV Archaeological Study Bible,* 391.

18. David Atkinson, *The Message of Ruth: The Wings of Refuge* (Leicester, UK: InterVarsity, 1991), 100.

19. Joyce G. Baldwin, "Ruth," in *The New Bible Commentary Revised,* ed. Donald Guthrie and J. Alec Motyer (Grand Rapids: Eerdmans, 1970), 281.

20. Genesis 35:2; Deuteronomy 8:4

21. Exodus 22:26; Isaiah 3:6

22. Isaiah 61:10

23. Moore, "Ruth," 348.

24. Hubbard, *The Book of Ruth,* 196.

25. Moore, "Ruth," 349.

26. Hubbard, *The Book of Ruth,* 196.

27. Hubbard, *The Book of Ruth,* 203.

28. F. C. Cook, ed., *Exodus to Esther,* vol. 2 of *Barnes Notes* (Grand Rapids: Baker, 1998), 476.

29. Hubbard, *The Book of Ruth,* 203.

30. Ellen van Wolde, *Ruth and Naomi* (Macon, GA: Smyth and Helwys, 1998), 69.

31. van Wolde, *Ruth and Naomi,* 75.

32. Kirsten Nielsen, *Ruth: A Commentary,* Old Testament Library (Louisville, KY: Westminster John Knox, 1997), 74.

33. Carol M. Bechtel, *Above and Beyond: Hearing God's Call in Jonah and Ruth* (Louisville, KY: Presbyterian Women, Presbyterian Church [USA], 2007), 50.

34. Sakenfeld, *Ruth: Interpretation,* 54.

35. van Wolde, *Ruth and Naomi,* 92.

36. Ruth 1:17

37. Ruth 2:12

38. Hubbard, *The Book of Ruth,* 196.

39. Romans 8:8

40. Psalm 130:3

41. Psalm 130:4

42. Exodus 20:20

43. John Piper, *A Sweet and Bitter Providence: Sex, Race, and the Sovereignty of God* (Wheaton, IL: Crossway, 2010), 13.

44. Sinclair B. Ferguson, *Faithful God: An Exposition of the Book of Ruth* (Bridgend, UK: Bryntirion, 2005), 102.

45. Ruth 1:16

46. Moore, "Ruth," 352.

47. André LaCocque, *Ruth: A Continental Commentary,* trans. K. C.

Hanson (Minneapolis: Augsburg Fortress, 2004), 86.

48. Psalm 9:10

49. Robert Lintzenich, ed., *Ruth, Esther,* in *Shepherd's Notes* (Nashville: Broadman and Holman, 1998), 28.

50. Moore, "Ruth," 352.

Chapter 9

1. Song of Songs 4:14

2. Walter C. Kaiser Jr. and Duane A. Garrett, eds., *NIV Archaeological Study Bible: An Illustrated Walk Through Biblical History and Culture* (Grand Rapids: Zondervan, 2005), 389.

3. Michael S. Moore, "Ruth," in *Joshua, Judges, Ruth,* vol. 5 of *New International Biblical Commentary* (Peabody, MA: Hendrickson, 2000), 349.

4. Robert L. Hubbard Jr., *The Book of Ruth,* in *The New International Commentary on the Old Testament* (Grand Rapids: Eerdmans, 1988), 208.

5. Victor Hugo, *"Boöz Endormi,"* in *Légends des Siècles,* trans. C. John Holcombe, Textetc.com, www.textetc.com/exhibits/et-hugo-1.html.

6. Marjory Zoet Bankson, *Seasons of Friendship: Naomi and Ruth as a Model for Relationship,* rev. ed. (Minneapolis: Augsburg Fortress, 2005), 85.

7. Matthew Henry, *Matthew Henry's Commentary on the Whole Bible* (Peabody, MA: Hendrickson, 1991), 2:210.

8. Hubbard, *The Book of Ruth,* 210.

9. Sinclair B. Ferguson, *Faithful God: An Exposition of the Book of Ruth* (Bridgend, UK: Bryntirion, 2005), 98.

10. F. B. Huey, "Ruth," in *The Expositor's Bible Commentary* (Grand Rapids: Zondervan, 1992), 3:537.

11. Moore, "Ruth," 354.

12. Gillian M. Rowell, "Ruth," in *The IVP Women's Bible Commentary* (Downers Grove, IL: InterVarsity, 2002), 151.

13. Hubbard, *The Book of Ruth,* 211.

14. Genesis 29:25, NASB

15. Ruth 2:5

16. Huey, "Ruth," 3:537.

17. Hubbard, *The Book of Ruth,* 211.

18. Iain M. Duguid, *Esther and Ruth,* in *Reformed Expository Commentary* (Phillipsburg, NJ: P and R, 2005), 172.

19. Ruth 2:12

20. Ellen van Wolde, *Ruth and Naomi* (Macon, GA: Smyth and Helwys, 1998), 83.

21. Duguid, *Esther and Ruth,* 172.

22. Dee Brestin, *The God of All Comfort: Finding Your Way into His Arms* (Grand Rapids: Zondervan, 2009), 197.

23. Hubbard, *The Book of Ruth,* 212.

24. Ezekiel 16:8

25. Psalm 147:3

26. Kirsten Nielsen, *Ruth: A Commentary,* Old Testament Library (Louisville, KY: Westminster John Knox, 1997), 75.

27. Edward F. Campbell Jr., *Ruth,* vol. 7 of *The Anchor Bible* (New York: Doubleday, 1975), 136.

28. Ferguson, *Faithful God,* 108.

29. Ferguson, *Faithful God,* 98.

30. Hubbard, *The Book of Ruth,* 213–14.

31. Deuteronomy 24:19

32. Isaiah 61:1–3

33. Katharine Doob Sakenfeld, *Ruth: Interpretation; A Bible Commentary for Teaching and Preaching* (Louisville, KY: Westminster John Knox, 1999), 61.

34. Joyce G. Baldwin, "Ruth," in *The New Bible Commentary Revised,* ed. Donald Guthrie and J. Alec Motyer (Grand Rapids: Eerdmans, 1970), 281.

35. André LaCocque, *Ruth: A Continental Commentary,* trans. K. C. Hanson (Minneapolis: Augsburg Fortress, 2004), 98.

36. Virginia Stem Owens, *Daughters of Eve: Seeing Ourselves in Women of the Bible* (Colorado Springs, CO: NavPress, 1995), 46.

37. Huey, "Ruth," 3:538.

38. Isaiah 43:1

39. James 1:5

40. John 16:24

41. Matthew 6:8

42. Proverbs 12:4

43. Proverbs 31:10

44. Carol Meyers, gen. ed., *Women in Scripture: A Dictionary of Named and Unnamed Women in the Hebrew Bible, the Apocryphal/Deuterocanonical Books, and the New Testament* (New York: Houghton Mifflin, 2000), 147.

45. Proverbs 2:1–5

46. Proverbs 31:10, NKJV

47. Miki Raver, *Listen to Her Voice: Women of the Hebrew Bible* (San Francisco: Chronicle, 1998), 149.

48. Hubbard, *The Book of Ruth,* 219.

Chapter 10

1. Grace Goldin, *Come Under the Wings: A Midrash on Ruth* (Philadelphia: Jewish Publication Society of America, 1980), 64.

2. Deuteronomy 33:27

3. Isaiah 47:4

4. Romans 8:29

5. Katharine Doob Sakenfeld, *Ruth: Interpretation; A Bible Commentary for Teaching and Preaching* (Louisville, KY: Westminster John Knox, 1999), 64.

6. André LaCocque, *Ruth: A Continental Commentary,* trans. K. C. Hanson (Minneapolis: Augsburg Fortress, 2004), 3.

7. Matthew Henry, *Matthew Henry's Commentary on the Whole Bible* (Peabody, MA: Hendrickson, 1991), 2:211.

8. Song of Songs 2:10, KJV

9. Gillian M. Rowell, "Ruth," in *The IVP Women's Bible Commentary* (Downers Grove, IL: InterVarsity, 2002), 151.
10. Elizabeth Ruth Obbard, *Ruth and Naomi: A Story of Friendship, Growth and Change* (Cincinnati: Saint Anthony Messenger, 2003), 74.
11. Luke 6:38
12. Robert Lintzenich, ed., *Ruth, Esther,* in *Shepherd's Notes* (Nashville: Broadman and Holman, 1998), 30.
13. Henry, *Matthew Henry's Commentary,* 2:211.
14. Ruth 1:21
15. Rowell, "Ruth," 151.
16. Robert L. Hubbard Jr., *The Book of Ruth,* in *The New International Commentary on the Old Testament* (Grand Rapids: Eerdmans, 1988), 226n1.
17. Ruth 2:20
18. Hebrews 10:37
19. Psalm 27:14

Chapter 11

1. 1 Corinthians 4:5
2. Matthew Henry, *Matthew Henry's Commentary on the Whole Bible* (Peabody, MA: Hendrickson, 1991), 2:211.
3. Michael S. Moore, "Ruth," in *Joshua, Judges, Ruth,* vol. 5 of *New International Biblical Commentary* (Peabody, MA: Hendrickson, 2000), 361.
4. Iain M. Duguid, *Esther and Ruth,* in *Reformed Expository Commentary* (Phillipsburg, NJ: P and R, 2005), 181.
5. T. J. Wray, *Good Girls, Bad Girls: The Enduring Lessons of Twelve Women of the Old Testament* (Lanham, MD: Rowman and Littlefield, 2008), 74.
6. Moore, "Ruth," 361.
7. Moore, "Ruth," 356.
8. Walter C. Kaiser Jr. and Duane A. Garrett, eds., *NIV Archaeological Study Bible: An Illustrated Walk Through Biblical History and Culture* (Grand Rapids: Zondervan, 2005), 393.
9. Moore, "Ruth," 356.
10. Leviticus 25:25
11. Deuteronomy 25:5–6
12. Ruth 3:11
13. Virginia Stem Owens, *Daughters of Eve: Seeing Ourselves in Women of the Bible* (Colorado Springs, CO: NavPress, 1995), 47.
14. Miki Raver, *Listen to Her Voice: Women of the Hebrew Bible* (San Francisco: Chronicle, 1998), 149.
15. John 14:2
16. Revelation 2:17
17. John H. Walton, Victor H. Matthews, and Mark W. Chavalas, *The IVP Bible Background Commentary: Old Testament* (Downers Grove, IL: InterVarsity, 2000), 280.
18. Deuteronomy 25:9–10

19. Katharine Doob Sakenfeld, *Ruth: Interpretation; A Bible Commentary for Teaching and Preaching* (Louisville, KY: Westminster John Knox, 1999), 73.

20. Deuteronomy 32:47

21. Psalm 119:103

22. Genesis 35:19

23. Ruth 2:5

24. Sakenfeld, *Ruth*, 78.

25. Genesis 38:26

26. Ruth 3:11

27. Sakenfeld, *Ruth*, 79.

28. Numbers 26:22

Chapter 12

1. Genesis 21:1–2

2. Genesis 25:21

3. Genesis 29:31

4. Genesis 30:22

5. 1 Samuel 2:21

6. Luke 1:24–25

7. Robert L. Hubbard Jr., *The Book of Ruth*, in *The New International Commentary on the Old Testament* (Grand Rapids: Eerdmans, 1988), 97.

8. Matthew Henry, *Matthew Henry's Commentary on the Whole Bible* (Peabody, MA: Hendrickson, 1991), 2:215.

9. 2 Corinthians 12:9

10. Psalm 118:24

11. John H. Walton, Victor H. Matthews, and Mark W. Chavalas, *The IVP Bible Background Commentary: Old Testament* (Downers Grove, IL: InterVarsity, 2000), 281.

12. Gillian M. Rowell, "Ruth," in *The IVP Women's Bible Commentary* (Downers Grove, IL: InterVarsity, 2002), 146.

13. Proverbs 22:1

14. Katharine Doob Sakenfeld, *Ruth: Interpretation; A Bible Commentary for Teaching and Preaching* (Louisville, KY: Westminster John Knox, 1999), 82.

15. Ruth 1:21

16. Hubbard, *The Book of Ruth*, 273.

17. Michael S. Moore, "Ruth," in *Joshua, Judges, Ruth*, vol. 5 of *New International Biblical Commentary* (Peabody, MA: Hendrickson, 2000), 370.

18. Romans 11:13

19. Romans 11:17

20. Isaiah 65:9

21. 1 Peter 2:9

22. 2 Corinthians 6:18

23. Ephesians 4:4–6

24. Marjory Zoet Bankson, *Seasons of Friendship: Naomi and Ruth as a Model for Relationship*, rev. ed. (Minneapolis: Augsburg Fortress, 2005), 126.

25. "Baptismal Covenant II, Congregational Pledge 2," *The United Methodist Hymnal* (Nashville: United Methodist, 2007), 44.

26. Hubbard, *The Book of Ruth*, 276–77.

27. John Piper, *A Sweet and Bitter Providence: Sex, Race, and the Sovereignty of God* (Wheaton, IL: Crossway, 2010), 108.

28. Hubbard, *The Book of Ruth*, 283.

29. Phineas Camp Headley, *Women of the Bible* (Buffalo, NY: Miller, Orton and Mulligan, 1854), 140.
30. Matthew 9:27
31. Matthew 21:9
32. 1 Samuel 13:14
33. Harold S. Paisley, *This Ruth* (Glastonbury, CT: Olive, 1995), 136.
34. Philippians 4:1, NKJV
35. 1 John 4:12

Before We Go
1. 1 Thessalonians 1:4, NCV
2. 1 Peter 5:10
3. Psalm 46:1

Discussion Questions
1. Marjory Zoet Bankson, *Seasons of Friendship: Naomi and Ruth as a Model for Relationship,* rev. ed. (Minneapolis: Augsburg Fortress, 2005), 18.
2. William Mackintosh Mackay, *Bible Types of Modern Women* (New York: George H. Doran, 1922), 230.
3. Sinclair B. Ferguson, *Faithful God: An Exposition of the Book of Ruth* (Bridgend, UK: Bryntirion, 2005), 45.
4. Phineas Camp Headley, *Women of the Bible* (Buffalo, NY: Miller, Orton and Mulligan, 1854), 128.

Study Guide
1. World Hunger Education Service, "2011 World Hunger and Poverty Facts and Statistics," WorldHunger.org, www.world hunger.org/articles/Learn /world%20hunger%20facts% 202002.htm.
2. Kenneth D. Kochanek et al., "Deaths: Preliminary Data for 2009," *National Vital Statistics Reports* 59, no. 4 (March 2011), US Department of Health and Human Services, www.cdc.gov /nchs/data/nvsr/nvsr59/nvsr59 _04.pdf, 2.
3. Centers for Disease Control and Prevention, "Reproductive Health: Infertility FAQ's," June 28, 2011, www.cdc.gov /reproductivehealth/Infertility /index.htm.
4. Iain M. Duguid, *Esther and Ruth,* in *Reformed Expository Commentary* (Phillipsburg, NJ: P and R, 2005), 136.
5. Vanessa L. Ochs, *Sarah Laughed: Modern Lessons from the Wisdom and Stories of Biblical Women* (New York: McGraw-Hill, 2005), 97.
6. Genesis 12:1
7. 1 Thessalonians 1:9
8. 1 Samuel 14:44
9. 1 Samuel 20:13
10. 1 Samuel 25:22
11. Larry Crabb, *Shattered Dreams* (Colorado Springs, CO: Water-Brook, 2001), 68.
12. John Piper, *A Sweet and Bitter Providence: Sex, Race, and the Sovereignty of God* (Wheaton, IL: Crossway, 2010), 15.

13. Elizabeth Ruth Obbard, *Ruth and Naomi: A Story of Friendship, Growth and Change* (Cincinnati: Saint Anthony Messenger, 2003), 37.

14. Gillian M. Rowell, "Ruth," in *The IVP Women's Bible Commentary* (Downers Grove, IL: InterVarsity, 2002), 150.

15. Katharine Doob Sakenfeld, *Ruth: Interpretation; A Bible Commentary for Teaching and Preaching* (Louisville, KY: Westminster John Knox, 1999), 43.

16. Matthew Henry, *Matthew Henry's Commentary on the Whole Bible* (Peabody, MA: Hendrickson, 1991), 2:207.

17. Sakenfeld, *Ruth,* 24.

18. Louise Pettibone Smith, "Ruth," in *The Interpreter's Bible* (Nashville: Abingdon, 1953), 2:831.

19. Acts 9:6

20. Marjory Zoet Bankson, *Seasons of Friendship: Naomi and Ruth as a Model for Relationship,* rev. ed. (Minneapolis: Augsburg Fortress, 2005), 81.

21. Marsha Pravder Mirkin, *The Women Who Danced by the Sea: Finding Ourselves in the Stories of Our Biblical Foremothers* (Rhinebeck, NY: Monkfish Book, 2004), 179.

22. Steve Zeisler, *A Conspicuous Love: The Enduring Story of Ruth, Romance and Redemption* (Grand Rapids: Discovery House, 1999), 137.

23. Henry, *Matthew Henry's Commentary,* 2:210.

24. Henry, *Matthew Henry's Commentary,* 2:211.

25. F. C. Cook, ed., *Exodus to Esther,* vol. 2 of *Barnes Notes* (Grand Rapids: Baker, 1998), 477.

26. Carol M. Bechtel, *Above and Beyond: Hearing God's Call in Jonah and Ruth* (Louisville, KY: Presbyterian Women, Presbyterian Church [USA], 2007), 53.

27. Edith Deen, *All the Women of the Bible* (New York: Harper and Row, 1955), 82.

HEARTFELT THANKS

A big hug to my editorial team, who offered kind words and wise counsel from the early drafts to the final typeset pages: Laura Barker, Carol Bartley, Sara Fortenberry, Bill Higgs, Glenna Salsbury, Holly Briscoe, and Matthew Higgs. In the words of Boaz, "May the LORD repay you for what you have done."

A special shout-out to my Sisters of the Mud, the three dozen women who joined me on our Women of the Bible tour of the Holy Land in 2011. We bonded as sisters from the time we met at the airport en route to Tel Aviv. The mud part came later, when we gathered on the shore of the Dead Sea and slathered mineral-rich mud on one another. Trust me, you do *not* want to see the photos. But oh the memories.

A warm *shalom* to Michelle and Natanel Cohen of Shabbat of a Lifetime in Jerusalem, who welcomed us into their home and into their hearts. Check out www.ShabbatOfALifetime.com for a taste of Jewish tradition and hospitality. Extra hugs go to Bev Henry, our fearless tour director, and to Hedva Ma'ane, our Israeli guide, whose passion for her country energized us all. (Good thing, because we walked our feet off!)

I also owe a huge debt of gratitude to my newsletter readers and Facebook followers who shared their Ruth In Real Life experiences. Your voices add so much to these pages, letting us see what a lived-out faith looks like. Thank you, dear ones. You've definitely still got it.

Finally, to the thousands of women who've heard me teach the book of Ruth and have encouraged me to write this verse-by-verse study, bless you for your patience. Our girl's story is finally told, thanks to your enthusiasm. I could never do what I do without you.

RIGHTEOUS RUTH RAP

Lyrics by Liz Curtis Higgs

The first time I taught a weekly Bible study on Ruth, I wanted a quick, fun way to *wrap up* the previous week's lesson. That's how the "Righteous Ruth Rap" was born. If you've seen me perform this on YouTube, you'll understand why more than one person has called me a Crazy White Woman. The shoe definitely fits. Now let's get snapping, girl.

My name is Lizzie;
It's time to get busy;
Turn to Ruth 1:1,
And we'll rap 'til she's done.

Naomi and her brood
Needed more food;
When to Moab they fled,
Hubby ended up dead.

Then her sons died too.
What's a mother to do?
Their wives were both heathen,
But at least they were breathin'.

Naomi started pinin';
Pretty soon she was whinin';
We've been there, baby,
And I don't mean maybe.

The women hit the road,
Their grief, a heavy load.
Weepy Orpah turned back;
Loyal Ruth stayed on track.

"I'm with you," said Ruth,
"And with God. That's the truth."
Naomi's words spent,
Back to Bethlehem they went.

"Look who's home!" said the sisters.
"And without their misters."
A decade full of sorrow;
Still, there's hope for tomorrow.

You may call Naomi bitter,
But she ain't no quitter;
Not with Ruth beside her
And the Lord to guide her.

Ruth went to glean barley,
Didn't ride no Harley;
She walked the whole way
And worked the whole day.

Then Boaz came along,
Both wealthy and strong.
Whose maiden is she?
Is she married? wondered he.

"Now listen, my daughter,
You can drink my water.
Hang as close as you can,
And watch those men."

Righteous Ruth bowed down,
With her face to the ground.
"What mercy!" she did cry.
"But I can't imagine why."

"You're a stand-up homey,
Takin' care of Naomi.
May you find a rich reward,
Stayin' close to the Lord.

"Sit with me," he said at dinner.
(Boaz knew he had a winner.)
Ruth gleaned without flack.
Then she took home a sack.

One day Naomi told her,
"Sprinkle perfume on your
        shoulder.
Put on your girly clothes,
But forget the pantyhose."

Ruth headed out the door,
Bound for the threshing floor.
She watched and she waited,
While her breath was bated.

Ruth had to find out
Is he hero or lout?
So she laid at his feet.
(Bet they smelled real sweet.)

"Who are you?" asked he.
"I am Ruth," answered she.
"Kindly share your blankie,
And we'll skip the hanky-panky."

Old Boaz was excited;
Yes, indeed, he was delighted.
If we're talking virtue-wise,
Young Ruthie took the prize.

Didn't wanna burst her bubble,
But there was a little trouble.

Some no-name schemer
Had the right to redeem her.

She lay by her hero's side,
Safe and comfy as a bride,
Then went home to m-i-l,
Where they had to sit a spell.

Boaz faced the other fellow,
Acting cool and mellow.
When the deal was said and done,
Boaz was the dude who won.

Then Ruth became his Mrs.;
Bet he showered her with kisses.
When he cried, "O, bed!"
She was glad they were wed.

All the men shouted, "Glory!
You fit right into our story."
Then the women named the
        child.
Don't you know Naomi smiled?

It was a happy-ever-after
Filled with pain and laughter.
Stood the lengthy test of time
And survived my crazy rhyme.

See, the girl's still got it,
Which is why I taught it.
If you like what you've heard,
You will find it in the Word.

God spread this whole jam
Between Judges and First Sam.
As for now, it's a wrap;
Go ahead, you can clap.

Want to see and hear "Righteous Ruth Rap" recorded live in Little Rock? You'll find it under "videos" at www.YouTube.com/LizCurtisHiggs. Go ahead, you can laugh.

About the Author

An award-winning speaker, LIZ CURTIS HIGGS has addressed audiences from more than sixteen hundred platforms, in all fifty states and fourteen foreign countries. Women of Faith, Women of Joy, Among Friends, Time Out for Women, Moody Women, Women of Virtue, Extraordinary Women, Win-Some Women, Women's Journey of Faith, Women Who Worship, Christian Women Communicating International—if it's a conference for and about women, Liz is honored to be there, encouraging her sisters in Christ.

She's also a best-selling author of nearly thirty books, with more than three million copies in print. Her popular nonfiction books include *Bad Girls of the Bible, Really Bad Girls of the Bible, Unveiling Mary Magdalene, Slightly Bad Girls of the Bible, Rise and Shine,* and *Embrace Grace.* More than forty-five hundred churches nationwide are using her video Bible study series, *Loved by God.*

Her fiction includes both contemporary and historical novels: *Here Burns My Candle,* a 2011 Retailers Choice Award winner; *Mine Is the Night,* a *New York Times* bestseller; *Thorn in My Heart; Fair Is the Rose; Whence Came a Prince,* a 2006 Christy Award winner; and *Grace in Thine Eyes,* listed in the 2006 Top Five Best Christian Fiction by *Library Journal.*

If you'd like to sign up for Liz's free e-newsletter, *Encouragement to Go,* visit her website, www.LizCurtisHiggs.com, where you'll also find her weekly blog and monthly Podcasts. And you can connect with Liz on Facebook at www.Facebook.com/LizCurtisHiggs and on Twitter at www.Twitter.com/LizCurtisHiggs.

VIDEO STUDY
with
LIZ CURTIS HIGGS

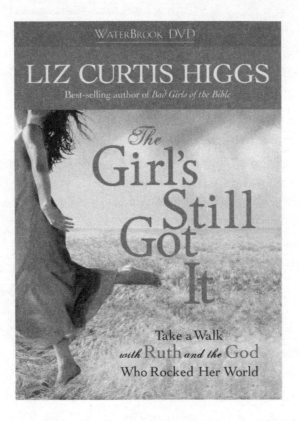

In short and engaging videos, Liz Curtis Higgs
shares fresh insights about the character of
Ruth—and connects her story to *your story*.
The flexible formatted DVD works perfectly
for Bible studies and small groups.

To learn more, visit www.waterbrookmultnomah.com.

Contemporary fiction.
Timeless truths. Changed lives.

With one million copies sold, the Bad Girls of the Bible series breathes new life into the ancient stories about the most infamous—and intriguing—women of the Bible, from Eve to Mary Magdalene. Workbooks and DVDs are also available.

Available in bookstores and from online retailers.

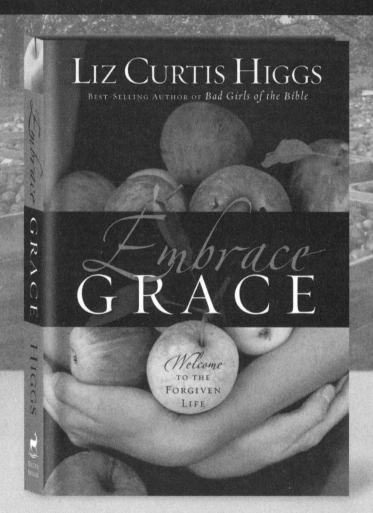